Catholic World Culture

Written by
Dr. Anne W. Carroll

Author of *Christ the King, Lord of History*

SETON PRESS
Front Royal, VA

Executive Editor: Dr. Mary Kay Clark
Editors: Seton Staff

© 2010 - 2020 Seton Press
All rights reserved.
Printed in the United States of America.

Seton Press
1350 Progress Drive
Front Royal, VA 22630
540-636-9990
540-636-1602 fax

For more information, visit us on the Web at http://www.setonpress.com.
Contact us by e-mail at info@setonpress.com.

ISBN: 978-1-60704-052-1

Cover: The *Pieta*, Michelangelo Buonarrotti

DEDICATED TO THE SACRED HEART OF JESUS

Contents

Italy
Chapter 1   The Mother Church of Christendom 1
Chapter 2   Genius in Marble 7
Chapter 3   The Artist of Mysteries 14
Chapter 4   Bride of Christ 21

Spain & Portugal
Chapter 5   The Catholic Queen 28
Chapter 6   God Alone Sufficeth 37
Chapter 7   Roses and Bread 44

France
Chapter 8   Eldest Daughter of the Church 50
Chapter 9   Spires in the Sky 56
Chapter 10   Saint in Armor 62

The Netherlands
Chapter 11   Martyrs and Miracles 69
Chapter 12   Portraits that Breathe 74

England & Ireland
Chapter 13   Kings and Crowns 80
Chapter 14   Prayers and Penance 87
Chapter 15   Wife, Mother, Foundress 93
Chapter 16   Trading Crowns 100

Scandinavia
Chapter 17   Conversions in the North 106
Chapter 18   Switzerland's Heroes 113

Germany & Switzerland
Chapter 19   Master of Music 120

Eastern Europe

Chapter 20	Earthly and Heavenly Loves	126
Chapter 21	Captive Cardinal	131
Chapter 22	Christ in Ukraine and Russia	139
Chapter 23	Jadwiga's Wedding Ring	146
Chapter 24	The Black Madonna's Fort	154
Chapter 25	Suffering Poland	160

The Far East

Chapter 26	Survival of the Faith	168
Chapter 27	Forbidden Country	178
Chapter 28	Teacher of Reality	187

The New World

Chapter 29	Roses in Winter	196
Chapter 30	Our Lord's Grandmother	203
	Bibliography	209
	Index	211
	Answer Key	215

Introduction

In this book you are about to embark on a journey around the world. It will be a journey of the imagination. We will visit many parts of the world, from Rome on the Tiber to Vienna on the Danube, from the island of Great Britain to the island of Japan, from the Alps of Switzerland to the Urals of Russia.

It will also be a journey in time. We will see England when it was still Roman Britain, France when it was still Gaul, Sweden in the fourteenth century and China in the seventeenth.

We will meet artists and composers, saints and popes, heroes and villains, men and women who left a mark on the world.

Our book is called *Catholic World Culture*, and culture may be defined as the presence of truth, beauty and goodness in the world, and more specifically, as those presentations of truth, manifestations of beauty and examples of goodness unique to a given country or nationality.

We know, of course, that the ultimate source of truth, beauty and goodness is God Himself. He is all truth, who can neither deceive nor be deceived. He is perfect beauty, to delight the eyes of men in the beatific vision through all eternity. He is infinite goodness, and the only way any of us can be good is through the help of His grace.

Therefore, we will judge the culture we study by certain standards. We will not simply present scattered examples with no relationship to each other, with no deeper purpose. We will try to see how these examples have served God and glorified His holy name.

Thus, we will specifically study the Catholic culture of the world. We will see how Catholic artists, saints and kings have brought truth, beauty and goodness into the world. We will study some people who were not Catholics, but we will see that their contributions to world culture were built on Catholic foundations or grew from Catholic roots. And we will see that troubles afflict the world when men and women stray from Catholic truth and Catholic channels of grace.

Since this book is a journey, you must be an active participant. If all you do is read the book and then promptly forget what you have learned, you have wasted your time. As you read, try to picture the events in your mind. Sometimes we provide pictures to help you, but most of the time you must rely on your own imagination.

You must also rely on your own ingenuity to seek out sources which will show and tell you more about the events you are studying. A book such as this can be only an introduction to the vast world of Catholic world culture. If you become especially interested in one topic, pursue that interest. Go to other books, find out more about it, learn as much as you can about what interests you. The author of this book hopes to expand your mind and fire your imagination, so that you can appreciate the Catholic culture of the world.

We encourage you to look in recent magazines and newspapers, as well as on Catholic internet sites, to learn about how Catholics are doing now in the countries you read about. For instance, you should discover that Italy, surrounding the Vatican, has the highest abortion rate of any country in the world; the Spanish government has taken over the Catholic schools of Spain; Hindus in India are trying to outlaw other religions; and in China, Catholic bishops are being arrested or killed. Please keep them and all struggling Catholics around the world in your prayers.

Now your journey is about to begin. You don't need money or a plane ticket: just time, enthusiasm and energy. Welcome aboard.

Chapter 1
The Mother Church of Christendom

We will begin our travels through the Catholic world with the most important city in that world, Rome. Our Church is sometimes called the Roman Catholic Church, because Rome was the city selected by the first head of the Church as his headquarters. St. Peter was the man chosen by Our Lord to be the head of His Church after He ascended into Heaven. When the apostles left Jerusalem to go out into the whole world to convert it, as Christ had told them to do, St. Peter chose Rome as the primary center of his missionary activity, a logical choice since Rome was the most important city in the world and he was the head of the Church. St. Peter was martyred in Rome by the insane emperor Nero and buried there, and ever since then Rome has been the city of the head of the Church, the Pope.

Peter was in Rome from approximately 42 A.D. to 67 A.D. In 64 A.D., a great fire lasting nine days demolished a major section of Rome. Already unpopular, Nero was blamed for the fire by many of the people; they accused him of having the fire set to clear a section of the city for a new palace. To deflect blame from himself, Nero accused the small and mysterious new sect of Christians of having started the fire. As a result, Christians were cruelly martyred. Some were fed to wild beasts; others were tied to posts, soaked with oil, and then set afire to serve as torches for Nero's evening banquets. The leader of the Christians was among those arrested. Peter was sentenced to death by crucifixion, but he did not consider himself worthy to die the way his Master had died. He asked the Roman soldiers to crucify him upside down, and so they did, killing him at Nero's Circus, an arena for chariot races, on a hill across the Tiber from the main part of Rome, in a section of the city called the Vatican. The Christians would not have been able to have an elaborate funeral. They would have had to bury Peter as quickly as possible, in a cemetery on the hill overlooking the place where he was martyred.

Through persecution after persecution, the Christians kept alive the memory of where Peter was buried until at last Christianity was declared legal in 313, by the Emperor Constantine, who became the first Christian Roman emperor. Constantine had a Christian mother, St. Helena, and he defeated his enemy Maxentius after seeing a vision of the cross in the sky with the words, "In this Sign, you will

St. Peter's Basilica in Rome.

Interior of St. Peter's Basilica in Rome.

conquer." After his victory he issued the Edict of Toleration, which legalized Christianity. He wanted to build Christian temples to overshadow the pagan temples; the first of which was the Church of St. John in the Lateran section of Rome, today still the parish church of the Pope. He also chose the site of St. Peter's burial for a major church.

Construction of the Vatican

The Vatican was not a favorable site for a church. There was poor drainage and terrible mosquitoes. The workmen were obliged to cut deeply into the rock of the Vatican Hill to make a level space and then to fill up the depression with tons of earth and rock scooped from the northern slope. One of the reasons we know that this site must be the location of St. Peter's martyrdom is that there could be no other reason why a church would have been built in such an unsuitable location.

Emperor Constantine did not want the church to look like a pagan temple, so he modeled it after the architecture of the law courts. Built between 326 and 333, in a style and size to command respect, it was called a basilica, a rectangular shape with columns dividing it into three lengthwise sections. A shrine for St. Peter's bones was placed at the end, raised above the pavement and surrounded with twisted columns. In 594, Pope Gregory the Great put the shrine below the pavement to protect it. Over the centuries, the basilica fell into disrepair, especially during the Babylonian Captivity when the Popes temporarily lived in France. Sheep and cows wandered in; wolves dug up graves; the walls were in danger of collapse. When the Popes came back from France, the southern walls had a six-foot tilt from the perpendicular.

Pope Nicholas V (1447-1455) decided that repairs could not save the church but that it must be entirely rebuilt, a task which took over a hundred years. The Pope responsible for the major portion of the rebuilding was Julius II (1503-1513). Julius was not an admirable pope. He spent more time leading armies than tending to the spiritual business of the Church. He wanted a magnificent tomb for himself; no existing church was big enough to hold it so he pressed ahead with the renovation of St. Peter's in order to have a place for his tomb. (Ironically, Julius is now buried in an out-of-the-way part of St. Peter's, with only a small stone set in the pavement to indicate where his grave is.) Julius laid the cornerstone of the new church. He was so enthusiastic that he climbed down into the excavation, but when it started to collapse, he quickly climbed out.

Pope Julius hired Bramante, an outstanding architect of the time, to design the new basilica. Bramante was cheerful and friendly, very generous and a spendthrift, so that he was always in debt and having to ask his friends for money. He studied classical buildings, but when he started to build anything himself, he was too impatient. He would demolish buildings hurriedly and put up replacements too hastily. His nickname was *Il Ruinante* (the Ruiner).

Bramante's concept for St. Peter's was a mighty building with a great open space around the tomb to honor the magnificence of the Papacy. His plan was to have four transepts (aisles) in the form of a Greek cross (a cross with four arms of equal size). In the center would be a gigantic dome, (a rounded roof) supported by four great piers. He plunged immediately into tearing down the existing structure. For several weeks he employed 2,500 workmen solely on destruction. He threw out tombs, statues, mosaics, candelabra, icons, and altars. He even suggested moving St. Peter's tomb, but the Pope absolutely refused. After all the destruction, the only construction he completed was the raising of the four piers (which support the dome to this day). The area encompassed by the piers was so enormous that a small church could fit into them. Bramante died in 1514, just after Julius II. In spite of his failings, he had a vision of the design as symbolizing the glory of the Papacy, and this vision was carried on.

The next major architect to be commissioned was Sangallo. He built a huge model of his projected design. It took him seven years and cost as much as a parish church. Critics said it looked like a wedding cake, and his plans were never put into effect.

When Paul III (1523-1549) became pope, he wanted to hire the renowned sculptor, Michelangelo, as the next architect for St. Peter's. Pope Paul went to Michelangelo in a splendid procession to ask him to complete the church, but Michelangelo was not interested. Twelve years later, when Michelangelo was seventy-five, Paul asked him again. Michelangelo had undergone a spiritual conversion. Wanting to work for the glory of God, he agreed to take on the task. He refused any new salary, saying that he would work "only for the love of God and in honor of the Apostle."

Michelangelo completed the apse (back section) which still exists today as he designed it. He took over Bramante's idea of a dome, but wanted to make it much higher and heavier. This plan was a much more difficult architectural problem: would it be so heavy as to collapse the whole church? A dome has three parts — the drum (base), the dome itself, and the lantern (decoration on the top) — but Michelangelo was able to complete only the drum. Afterwards, however, domes were built all over Europe because Michelangelo had shown it could be done.

Another architect, Giacomo Della Porta, finished the dome. He used Michelangelo's basic design but made it higher and lighter. He had drawn out a full-sized design for the dome. The only place to put it so it could all be seen at once was on the floor of the Church of St. Paul's Outside the Walls, where the Pope came to survey it and approve.

Carlo Maderno, the next architect, discarded the Greek cross plan and lengthened the nave (center aisle) to its present overall size of 211½ meters, a Latin cross design (three short arms and one long arm). His innovation was criticized because the nave hides the dome from anyone standing near the church, but it was necessary for the large crowds which the church had to accommodate.

The design of the interior was entrusted to Gian Lorenzo Bernini, a well-known artist and

Baldachino over the main altar

Veronica by Francesco Mochi

sculptor of the day. Bernini was flamboyant; he liked to pull tricks and he liked a show. Once, he was commissioned to sculpt a bust of a cardinal. When the cardinal arrived to examine the completed work, Bernini, with a crestfallen expression, showed him a seriously flawed sculpture. Just as the cardinal was wavering between dejection and anger, Bernini pulled out the real sculpture, perfectly executed.

Bernini was a dedicated Catholic who gave his whole life to art for the glory of God. For the interior of St. Peter's, Bernini chose the baroque style (an ornate, highly decorative style), because that showed the triumph and glory of Catholicism, in contrast to the soberness and lack of decoration of Protestant churches. Bernini used the twisted column design from the original basilica to support the baldachino (canopy) over the altar. The baldachino was extremely heavy and foundations had to be sunk deep underneath because it was as tall as a three-story building. Each of the columns was in three parts. The bottom part was fluted. The top two parts were covered with sculpted olive foliage.

Among the leaves, angels play. The four columns rest on plinths (bases) made of white marble. The plinths bear carvings of the face of one of the Pope's nieces during the different months of her pregnancy. Anxiety, fear, agony and ecstasy and other appropriate moods are represented. Finally, the small head of a newly born baby boy appears.

Bernini was also responsible for the erection of the four colossal statues on the Bramante piers. For the statues, which overlook the altar where the Holy Sacrifice of the Mass is offered, he chose four saints who would carry out the theme of the cross: Longinus, who stabbed Christ's side with a lance and later converted to Christianity; Veronica, who wiped Christ's face with her veil; Helena, who found the True Cross; and Andrew the Apostle who was martyred on an X-shaped cross. Each of the saints is depicted holding his or her symbol: Longinus with a spear, Veronica with a veil, Helena with a cross, and St. Andrew with an X-shaped cross.

Bernini designed the most beautiful chapel in St. Peter's, the Cattedra Chapel, so called because the chair used by St. Peter is there. *Cattedra* is the Latin word for chair or throne, and it is the root word of our word "cathedral," which is the location of a bishop's throne or seat of authority. Bernini also completed the outside of the church by designing a curving facade with 284 columns, with two wide arms symbolizing the Church's embrace of all men.

Since the time of Bernini, almost every pope has left some mark on St. Peter's. One such major addition was the thirteen statues on the roof: the eleven apostles, the Risen Christ, and St. John the Baptist.

All of us who are Catholics should praise God for the talents of the great artists and architects who have given us this beautiful edifice that serves as the Mother Church of Christendom.

Chapter 1
Review Questions

A. Write the definitions for the following terms:

1. basilica _____

2. transepts _____

3. Greek Cross _____

4. apse _____

5. dome _____

6. lantern _____

7. nave _____

8. Latin Cross _____

9. baroque _____

10. baldachino _____

11. plinth _____

12. Cattedra _____

B. What is historically significant information about the following? In other words, who were these people or what position did they hold? What did these people do that influenced future historical events? Example: Nero was a Roman emperor and a hateful dictator, but it was his burning of the city of Rome and blaming the Christians that was historically important because of the events that followed: the persecution and crucifixion of Christians.

13. St. Peter _____

14. Constantine _____

15. Nicholas V _____

16. Julius II _____

17. Bramante _____

18. Sangallo _____

19. Paul III _____

20. Michelangelo _____

21. Della Porta _____

22. Maderno _____

23. Bernini _____

24. Longinus _____

25. Helena _____

26. Andrew _____

27. Give the year and describe the martyrdom of St. Peter. _____
    _____
    _____
    _____

28. Why is St. Peter's Basilica built where it is? _____
    _____
    _____
    _____

29. Why did the original St. Peter's need to be rebuilt? _____
    _____
    _____
    _____

30. What are the thirteen statues on the roof of St. Peter's? _____
    _____
    _____
    _____

Chapter 2

Genius in Marble

Michelangelo Buonarrotti lived for eighty-nine years, and in that time he was the world's finest painter, sculptor, and architect. Once he said: "Painting and sculpture have ruined me. . . . It would have been better if in my youth I had hired myself out to make sulfur matches." As we retell his life, see if you can think why he would have made such a statement.

Michelangelo was born March 6, 1475, in Florence. He had ordinary parents and four ordinary brothers. After his mother died when he was six, he lived with a family of stonecutters until his father remarried four years later. During this time he learned to handle a chisel and fell in love with stonecutting. When he went back to his father, he was sent to school, where he learned to read and write but spent most of his time drawing pictures. He was stubborn and persuaded his father to let him be apprenticed to a painter when he was thirteen. His earliest drawings show his superiority to the other pupils and even to the master.

Lorenzo di Medici, leader of the family that ruled Florence, called for good sculptors. Michelangelo was sent. Lorenzo gave him a piece of marble, and Michelangelo began to copy the head of a marble faun (a mythological creature). He carved the mouth wide open to show all the teeth. Lorenzo was delighted but said jokingly that he did not think a faun as old as that would have such a perfect set of teeth. Michelangelo took him seriously. He broke out a tooth and filed down the gum to make it look shrunken. Lorenzo was so impressed that he persuaded Michelangelo's father to let him live in his palace. Thus was the young boy introduced into the highest cultural and intellectual company of Florence.

When Lorenzo died in 1492, Michelangelo was heartbroken but persevered in his work. He went to the Santo Spirito hospital secretly to study anatomy through dissection, which was illegal at the time. His first commission was from Lorenzo's son Piero, who paid him to make a snow-giant after a rare tremendous snowfall on January 20, 1494. Later that year, France invaded Florence. Michelangelo fled to Bologna, which had just enacted a law that foreigners had to pay a special tax. Michelangelo did not pay and was sent to jail. Fortunately, the young artist was rescued by an art lover who had heard of his misfortune. While in Bologna Michelangelo sculpted statues for St. Dominic's tomb; these statues are his earliest existing sculptures.

When peace returned in 1495, Michelangelo returned to Florence. Another Lorenzo di Medici got the idea of using Michelangelo's talents to make some money.

Lorenzo di Medici
(from his tomb)

He had Michelangelo carve a cupid as if it were worn and paid him thirty ducats for it. Then Lorenzo took it to Rome, passed it off as an antique, and sold it for 200 ducats. Cardinal Raffaelo was suspicious and sent a friend to Florence to investigate. He found Michelangelo and asked him to do a drawing for him. He could immediately see that the style was the same as that of the cupid. When the friend told Michelangelo that Lorenzo had gotten 200 ducats for the cupid for which Michelangelo had received only thirty, he willingly confessed his part in the fraud.

Then Michelangelo went to Rome. He signed a contract on August 26, 1498, to carve "the finest work in marble which today can show." Most people believe that he fulfilled his part of the contract by his *Pieta*, carving an exquisite statue of Our Lady holding the crucified body of her Son. The veins of the Christus are distended as though he were alive; the body looks as if it is sleeping, to emphasize Christ's love for us, rather than His agony. Mary is depicted as younger than her Son, symbolizing the youthful innocence and purity of her Immaculate Heart. In order to make the depiction of Mary holding Christ seem graceful and natural, she is much bigger than life; if she stood she would be seven feet tall. Each detail of the sculpture, from the folds in Mary's veil to the knuckles of Christ's hands, is lifelike and realistic. One interesting detail was added later. After the statue was put in place, Michelangelo overheard some people discussing it and attributing it to other artists. He went back at night and carved his name on Mary's sash so that no one could ever mistake who the artist was.

The *Pieta* shows Mary serene in offering Christ to the Father, and Christ serene in death. Michelangelo once wrote: "If life pleases us, death, being made by the hands of the same Creator, should not displease us."

Michelangelo was only twenty-three when he completed the *Pieta* (on front cover).

In 1501, he went back to Florence because he was homesick. He discovered an eighteen-foot chunk of marble which somebody had cut into and then abandoned. No one else wanted to tackle a piece of marble so big. So Michelangelo took the piece and carved the seventeen-foot tall statue of *David,* symbolizing the ideal man, putting into practice a belief he then held that contemplation of physical beauty would bring a man closer to God.

At the same time as he worked on *David,* he completed a commission to carve fifteen statues of saints in three years. He always took on more work than he had time to complete, barely taking time to eat or sleep. Sometimes he wore his boots for so long that when they were finally pulled off, the skin was peeled off as well.

When the statue of *David* was moved to the Piazza in Florence, it took four days, forty

St. Peter by Michelanglo
in the Siena Cathedral

men and fourteen rollers. He then completed the *Bruges Madonna,* an ethereally beautiful statue of the Blessed Mother with the infant Christ.

In the year 1505, Michelangelo was summoned to Rome by Pope Julius II, who hired him to carve statues for his tomb, which was to be 36 feet long, 24 feet wide and 36 feet high, with forty statues bigger than life-size. Michelangelo agreed to complete it in five years. He soon realized that the task was impossible, writing at one point: "If I were to remain in Rome, my own tomb would be prepared before that of the Pope." As time went on, Julius stopped coming to see the progress and sent no money. Michelangelo went to see him to demand payment, but was refused admittance. Michelangelo went off in a huff to Florence, ignoring all of Julius' frantic summonses. Finally the Pope apologized and persuaded Michelangelo to make a ten-foot tall bronze casting of him. Michelangelo did not understand the casting procedure, and it was more expensive than he expected. He hired three assistants, but could afford only one bed, so that they had to sleep by turns. The weather was miserably hot and the plague broke out. He fired one assistant and another quit. Finally he finished the statue. Only three years later, though, the Pope's enemies toppled the statue and melted it down.

Painting the Bible in Pictures

In 1508, Michelangelo abandoned everything else to work on the Sistine Chapel ceiling. The fact that he received the commission was the result of Bramante's scheming. Bramante was making little progress on St. Peter's. He was jealous of Michelangelo and wanted to discredit him. So he thought of a plan. The Pope wanted the Sistine Chapel painted. Bramante knew that such a project was practically impossible, that Michelangelo would dislike doing it, and would in all likelihood fail if he tried. Bramante convinced the Pope that Michelangelo was the only man for the job.

Moses by Michelangelo

Michelangelo tried to get out of doing it, but he could rarely refuse a commission and finally agreed.

The task was superhuman. The ceiling was 132 feet long, 44 feet wide and 68 feet high. He had to paint while lying on his back on a scaffolding above the floor. The ceiling was vaulted instead of flat. Paint fell on his face and eyes. His back, neck and eyes hurt. For weeks after finishing the project, he could not read anything unless he held it over his head.

The method chosen was *fresco* (painting on wet plaster). At first, the plaster was too wet and mold grew on it. He had to scrape all the paint off and do it again. He started with five assistants, but eventually dismissed them all,

Esther); the slaying of Holofernes by Judith; and the brazen serpent in the desert (which saved the Jewish people from the poisonous serpents). All along the outside are prophets and sybils (pagan prophets), set in niches which look as if they were sculpted, though all was done by paint.

The Sistine Chapel is a Bible in pictures, showing the power of God and His Divine Providence at work in His creation.

After Pope Julius died, Michelangelo worked on the Pope's tomb and completed *Moses,* the ideal man of maturity as *David* is the ideal youth. Moses is seated, holding the Ten Commandments, his eyes showing the anguish he feels that his people have broken their covenant with God by worshipping the golden calf.

Later, Michelangelo returned to the Sistine Chapel to paint *The Last Judgment* on the back wall. This painting shows a harsh Christ, with even the Blessed Mother afraid of Him. The rising and falling movement conveys a feeling of action. In the lower right-hand corner is a man with a snake wrapped around him. His face is that of a cardinal who had once annoyed Michelangelo with criticisms about his paintings. When the cardinal saw his portrait in the depths of hell, he complained to the Pope. The Pope told him that the keys of Peter extended only to Purgatory, not to Hell, so there was nothing he could do about it. One of the saints in Heaven is St. Bartholomew, holding his skin, since he was martyred by being flayed. The skin falls into a self-portrait of Michelangelo.

Then Michelangelo worked on St. Peter's. At the age of eighty-five he could still inspect the building on horseback. At almost ninety, he rode every evening in good weather and walked every day in good or bad weather. On February 12, 1564, he spent all day on the Rondanini *Pieta*. On February 14, he went riding, though the weather was cold and rainy. On February 18, he died.

Judith with the head of Holofernes

destroyed the parts they had painted, barred the chapel to all visitors except the Pope, and did the rest by himself. He took two years to do the first half and one year to do the last half.

The ceiling depicts the story of the creation and fall of man. In the center section are nine paintings from the first book of the Bible, Genesis: the creation of light and darkness; the gathering of the waters; the creation of the sun, moon and planets; the creation of Adam; the creation of Eve; the temptation and expulsion of Adam and Eve from the Garden; the Deluge; the sacrifice of Noah (Noe); and the drunkenness of Noah. The largest and most magnificent painting is the creation of Adam. The finger of God is just being removed from the finger of Adam, who has just come into existence, a beautiful human being created in the state of grace. Angels look on and Eve is depicted as being still in the mind of God.

In the four corners are four biblical scenes showing the triumph of God and His people over their enemies: David and Goliath; the hanging of Haman (Aman) (from the book of

How vain will then appear that favored
   art,
Sole idol long and monarch of my heart,
For all is vain that man desires below.
And now remorseful thoughts the past
   upbraid,
And fear of twofold death my soul alarms,
That which must come, and that beyond
   the grave:
Picture and sculpture lose their feeble
   charms,
And to that Love Divine I turn for aid,
Whom from the Cross extends His arms to
   save.

Thus did the greatest artist the world has even known humble himself before his Divine Master, whose glory he had so beautifully portrayed.

Last Judgment

Michelangelo's philosophy of art is contained in the following quote: "True art is made noble and religious by the mind producing it." And the mind, the soul, becomes ennobled by "the endeavor to create something perfect, for God is perfection, and whoever strives after perfection is striving for something divine."

Toward the end of his life he wrote this poem:

Well-nigh the voyage now is overpast,
   And my frail bark, through troubled seas
      and rude,
Draws near that common haven where at last
Of every action, be it evil or good,
Must due account be rendered.
   Well I know

St. Bartholomew

11

Chapter 2
Review Questions

1. Define fresco. _____
   _____

2. Define apprentice. _____
   _____

3. Describe the *Pieta*. _____
   _____

4. Describe *David*. _____
   _____

5. Describe the *Bruges Madonna*. _____
   _____

6. Describe the ceiling of the Sistine Chapel. _____
   _____

7. Describe *Moses*. _____
   _____

8. Describe *The Last Judgment*. _____
   _____

9. When was Michelangelo born? Where did he live? How did Michelangelo begin stonecutting?
   _____

10. How did Michelangelo happen to begin painting? _____
    _____

11. How old was Michelangelo when he studied painting? _____
    _____

12. What did Michelangelo's earliest paintings show? _____
    _____

13. What did Michelangelo study secretly? _____
_____

14. Where do we find Michelangelo's earliest existing statues? _____
_____

15. How old was Michelangelo when he finished the *Pieta*? _____
_____

16. What was Michelangelo's philosophy of art? _____
_____

17. Michelangelo said that "… God is perfection, and whoever strives after perfection is striving for something _____."

18. Read the poem that Michelangelo wrote. What is he saying about art in his poem?
_____
_____
_____
_____

19. Michelangelo had several things happen to him, (and even things that he did), which we would consider "unfortunate." What were some of those things?
_____
_____
_____
_____

20. Although Michelangelo had unfortunate things in his life, what kind of a person do you think he really was? Upon what do you base your opinion?
_____
_____
_____
_____

Chapter 3
The Artist of Mysteries

Leonardo da Vinci was born April 15, 1452, in Vinci, Tuscany (northern Italy). He was the illegitimate son of Piero da Vinci, of the upper middle class, and Catherine, a peasant woman. He lived with his mother until he was four, then was admitted to his father's house. Nothing is known of his boyhood; Leonardo never talked about it. We do know that he was exposed to the beautiful Tuscan countryside, which may have sparked his interest in landscapes. Vinci is on the side of Monte Albano, which descends toward the Arno Valley.

At fifteen, Leonardo was apprenticed in Florence to Andrea Della Verrocchio, a well-known artist. His gentle love of animals made him a vegetarian, and he would sometimes buy all the birds in a pet shop to set them free. A good singer and harp player, he was known as a charming young man who nevertheless kept much to himself. He once wrote: "If you are alone, you belong entirely to yourself. If you are accompanied by even one companion you belong only half to yourself."

Leonardo learned modern techniques of painting and perfected one in particular. Fifty years earlier, Brunelleschi had developed linear perspective. The effect of depth was achieved by the use of lines converging on a central vanishing point. Leonardo learned this technique but went beyond it. He achieved perspective by *chiaroscuro*, the use of light and dark to create three dimensions.

One of his earliest works was part of a larger work by Verrocchio, the *Baptism of Christ*. Leonardo painted a kneeling angel and part of the landscape. These earliest paintings revealed characteristics which would be found in later works: precise detail, puzzling expressions on faces, other worldly colors.

Da Vinci's *Annunciation* (1472) was his first complete painting. Noteworthy are the realistic detail of the plants in the foreground

Baptism of Christ by Verrocchio with detail by Leonardo

The Annunciation by Leonardo da Vinci

(Leonardo was fascinated with growing things) and the sense of real communication between the angel and Our Lady.

In 1481-82, Leonardo did his first major work, the *Adoration of the Magi*, an altarpiece. He showed how the awesome event of the Incarnation affected all men by including the whole sweep of humanity in his painting: young, old; poets, warriors; believers, doubters. The crumbling architecture symbolizes the decay of paganism. The palm in the center represents the tree of life, symbolizing the life-giving powers of grace. Mary, Joseph and the Christ Child are in the center, and the other figures advance and recede.

Futuristic Inventions

Leonardo felt he had no future in Florence because he did not get along with the powerful Medici family, so in 1482, he went north to Milan, which Lodovico Sforza had just conquered. Leonardo offered to be a military engineer for him, writing: "I have plans for destroying every fortress or other stronghold unless it has been founded on rock. I will make covered chariots, safe and unassailable. I can make cannon, mortars, and light ordnance (weapons), of very beautiful and useful shapes, quite different from those in common use." Leonardo had a lifelong interest in inventions and his sketchbooks are filled with the ideas that he presented to Sforza. For example, he designed a tank: a turtle-shaped armored car fitted with cannon, to be propelled by eight men within, using cranks and gears. An enemy would have been hard put to penetrate the armor, but it is doubtful that human muscle could have moved the heavy machine very far. He also designed a chariot armed with scythes with a mechanism that rotated the blades horizontally. Another of his ideas was a multibarreled cannon in which thirty-six guns were mounted in three tiers of twelve each; while one tier was being fired, the second was cooling and the third was being loaded. He also sketched a shrapnel-like bombshell that would explode on impact, scattering metal fragments. Sforza was not much interested in Leonardo's inventions, and none of them were ever built.

Sforza was not really interested in Leonardo's paintings either. The main commission he gave the artist was to do a huge statue of a horse. Leonardo worked on it off and on for sixteen years with meager pay. He finally built a twenty-six-foot clay model. Some pranksters shot it with arrows, rain water got inside, and it disintegrated.

After a plague, Leonardo suggested widening Milan's streets, making the buildings lower to let in the sunlight, and diverting streams to carry off the sewage. His hygienic plans were ignored.

Da Vinci wrote down everything that interested him in random order. His notes were like a loose-leaf encyclopedia with all the pages shuffled. He designed machines for making files, a rolling mill to produce sheet iron, and a cloth-shearing machine which would have doubled Milan's textile output. Sforza ignored them all and had him design costumes and scenery for court plays and install a bathtub. In 1499, Sforza was conquered by the king of France, and Leonardo returned to Florence.

Da Vinci's Masteriece

Leonardo left behind in Milan his masterpiece: *The Last Supper*. He had worked on the painting, which was originally intended as a wall decoration for the refectory (dining room) of the Monastery of Santa Maria, from 1495-1498. He solved the serious composition problem of thirteen men seated at a straight table by grouping them in four sets of three each with Christ in the center. He solved the problem of isolating Judas without the expedient used by earlier artists of seating him on the opposite side of the table. Leonardo's Judas is smaller and darker than the other apostles, pulling away from Christ and clutching a money bag. He showed emotions through the whole body, not just the face. Said Leonardo: "The painter has two objectives, man and the intention of his soul. The first is easy, the latter hard, because he has to represent it by the movements of the limbs." He used live models for all except Christ. He searched a long time for Judas, wandering the streets of Milan. The prior of Santa Maria complained at the delays, so Leonardo told him that the prior himself would do nicely as a model for Judas. The prior lodged no more complaints. All the time Leonardo was in Milan, the painting was uppermost in his mind. Some days he would be working on a horse statue for Sforza, then suddenly run over to the priory to add just a touch or two. He would spend days just looking at the painting. He surrounded the apostles with objects in everyday use to make the painting more immediate. The painting's perspective draws the viewer into the painting to feel as if he were a part of it.

The Last Supper

Leonardo Self-Portrait

The painting captures the moment when Christ has just announced that one of the disciples will betray Him. Judas is silent, staring, alone. The other disciples are questioning, arguing, denying. The light from the arched window forms a halo for Christ. He wears a red robe to symbolize the Passion. His arms are spread wide, His hands open. He is offering Himself for the salvation of mankind.

Unfortunately, *The Last Supper* has seriously deteriorated. The wall on which it was painted had been hastily rebuilt, filled with moisture-retaining rubble. Almost as soon as Leonardo finished, the paint began to flake. The area was subject to floods, and the dampness caused further deterioration. Restoration attempts by inept artists harmed the paintings of Peter, Andrew and James the Less. During World War II, Allied bombs destroyed the refectory but the painting escaped unharmed. A restoration was started in 1946 to remove all the accretions of the years and to restore Leonardo's original work, flake by flake. A special clear shellac was applied to make the paint adhere to the wall. The restoration was completed in 1954. Another restoration got underway in the 1980s, using the most modern techniques to discover Leonardo's true intentions.

Leonardo applied his talents to many endeavors. Besides his proposed inventions for Sforza, Leonardo designed a flying machine. It was based on human motor power, and a man simply could not supply enough power to lift it off the ground. Leonardo also designed a parachute. He discovered the distribution of leaves, the orientation of certain plants toward the sun, and the downward growth of roots attracted by gravity and he came close to discovering the laws of inertia. He was the first to do anatomical drawings, some of which are accurate enough to be used today. In addition, in his notebook on optics, a note reads, "Make glasses in order to see the moon large."

He returned to Florence, where the Servite monks asked for an altarpiece. He designed the painting *Virgin and Child with St. Anne*, although he never finished it. The composition was unusual. The Blessed Mother as an adult woman is actually sitting on St. Anne's lap, but the picture does not seem at all odd. Instead it has a sense of warmth and unity. The Christ Child plays with a lamb, symbolizing that He is the Lamb of God.

Leonardo could find no permanent patron in Florence, so he occupied himself by becoming a military engineer for Cesare Borgia, in spite of his professed hatred for war. He designed fortifications, drained marshes and made military maps.

He received a commission to decorate one wall of the council chamber in Florence. (The artist for the other wall was Michelangelo.) Leonardo chose a scene from a Florentine military victory, the Battle of

Mona Lisa

Anghiari. He put the paint on the wall, but he experimented with a new technique which was a failure. Within sixty years the paint had run off the wall in huge globs.

He was appointed to the committee to decide where to place Michelangelo's *David*, though Leonardo did not really like Michelangelo. He once wrote: "The sculptor in producing his work makes a manual effort in striking the marble or stone, whichever it is, to remove what is superfluous and extends beyond the figure shut in it. This demands a wholly mechanical exercise that is often accompanied by much sweat and this combines with the dust and turns into a crust of dirt. His face is covered with this paste and powdered with marble dust, like a baker, and he is covered with tiny chips as if it had snowed on him. His lodgings are dirty and filled with stone splinters and dust."

At this same time, Leonardo worked on the *Mona Lisa*, a portrait of a Florentine woman. The painting took three years. The background was typically Leonardo: accurate depictions of nature, but mysterious and otherworldly. The woman has always been a puzzle. Is she smiling? Is she planning some mischief? Is she innocent or guilty? Some critics think she represents Eve, who was both innocent and guilty: created in the innocence of sanctifying grace but guilty of original sin.

Because so many of his works were unfinished, people began calling him a failure. In 1513, he went to Rome. Although Leo X gave him thirty-three ducats a month, almost everyone ignored Leonardo as out of date and gave all attention to an upcoming young artist named Raphael. Depressed, Leonardo did a harsh self-portrait and a wild drawing of the Deluge, with frightening swirls of water engulfing the world.

Suddenly his life changed when he received a summons from King Francis I to come to France. The king gave Leonardo a house and income in exchange for nothing more than his conversation. Leonardo was there for three years, then died peacefully in 1519. Wrote one critic of him: "Leonardo was a searcher after unfathomable things, a painter of disquieting smiles that suggest the riddles of human personality, and of hands that point to mysteries beyond the earth."

Though most of his paintings remain mysterious, his greatest painting is *The Last Supper*, which treats of the great supernatural mystery of Christ's love, as He gave Himself in the Eucharist and on the Cross.

Chapter 3
Review Questions

1. When did Leonardo da Vinci live? What was his native country? In which two cities did he do most of his work?

2. Give significant information about Verrocchio. What did he do to influence future events?

3. Why is Lodovico Sforza important?

4. Who was Francis I? What did he do to influence future events?

5. Describe the *Annunciation*.

6. Describe the *Adoration of the Magi*.

7. Describe the *Last Supper*.

8. Describe the *Virgin and Child with St. Anne*.

9. Describe the *Mona Lisa*.

10. What are some interesting facets of Leonardo da Vinci's personality?

11. List at least five of Leonardo da Vinci's inventions.

12. What was the damage done to the *Last Supper*?
    _____
    _____

13. How is the *Last Supper* being restored? _____
    _____

14. How old was Leonardo da Vinci when he began learning from an artist?
    _____

15. What special technique did Leonardo da Vinci learn from his teacher?
    _____

16. What were three characteristics of Leonardo da Vinci's paintings discovered in his earliest paintings? Include chiaroscuro.
    _____
    _____
    _____

17. What kind of models did Leonardo use for his paintings?
    _____

18. We know that Leonardo was interested in landscapes when he was young. How does the painting of Mona Lisa show this interest?
    _____
    _____

19. Which pope gave money on a regular basis to Leonardo da Vinci?
    _____

20. Some historians believe that Leonardo da Vinci was one of the greatest thinkers who ever lived. Would you agree? Why or why not?
    _____
    _____
    _____
    _____

The Mystic Marriage of St. Catherine by Fra Bartolommeo

Chapter 4
Bride of Christ

Some of the greatest writings in Italian came from the pen of the twenty-fifth child of a Siennese cloth dyer named Benincasa. Born in 1347, St. Catherine of Siena grew up to be a mystic, a Doctor of the Church, and a saint.

When Catherine was young, she was the joy of her family, always lively and happy. When she became a teenager, she often would go by herself to pray. She did not feel called to marry and raise a family as most other young girls did, and she would not dress up and go to parties. Neither did she want to be a nun. Finally, at the age of sixteen, she received permission to become a member of the Third Order of St. Dominic. She wore the black and white habit of a Dominican nun, but she remained a layperson. For three years she never left her room except to go to Mass and confession; she spoke to no one except her confessor. She trained herself to live on a spoonful of herbs a day and to sleep only a few hours at night. She concentrated totally on Christ to learn His will for her.

Satan subjected her to many temptations to try to break her will. She would fight against these temptations with all her strength. After one particularly difficult struggle, God revealed Himself to her. She asked where He had been when she was fighting with Satan. He replied, "I was never closer to you than at that time."

Her Mystical Marriage

During the carnival season (just before Lent) one year, when the people gave themselves up to riotous feasting, Catherine prayed and did penance in her room for the sins that were being committed. She begged Christ to forgive all those who offended Him. The Lord appeared to her and said: "For My sake you have thrown away the vanity of this world. You have regarded the lusts of the senses as nothing and chosen Me as the only joy of your heart. Therefore now, while all the others here in your house feast and enjoy themselves with good food and drink, I will celebrate the solemn marriage feast with your soul." With Christ there appeared His Mother, St. John the Evangelist, St. Paul, and King David bearing a harp. As was the custom at betrothals, the mother, the Virgin Mary, stepped forward and took Catherine's right hand. She lifted it up towards Jesus, and bade Him bind His bride to Him in faith as He had promised. Jesus put a beautiful ring on her finger; it was adorned with a brilliant diamond surrounded by four large pearls. He spoke the solemn words which the bridegroom says to his bride: "I here betroth you as My bride in perfect faith, which for all time shall keep you pure and virgin, until our marriage is celebrated in Heaven with great rejoicing. My daughter, from now on you must undertake without protest all the works I come to demand of you; for armed with the power of faith, you shall triumphantly overcome all your opponents." The vision disappeared. Afterwards Catherine could see this ring on her finger, though it was invisible to all others. This mystical phenomenon is known as the "mystical marriage," a total consecration to Christ.

Serving Christ and Neighbor

Shortly after the mystical marriage, Christ appeared to her and told her to return to her family, take up her role as daughter and sister, and be of service to her family and her community. Catherine did not want to leave her life of prayer and was also afraid that she would be too weak to fulfill Christ's plans for her. Christ gave her the strength, and in obedience she left her room, walked downstairs, and for the first time in three years joined her family at the dinner table.

While still maintaining a deep prayer life, Catherine began a life of action, totally in service to others. She cared for her family, doing all the disagreeable jobs without a word of complaint. She went out into the community to nurse the sick, help the poor, and counsel the troubled. She continued to have ecstasies and would often be an object of ridicule. Gradually, though, her sanctity became so apparent that she gathered disciples around herself who came to her for spiritual advice and who followed her example of service to the poor.

Tirelessly, Catherine put herself at the service of all who came to her with their sorrows and difficulties. Young men railed at her for causing their friends to desert their sinful lives. She met them with friendliness; it was impossible to frighten her. It often happened that after leaving her they went to confession, and returned to Catherine to beg her to be their spiritual mother. In the hospitals she cared for those with the most disgusting diseases, often receiving no thanks for her generosity.

One morning, two robbers were being driven to the place of execution. As they stood in a wagon, the executioner's apprentices stabbed them with red-hot iron forks. Instead of crying for pity, they shouted curses and blasphemed God. Seeing them, Catherine knelt to pray, saying to Christ: "You saved the robber who hung on the cross beside You even though he was justly condemned for his crimes; save these

Papal Palace in Avignon

two miserable men who were created in Your image and redeemed by Your Precious Blood." As she continued kneeling, Christ granted her a vision of the two robbers. She saw them dragged through the streets to the place of execution. In the air around the two robbers, devils swarmed like mosquitoes, urging them to blasphemy and despair. Catherine's soul also floated round the criminals, and with love and tenderness she urged them to repentance. The carts drove up to the gate, and under the shadowy arch stood Christ, crowned with thorns and bleeding from the scourging. Catherine saw Him, and the two robbers saw Him too. Suddenly their curses ceased. They called for a priest. They wept from repentance as they confessed their sins and met death calmly and happily.

Her followers increased; they came to be known as the *Bella Brigata* (Happy Brigade). They were attracted to Catherine by her high spirits as well as her asceticism, by her practical common sense as well as by her spiritual insight and by her serenity and personal charm. She showed them how to love Christ in the midst of a busy life. She taught them the meaning of living in the awareness of the presence of God, of making every action a prayer. She taught them that if they wanted to reform the many evils in their society, they must reform themselves first.

Siena was ravaged by the plague, the Black Death; about a third of the inhabitants died of it. Tirelessly Catherine went from hospital to hospital, in and out of homes where the sick lay, to nurse them, pray for them, console them, and wash and clothe the bodies for burial. One of her good friends and supporters, Signore Matteo, caught the plague.

Catherine's disciples were sure he was dying. Her confessor, Blessed Raymond of Capua, said to her, "Mother, can you let this man die whom we are so fond of and who does so much good?" Catherine shook her head, "What are you saying? Do you think I am like God and can save a mortal man from death?"

Raymond replied, "You can say that to those who may believe it, but not to me who knows your secrets. I know well that you obtain from God all that you ask for with your whole heart."

Catherine smiled, "Rejoice then, for he will not die this time."

Raymond went into Matteo's house and there he sat in bed eating vegetables and raw onions, not exactly the diet for a man on the point of death.

Catherine called out, "Get up, Signore Matteo, get up. This is not the time to lie and laze in bed." Suddenly Matteo felt all pain and fever leave him. He jumped up, and Catherine fled, embarrassed because everyone was praising her. When he had finished his supper, Matteo returned to the hospital to care for those who were really sick.

On Laetare Sunday, 1375, Catherine had just received Holy Communion. She went into an ecstasy and was motionless for a long time. Suddenly it was as though she were lifted up; she knelt with closed eyes, her face shining with supernatural bliss. She stretched out her arms, with the palms of her hands outwards; then she fell suddenly to the ground as though mortally wounded. When she recovered consciousness, she whispered to Raymond, "Father, know that by the grace of Our Lord Jesus I now bear His stigmata on my body." The *stigmata* are the five wounds of Christ — the two nail wounds in the wrists, the two nail wounds in the feet, and the lance thrust on the side — borne on the body of one who loves Him. These wounds are a reminder to all of the great suffering Christ endured for our sins and they give the person who has the stigmata the chance to suffer with Christ. Catherine described her reception of the stigmata as follows: "I saw Our Savior on the Cross lean down toward me in a bright light. Then I saw how five jets of blood came from the five wounds and streamed toward my miserable body. The jets of blood changed to shining light, and as rays of light they struck my hands, feet, and heart."

A Doctor of the Church

The greatest evil afflicting the Church at this time was the Babylonian Captivity. Under the dominance of French political power, the Papacy had moved to Avignon, which was a papal territory surrounded by France. As the bishop of Rome, the Pope was the symbol of the universal Church. In France, though he was still the infallible Vicar of Christ, he was also too much under the control of the French king.

Catherine wrote to the Pope, begging him to restore unity to the Church, to rid it of corruption and greed. When the Pope did not heed her pleas, she went to Avignon herself in June 1376. Pope Gregory XI was deeply impressed by her obvious sanctity. Gregory was basically a good man who cared for the Church, but he was too weak to make the decision on his own to leave Avignon. Others in the papal court were not so pleased by Catherine's arrival; she was ridiculed and humiliated. The Pope listened to her, though, and drew from this frail woman the strength he needed. Following Catherine's advice, he left Avignon on September 13. When he arrived in Rome, showers of flowers and confetti greeted him. Thanks to Catherine, the Pope had come home.

There was still much work for Catherine. Gregory died within a year; the new Pope, a Roman, was not accepted by the French cardinals, who elected an antipope and went into *schism* (refusal to accept the true Pope's authority). Catherine had to work harder than ever to persuade the new and valid Pope, Urban, to govern the Church rightly. She simply accepted this new burden as another cross to bear with love for her Bridegroom. For a year she

Pope Gregory XI returns to Rome, led by St. Catherine

lived only on the Blessed Sacrament; she took less than an hour's sleep every night while she sent her letters all over Europe. Just thirty, her body had become a fragile, almost transparent vase, lighted from within by her burning soul. She was almost constantly in pain but not a word of complaint was heard.

It was during this time that St. Catherine dictated the glorious book known as *The Dialogue of St. Catherine*, a book which earned her the title Doctor of the Church (one who has contributed greatly to the wisdom of the Church). The book was written in the form of a dialogue between God and the soul. Here is a typical quotation:

> Now what greater joy can the bride have than to be conformed to her Bridegroom, and clothed with like raiment? So, since Christ crucified in His life chose naught but the Cross and pain, and clothed Him in this raiment, His bride holds herself blessed when she is clothed in this same raiment; and because she sees that the Bridegroom has loved her so beyond measure, she loves and receives Him with such love and desire as no tongue can suffice to tell.

In January 1380, while dictating a letter to Pope Urban, Catherine suffered a stroke. For the next four months, she endured great pains, offering them all to Christ for the sake of the Church. On April 29, she went into her death agony. She prayed for the Church and for all her spiritual children with such intense love that her disciples thought their hearts would break. "Beloved," she cried, "You call me, I come. Not through any service of mine, but through Your mercy and the power of Your Blood." She made the Sign of the Cross. Then, bowing her head, she said, "Father, into your hands I commit my spirit." As Catherine of Siena died, her face became as beautiful as an angel's, radiant with tenderness and happiness.

Chapter 4
Review Questions

1. Why is Siena important in history? _____

2. What was the Bella Brigata? What did St. Catherine teach them? _____

3. Who was Raymond of Capua? What did Catherine tell him? _____

4. What kind of a man was Pope Gregory XI? What made him leave Avignon?

5. Describe the mystical marriage of St. Catherine. _____

6. Define stigmata. _____

7. Define schism. _____

8. What is a Doctor of the Church? _____

9. Tell about St. Catherine of Siena's early life. Where did she live? When did she live?

10. After the mystical marriage, what did Christ ask Catherine to do?

11. What was the work that Catherine did to serve others in the community?

12. What miracles are associated with St. Catherine?

13. Tell about the event when St. Catherine received the stigmata.

14. What did St. Catherine do about the Babylonian Captivity?

15. What is the title of the book St. Catherine wrote?

16. What is her book about?

17. Tell about the death of St. Catherine of Siena.

18. What did Christ mean when He told St. Catherine, after a time of great temptation, "I was never closer to you than at that time"?

19. How did Catherine's life show the interrelationship of love of God and love of neighbor?

20. If you know about Blessed Teresa of Calcutta, can you think of similarities between her and St. Catherine?

Chapter 5
The Catholic Queen

More than any other person, Queen Isabel deserves the credit for making Spain a great nation. She also richly deserves the title "The Catholic Queen," which was bestowed upon her by the Pope.

Isabel was the daughter of King Juan II of Castile and his second wife, Isabel of Portugal. She was born in *Madrigal de Las Altas Torres* (which in Spanish means, Song of the High Towers), on April 22, 1451. King Juan was dominated by Don Alvaro de Luna, the constable of Castile, an evil genius who looted the crown, gave Church benefices to unworthy friends, was insolent and arrogant, and was responsible for the moral decay in court life. Queen Mother Isabel and Alvaro de Luna were at odds. He may have poisoned her when she was in confinement for Isabel's birth. The queen recovered but was left a victim of chronic nervous depression.

In 1454, Prince Alfonso was born. The queen persuaded the king to have Don Alvaro executed after he murdered one of her friends by throwing him out of a window. The king suffered much remorse and himself died in July, 1455. His son by his first marriage, Enrique IV (Henry IV), became king.

The queen took her two children to Arevalo, a city in the Avila region of Castile. Enrique gave her only a small allowance, and they were often in want. Isabel was a spirited child and learned to ride and hunt as well as any boy.

An Incorruptible Isabel at a Corrupt Court

Enrique's court was the most corrupt in Europe. A favorite daily pastime at his table was the invention of blasphemies. He was unfair and would go unpredictably from excessive leniency to excessive severity. Public and private morality were at a low point. He even gave bandits permission to collect taxes.

The king ordered the royal children, Isabel and Alfonso, brought to court in 1462 to get them under his control. Isabel's mother, who remained at home, slipped over into

Ferdinand and Isabella

insanity, but at the corrupt court, Isabel was incorruptible.

In July 1465, the Marquis de Villena led a rebellion against Enrique. Enrique easily yielded; he agreed to give Villena more power and to marry Isabel to Villena's brother, Don Pedro Giron. Giron was forty-three years old, Isabel fifteen. He was one of the most corrupt and evil men in Spain, even looking the part with his sinister black mustache. Isabel was horrified at the thought. Her best friend, Beatriz de Bobadilla, grabbed a dagger and said, "You will never marry that monster, for I swear before God that if he comes to take you, I will plunge this in his heart."

Isabel replied, "No, God abhors violence." She fasted for three days and prayed before the crucifix, "Dear God, compassionate Saviour, do not let me be given to this man." However, her uncompassionate half-brother, the king, would not listen to her pleas and instead sent for Pedro to come to the court in haste. The city was in a bustle, with gowns and decorations being prepared for the wedding. However, on the first evening after he began his trip, Giron fell into a choking fit. Three days later he was dead. Isabel was saved.

Rebellion broke out anew in 1468. In July, Isabel received word that her brother Alfonso was very ill. She rode out to meet him, but he was dead before she arrived. Isabel decided to stay at the convent of St. Ann in Avila rather than return to court. Archbishop Carrillo of Toledo arrived with noblemen to offer her the crown of Castile and Leon. Isabel refused because Enrique was the lawful king, saying, "If I should gain the throne by disobedience to him, how could I blame anyone who might raise his hand in disobedience to me?"

Villena now persuaded the king to marry Isabel to the weakling King Alfonso of Portugal (known as Alfonso the Fat) to get her out of the country. Enrique told her to consent or be imprisoned. Archbishop Carrillo, now her closest supporter, urged her to make excuses to delay the Portuguese marriage while he arranged a marriage with young Prince Ferdinand of Aragon, the Spanish kingdom second only to Castile in prestige and power.

Isabel's two messengers reached Zaragoza in Aragon on September 25, 1469. This was not a good time to find a bridegroom. Ferdinand was fighting for his father against rebels, his mother had just died, and his father was going blind from cataracts. Ferdinand agreed to the marriage but said he would come later, as soon as affairs settled down in Aragon. As a pledge, he sent Isabel a necklace of pearls and rubies.

Villena's spies found out where Isabel was. Villena sent 400 cavalry to arrest her. She was alone and had not heard from anyone in days. She heard shouts and many horses' hooves in the streets and expected the worst. She fell on her knees, commending her life to God's care. The door flew open to admit a figure in armor with rattling spurs. It was the Archbishop, arriving with 300 horsemen just a few hours ahead of Enrique's troops. Carrillo had been unable to raise any army and told Isabel that it was imperative that she marry Ferdinand as soon as possible. She sent a swift messenger to Ferdinand pleading, "For the love of God, come."

Ferdinand could not resist her plea. Knowing that Enrique's troops guarded the border to prevent his entry, he disguised himself as a muleteer and took two friends disguised as merchants. As Enrique rode north, a small caravan of merchants came west. They traveled unusually fast, well into the night. The young muleteer was especially handsome, but seemed nervous, pacing the courtyard at night. The second night out, he reached Burgos, the first friendly castle. It was late at night and the castle was locked. Ferdinand ran ahead and knocked. The guards in the castle, expecting the worst, pelted him with rocks. He shouted: "Do you want to kill me, you fools? It is Don Fernando. Let me in." The next morning, he was escorted to Leon. He changed clothes and rode to Valladolid, where Isabel awaited him, arriving on October 11. The next day Isabel wrote to Enrique, announcing her intentions and begging his blessing. On October 18, the young couple was married.

Enrique left them alone, and they knew peace and happiness. In October 1470, their first child, little Isabel, was born. Throughout Spain, conditions were worsening: famine, outlawry, and disease were rampant.

In 1474, Villena died. Enrique, now at a loss, died soon after on December 12, 1474. Isabel dressed in mourning and went to the Church of St. Michael in Segovia for Mass. Although flags were lowered and covered with black, the people cheered her. She agreed to be crowned the next day, the Feast of St. Lucy. The town was full of well-wishers on the frosty December morning. Isabel was dressed in white brocade trimmed with ermine and rode a white horse. In front of Isabel rode a herald who held, point upward, the Castilian sword of justice, symbol of her authority. Then came two pages bearing on a pillow the gold crown of King St. Fernando. She slowly mounted a high platform hung with rich colors. Trumpets blew. Speeches were made. As she was crowned, all the church bells rang and muskets were fired. Dignitaries knelt before her to kiss her hand and swear allegiance. Isabel then walked to the cathedral where she knelt before the altar to pray.

Earning the "Los Reyes Catolicos" Title

Isabel and Ferdinand now confronted a Castile that was on the brink of disaster. They had no money and no troops; they faced anarchy, corruption in the Church, corruption in the government, nobles too powerful, currency and economic affairs in chaos, the Moslems still controlling the province of Granada and raiding across the border, and Portugal attacking as Alfonso the Fat hoped to conquer Castile.

Their first task was to defeat Portugal. Alfonso's army was poised on the border with much support from Spanish nobles, who feared Isabel would take away some of the power they had gained from the weak Enrique. Carrillo turned against Isabel. The Archbishop was worldly. He was jealous of Cardinal Mendoza (whom she had appointed Chancellor) and wanted more land.

Isabel, now pregnant again, rode from town to town to get help. She raised troops, money and supplies. Isabel put her trust in God and spared herself not at all, riding tirelessly. At the end of June she took personal command of several thousand troops and drilled them expertly. They were animated by her spirit and her faith. Eventually, she had assembled an army of 42,000 in Valladolid. Ferdinand trained them while she gathered supplies. In July, Ferdinand marched them south. Isabel made her headquarters at Tordesillas to maintain Ferdinand's line of communication. There she suffered a miscarriage. Then a nobleman in the area went over to Alfonso's side, leaving Ferdinand isolated. He was forced to retreat and the army broke up. Isabel had to start all over.

Cardinal Mendoza suggested that the churches of Castile melt down their treasures of silverplate to pay for a new army, as a loan with no security except Isabel's word. They followed his suggestion. By December 1, Ferdinand had a new army of 15,000 well-trained men. He commanded the troops in the field, but the overall strategy was Isabel's. She positioned the troops and ordered the attacks. In the camps she insisted on high moral standards and daily Mass. No soldier is known to have objected.

Alfonso, with a greatly superior force, surrounded and besieged Ferdinand. Isabel, studying the situation, saw a small fort that wasa essential to Alfonso's line of communications. She sent a force in a secret surprise attack. They took the fort, cutting Alfonso's communications. Alfonso asked for a secret meeting with Ferdinand across the river that separated the armies. On the way across, Alfonso's boat sprang a leak and he nearly drowned. Alfonso asked for a fifteen-day truce. Mendoza, speaking for Isabel, refused. The next morning (March 1, 1476), the Portuguese were seen to have broken camp during the night and were sneaking away. Ferdinand ordered a pursuit. The Portuguese broke through Ferdinand's right wing, but Mendoza led a charge and captured Alfonso's standard. The right reformed and attacked in the dark. The Portuguese were routed and the soldiers cheered, "Castile for King Ferdinand and Queen Isabel!" Ferdinand showed mercy to the defeated soldiers. Isabel had been praying fervently, scarcely eating or sleeping. She ordered the clergy of Tordesillas to march through the streets singing the *Te Deum* (Hymn of Praise) in thanksgiving. She herself went barefoot to the monastery of St. Paul to give thanks.

Having defeated a foreign enemy, Isabel and Ferdinand now turned toward an internal enemy, the bandits. They decided to revive the *Santa Hermandad* (Spanish for Holy Brotherhood). The Santa Hermandad was a domestic police force set up in each town to keep law and order. Every 100 families would pay for one horseman, his arms and equipment. The Hermandad was especially popular among the poor because now they had protection from bandits. Soon banditry was wiped out in Castile.

Isabel rode from town to town to hear complaints and order reconciliations and restitutions. She was impartial and incorruptible. For example, in Medina del Campo, a poor woman came to her to complain that her husband had disappeared after a visit to a wealthy nobleman. The man's body was found on the nobleman's property. The wealthy man offered Isabel a bribe of 100,000 ducats to overlook the case. Isabel investigated, found the man guilty and had him executed.

On another occasion, Isabel had left her baby daughter with friends in Segovia. Suddenly she received word that baby Isabel and a handful of loyalists were besieged in the castle tower by town rebels who resented the rule of the mayor whom Isabel had appointed. She had no time to assemble troops, so with three friends, she rode sixty miles through the hot dust of day and the chill of night, arriving at dawn. The rebel leaders met her at the gate and said she might enter if the others remained outside, since her companions were friends of the hated mayor. Isabel said: "Tell those cavaliers and citizens of Segovia that I am Queen of Castile and this city is mine, for the King my father left it to me, and to enter what is mine I do not need any laws or conditions that they may lay down for me." She rode calmly into the city through the mob, which parted to let her by. She called the rebels forward and asked their grievances. They wanted to get rid of the official, Cabrera. Isabel agreed to remove him from office temporarily, pending an investigation. The people shouted "Viva la Reina!" (Long live the Queen), and the rebel leaders were driven off. She later found the charges unfounded and restored Cabrera to office, with the people remaining in full support of Isabel.

On June 30, 1478, Isabel gave birth to her son, Juan. She moved to Toledo, where her daughter Juana was born on November 6, 1479.

In 1481, Isabel sent her fleet to fight the Turks in the Mediterranean. With Ferdinand, she traveled to Aragon to have Prince Juan acknowledged as the heir to the throne. (In Aragon, only a son could inherit the throne.) In ten months she rode 2,000 miles on horseback, though she was expecting another child in the summer of 1482.

At Christmastime in 1481, the Moslems raided across the border, slaughtering and enslaving Christians. Isabel made up her mind to rid her kingdom of the Moslems at last and complete the war, known as the *Reconquista* or Reconquest, begun over 700 years before. There were three million Moslems still in Spain. Their capital was the high-walled city of Granada, set on a mountain slope surrounded by twenty fortified mountain cities. Isabel's armies would have to take the forts one by one. The first big victory was the siege of Alhambra. The Christians took the city and drove the Moslems out. Then the Moslems diverted the river so that no water was available to the city. The Spaniards were in danger of dying of thirst. Isabel sent out a plea for help. A relief force rode to the rescue just in time.

Isabel planned strategy right up to the time of the birth of her daughter, Maria. Ferdinand rode out with a small but enthusiastic army to attack the city of Loja. The Moslems defeated them because they did not have enough big guns, so Isabel had a new task: acquiring artillery. In 1483 more defeats came. Isabel prayed for guidance and rode from castle to town, restoring shattered morale. Nothing at all could cause her to give up because she knew that the war was just. The Moslems had been attacking Christians for 800 years.

At the end of 1484, the Marquis of Cadiz captured Zahara by scaling the walls while the Moslems were asleep during the noon siesta. In 1485, Isabel planned a systematic siege warfare to replace scattered raids and forays. She assembled an army and equipment. She organized the "Queen's Hospital," with field nurses to care for the sick and wounded, a novel idea in warfare. Thanks to Isabel's new equipment the army was victorious. Many Christian prisoners, ragged and starving, were released. Isabel received them on the steps of the cathedral, and they cheered their queen and liberator.

A Christian force was ambushed in the mountains. Isabel decided to besiege two neighboring castles in strategic locations. The passage to the castles was too narrow for the cannon. Though she was six months pregnant, she rode out to inspect the passes. Since they could not move the cannon through the mountain, she decided to move the mountain. She brought in 6,000 men to dig and blast a road. Working day and night they built a nine-mile road in twelve days. The Moors had been laughing at the Christians. They woke up to see the Spanish guns pointing at their walls. On December 15, Isabel's last child, Catherine, was born.

In January 1486, Isabel was in Cordoba. A man in frayed clothing arrived and asked for the king and queen. His name was Christopher Columbus, and Isabel was attracted by his plan to sail west to reach the Far East. Defeating the Moslems came first, though, and she had to tell him she could not help him at that time.

In 1488, the Christian armies were less successful, and Spain was swept by the plague. Isabel spent the winter in prayer and fasting. In 1489, she pawned her jewels and heirlooms to raise more money. Ferdinand was at Baza and wanted to retreat in the face of a superior force. Isabel said no, and the men supported her decision. The Moslems came out on the walls of the city to catch a glimpse of the legendary queen. Before the end of the year, Baza surrendered.

In 1490, she led her armies on to Granada. In April, the queen's oldest daughter Isabel celebrated a proxy marriage to Prince Alfonso of Portugal. The younger Isabel had seventy maids of honor and the ceremony

Christopher Columbus

The Fall of Granada, in the Royal Chapel

was accompanied by jousting and a festival. Isabel left in November to go to Portugal. Her marriage was happy.

On April 11, 1491, 50,000 men left Cordoba for the final campaign. Young Juan was knighted and rode with his father. In July, Isabel's tent caught on fire. The fire spread rapidly but fortunately was put out in time. Isabel decided to replace their camp of tents with a city of stone near Granada under the eyes of the Moslems. The city was finished in three months and named *Santa Fe* (Holy Faith). On the topmost tower were placed a silver cross of the Crusade and the banners of Castile and Aragon. The building of the city showed Isabel's determination and demoralized the Moslems.

By November, Granada was so low on food that the Moslems asked to begin negotiations. Isabel gave generous peace terms, saying that they could keep their language, costumes and property. The Moslem leader, Boabdil, formally surrendered on January 2, 1492. The cross and flags were put at the highest point in Granada as all the Spaniards knelt in the dust. Four days later, on the Feast of Epiphany, Isabel, Ferdinand, and their children led a triumphal procession into the city. For the first time in 770 years, Christians were in authority in Granada.

Victorious Spain

All Europe rejoiced in Spain's victory. For almost the first time since she was crowned, Isabel had leisure time. Then in July came a great sorrow. After just six months of marriage, her son-in-law Alfonso was killed by a fall from a horse. Young Isabel was inconsolable. Then Columbus reappeared. Isabel still had no money but the Santa Hermandad offered to loan the money necessary to finance his voyage. She signed an agreement naming Columbus "Admiral of the Ocean Sea." Columbus' ship sailed with a flag with the initials of Ferdinand and Isabel on it.

Cardinal Mendoza died and she appointed Cardinal Ximenes to take his place. Ximenes was humble and saintly. He and Isabel worked to reform the Church in Spain, getting rid of such evils as the selling of indulgences. By anticipating the complaints of Martin Luther, Isabel and Ximenes spared Spain the evils of the Protestant Revolt.

In March 1493, Isabel received the first reports from Columbus. She and Ferdinand stood as godparents for the baptism of the Indians he brought back with him. In 1496, they celebrated the double wedding of Juan and Juana to Margaret and Philip, the children of the Holy Roman Emperor. Juana was sulky and moody, Philip selfish and irresponsible. Their marriage was stormy and tragic. Margaret and Juan were deeply in love and a delightful couple. Young Isabel returned to Portugal to marry Alfonso's cousin Manuel. Then Isabel began receiving disturbing reports that Juan was ill. He died October 3, 1497. He died at peace with God, but this was probably Isabel's greatest sorrow.

During the last seven years of her life, Isabel knew illness, anxiety, and penance. In 1497, the Pope bestowed on Ferdinand and Isabel the title "*Los Reyes Catolicos*" (The Catholic Sovereigns). In 1498, her oldest daughter died an hour after giving birth to her son Miguel. Isabel cared for the baby, who was the heir to her throne, but he died at the age of two. In 1500, Maria married Manuel. She lived to be thirty-five and had a happy marriage with six sons and two daughters. Juana's moodiness slipped into insanity, causing Isabel much grief. In 1500, Juana's oldest son Charles was born; he would eventually be Isabel's heir. In 1499, Catherine and Prince Arthur of England were married by proxy, though Isabel delayed sending her youngest daughter away. Catherine finally left in November 1501, but six months later Arthur was dead and Catherine was betrothed to his brother Henry. Isabel did not live to see the sufferings Henry VIII would inflict on her youngest daughter, Catherine of Aragon.

Queen Isabel died on November 6, 1504, wearing the humble habit of a Franciscan nun. As she lay dying she said to Ferdinand, "Do not grieve for me; I am very tired and ready to go." She left as her legacy Spain: a country which she almost single-handedly forged out of chaos and saved from its enemies and endowed with the deep religious spirit which characterizes it to this day.

After Isabel's death, Ferdinand was never the same. He married again, but had no children. When he died in 1517, he was succeeded by his grandson Charles. Charles I of Spain inherited the best characteristics of his grandmother Isabel, following her example of always putting service of God and the welfare of his people before all else.

The Royal Chapel in Granada. Queen Isabel and Ferdinand are buried on the right, Juana (their daughter) and Philip (their son-in-law) on the left.

Chapter 5
Review Questions

1. Why did the Pope bestow on Queen Isabel the title "The Catholic Queen"?

2. When and where did Isabel live? What were the problems of Isabel's childhood?

3. Who was Juan II? Was he a good father? A good husband? A good king?

4. How did God save Isabel from being married to Don Pedro Giron?

5. What bad things did Don Alvaro de Luna do? Why did the king finally execute him?

6. Who was Enrique IV? What were some of the bad things that Enrique did or allowed?

7. Who was the Marquis de Villena? After his brother died, why did he want Isabel to marry Alfonso of Portugal?

8. Why did Isabel refuse to rebel against Enrique?

9. Explain how Archbishop Carrillo helped Isabel to escape marriage to King Alfonso.

10. Describe Ferdinand's adventures as he rides to meet Isabel to marry her.

11. Why was the kingdom of Aragon important?

12. Describe the coronation of Isabel.

13. What were the problems Ferdinand and Isabel faced as they ascended the throne of Castile?

14. How did Queen Isabel and King Ferdinand defeat Alfonso the Fat?

15. How did King Ferdinand and Queen Isabel eliminate banditry?

16. How did Queen Isabel establish justice in Castile?

17. What did the Moslems do in 1481 which caused Isabel to go to war?

18. Why were the Moslems defeating Ferdinand in 1483? What did Isabel do about it?

19. What was Queen Isabel's systematic plan to win against the Moslems in 1485?

20. Why was the building of the city of Santa Fe so important?

21. Why did the Moslems agree to surrender in 1491? What were the generous peace terms of Isabel?

22. How did Isabel work to reform the Church in Spain?

23. What were the consequences of the reform of the Church in Spain?

24. What was the legacy Queen Isabel left for Spain?

25. Why were Queen Isabel and King Ferdinand given the title "Los Reyes Catolicos"? What did they do to earn the title?

Chapter 6
God Alone Sufficeth

Not long after Queen Isabel died, another Spanish woman was born who would accomplish as much in the spiritual realm as Isabel did in the political. This woman was St. Teresa of Avila.

St. Teresa was born on March 28, 1515. Her parents were Don Alonso Cepeda and his second wife, Beatriz de Ahumada. Don Alonso had two children by his first wife: a son, Juan, and a daughter, Maria. His first wife died after three years of marriage, and in 1509, he married Beatriz when he was thirty and she fourteen. Their children were Fernando, Rodrigo, Teresa, Lorenzo, Antonio, Pedro, Jeronimo and Juana. The family was fairly well off with many servants. Avila had provided many brave men to fight in Spain's armies and Teresa loved to hear battle stories. She was closest to Rodrigo, and the two would hide in the garden for religious discussions. Teresa had an attraction to the idea of martyrdom, probably based partly on the fact that the finest church in Avila had the relics of three child martyrs of Rome: Vincent, Cristeta, and Sabina.

A Reluctant Beauty

When Teresa was seven, she decided that she wanted to be a martyr, and the quickest way to do that was to go to North Africa where, she was sure, the Moslems would kill her. She persuaded Rodrigo, who was more reluctant, to run away with her. At daybreak they slipped out the gates, with a few crusts of bread tied up in a handkerchief. At a hill outside Avila, at a spot known as Cuatro Postes (Four Pillars), they ran into their Uncle Francisco who promptly took them home. Rodrigo, whose feet hurt already, blamed Teresa for the whole thing: "It was *la niña* (the little girl) who dragged me into it." Both children were soundly punished.

Teresa then decided that she would turn herself into a nun. She tried to build a cloister with stones from the garden, but it collapsed. The cloth disappeared from the house – she was making herself a nun's habit. Teresa's impatient longing for instant sanctity succeeded only in getting her into trouble.

By the time she was fifteen, she was known as one of the most beautiful girls in Avila. More frivolous and less pious than in her younger days, she loved to dress up and to be flattered, and she fancied herself in love with a handsome young man, Pedro. To put a stop to her flirtations, her father sent her at sixteen to the convent of the Augustinian nuns for an education and discipline. Teresa was angry and did not want to go. Once there, she still kept in contact with her worldly friends. Gradually, though, she began to face up to her selfishness, struggling to surrender her self-will to God. She began to worry, "Should I be a nun or a wife?"

St. Therese of Avila, by Rubens

The nervous strain and exhaustion made her ill as she tried to think of reasons why she should not be a nun. She returned home, kept house for her family, and debated with herself about her future. She knew that God was calling her, and she could not avoid His call. Finally, she decided to stop debating. At the age of twenty, with no warning to anyone, she left home and went to the Carmelite Convent of the Incarnation.

After she entered the convent, Teresa convinced herself that her spiritual life would be taken care of. Although she prayed, wore the habit, and obeyed the rules, she was still far too selfish and self-willed. She recognized sins in herself, but did not know how to overcome them. So she began extravagant penances and made herself ill. She suffered terrible pain, much of it brought on by nervousness, and lost weight. She had prolonged fainting fits. Finally, everyone was sure she was going to die. Her father took her to a doctor in Becedas, hoping for a miracle cure. The treatments she was given there almost had the opposite effect. She was rubbed with scorpion oil, bled, and burned with poultices. Finally her uncle, Don Pedro, took her into his house. He taught her to pray, to rely on God instead of herself, to meditate on the Passion. Though her health showed no improvement, she was happy and at peace.

Returning home, she sank into unconsciousness and was given the last rites. The doctor held a mirror in front of her mouth. No breath clouded the mirror, so he pronounced her dead. The nuns prepared her shroud and dug her grave. While the death watch was kept in her room, she suddenly opened her eyes and asked, "Why did you call me back?"

Though she lived, she remained bedridden for nine months more, suffering great pain. Then she begged to return to the convent. The nuns granted her appeal, but she remained for three years in the infirmary, paralyzed. Her sufferings purified her of self-love. Slowly she forced herself to get out of bed and crawl. She prayed to St. Joseph. One day, she felt she could walk. She pulled herself up and began walking around. Everyone felt that a miracle had occurred. (She was twenty-six years old at this time.)

Teresa now became very popular as everyone felt that she was especially favored by God. Still retaining her beauty and charm, she gradually began slipping back to her worldly ways and virtually ceased to pray. As a child she had wanted instant sanctity; now she was learning that holiness does not come easily. The convent itself did not help her spiritually because it was very worldly, with most of the young women there not having a religious vocation. They received and paid visits and made little pretense at prayer or penance.

A modern painting of St. Teresa receiving inspiration from the Holy Spirit as she writes, "either to suffer or to die," a reflection of her desire to suffer for God on earth and to be united with Him in death.

God did not leave Teresa alone. Her father's holy death reminded her of the importance of prayer. A vision of the *Ecce Homo* (Christ as He appeared after the scourging and crowning with thorns) tore her away from worldliness. She turned wholeheartedly to Christ and began to receive many spiritual favors, such as ecstasies and visions.

Her new dedication to Christ did not mean that her life would be smooth henceforth. Far from it. The other nuns criticized her and ridiculed her. Her first spiritual director told her that her spiritual favors were from the devil.

Reforming the Religious Life

Teresa would not let the taunts of others turn her from God. She knew that Christ had given her these blessings not because of any merits of her own but because He had work for her to do. The Carmelite Order needed to be reformed, to return to spirituality, to reject worldliness, and Christ had chosen Teresa to be the instrument of the reform.

She realized that she would have to begin the reform by starting her own convent, so she took the first step of buying a small house to be transformed into a convent. Many difficulties arose. Once, even a wall fell down. Finally, at dawn on August 24, 1562, a bell rang for the first time at the house, now transformed into St. Joseph's Convent. Teresa and thirteen nuns gathered for their first Mass, having vowed to live in total poverty.

Teresa and her nuns were delighted to be practicing the prayer and penance of the original Carmelite rule. They were not to be left in peace, however. The Prioress at the Incarnation ordered her to return. Teresa, with soldier's blood in her veins, prized obedience above all other virtues. Leaving her nuns at their frugal meal, she returned to the Incarnation. The prioress expected a rebel; instead, Teresa was all humble obedience. Eventually the uproar died down, and after six months, Teresa was permitted to return.

Teresa left her shoes before the statue of the Virgin in San Vicente Church to symbolize that she was dead to the world; hence her order was known as the discalced (barefoot) Carmelites. Their religious life was based on enclosure (they never left the convent), silence and recollection. Teresa emphasized the virtues of mutual charity, detachment from material things and humility. The nuns earned the money for their expenses by spinning, and Teresa worked as much as the rest. Once when Teresa was frying eggs in the kitchen, she went into an ecstasy. One of the nuns saw her and cried, "Our Mother will upset the little oil that's left to us on the fire!" But she did not. She fried the eggs perfectly.

Once a bishop came to visit. He had a beautiful crucifix with him. When he was ready to leave, the nuns prayed, "Jesus crucified, stay with us." Teresa was embarrassed that her nuns wanted the crucifix, but the bishop was charmed. He let them keep it.

The nuns wanted permission to wear rough serge cloth next to their skin as a penance, but the superiors were afraid of an infestation of lice. So the nuns made up a prayer and sang it, asking the Lord to deliver them from lice and all crawling creatures. Their prayer was answered.

After dinner the nuns had recreation, when they would sing, dance, and recite poetry. After the nuns went to bed, Teresa would go round the cloister, blessing each nun. She was the last to bed, staying up in her small cell to write the books which made her a Doctor of the Church.

The Founder of Numerous Convents

After a visit with a priest from the New World, Teresa realized that the world was full of souls to be saved and that her responsibilities extended to much more than one convent. The Master General of the Carmelites, after a visit with the Pope, authorized her to found convents all over Castile, including houses for men. She had no money, but that did not stop her.

Teresa's first new foundation was in Medina del Campo, where she went with six nuns. The townspeople called her crazy. She had to sneak into her new house because the Augustinians living nearby did not want her there. The house itself was falling apart, and Teresa had to supervise the reconstruction herself.

At this time she met the twenty-four-year-old John of San Matias, who was to become St. John of the Cross. (San Juan de la Cruz), the reformer of the male Carmelites. He and Teresa became fast friends. Amidst all her other duties, she also found time to write to King Philip II, urging him to be firm against heresy.

In 1568, she founded convents at Malagon and at Valladolid as well as the first friary for men. In 1569, she founded houses at Toledo and Pastrana, in 1570 at Salamanca, in 1571 at Alba da Tormes, in 1574 at Segovia, and in 1575 at Beas. None of these foundations were easy, as she faced constant opposition. Her talent for leadership and her total trust in God pulled her through. She was left with three ducats, but she said, "Teresa, three ducats, and God equal everything." She bought two mats, one blanket, and two pictures for the chapel. The next morning, they rang the bell for Mass.

On October 6, 1571, Teresa was ordered back to the Incarnation Convent as prioress. However, the 130 nuns there were angry at the thought of losing their comforts. Teresa took the statue of St. Joseph with her as she did to all her foundations. When she entered, she was booed. She calmly placed a statue of the Blessed Mother in the prioress' chair and said that Mary would be prioress. The nuns responded to her gentleness and compassion, her motherly love for them. She installed John of the Cross as confessor, and he taught them how to pray. He was also Teresa's spiritual director and further redefined her spiritual life. It was at this time that she reached the spiritual peak of the mystical marriage, the closest union with Christ possible on this earth. On the Feast of the Trinity, she and John were speaking of the Trinity when suddenly they soared to the ceiling in ecstasy.

She had many adventures with her foundations. On her way to Beas, she had to pass over a narrow mountain pass in a mulecart. The way was dangerous and the day foggy. As the nuns prayed in the cart, they and the driver heard a voice saying, "Stop! Go back." They could not see the person speaking but they took his advice. They narrowly missed falling over the side of the mountain thanks to this warning. Teresa was sure that it was St. Joseph who had warned them.

In 1577, the nuns at the Incarnation freely elected Teresa as prioress. The priest who was Provincial (in overall authority over the convents of the area) was furious. He said that everyone who voted for Teresa was excommunicated. He crushed the ballots with his fist, then stamped on them and burned them. The nuns refused to give in, and Teresa remained as prioress.

Tomb of St. John of the Cross

At this point John was arrested by the Carmelite friars who did not want to reform. In Avila, Teresa prayed for John. Then Teresa herself fell down the stairs and broke her arm, but she offered it all up for John's safety.

The Seven Mansions

At this time Teresa wrote her masterpiece, *Interior Castle*, describing seven mansions, or stages, of the spiritual life. The entrance gate to the castle is prayer. The first mansion has snakes and vipers. The soul is in a state of grace, but still is struggling against temptations to mortal sin. In the second mansion, the soul prays faithfully, but is still tempted toward venial sins. In the third mansion, the soul avoids most sins, but the soul is still much too concerned with self and gives way to many imperfections. The big change comes between the third and fourth mansions. In the fourth mansion the soul is freed from selfishness and begins to receive spiritual favors. In the fifth, the soul concentrates on prayer, something like a mystical engagement. In the sixth mansion, the soul experiences ecstasies and many gifts; effort is not needed for prayer. The seventh mansion is total union with God, the "mystical marriage." God works in the soul with no effort on the soul's part. Teresa herself had achieved the seventh mansion, and her book has guided many other souls along their spiritual pilgrimage toward union with God.

In 1578, Teresa was still suffering from her broken arm and from worries about John, who was confined in a tiny cell, prevented even from writing. After nine months of imprisonment, the Blessed Virgin Mary appeared to him and showed him an escape route. He had to tie strips of cloth together so that he could climb out of a window. He escaped from his pursuers by going into a cloister and hearing confessions.

Though old and ill, Teresa visited all of her convents during 1579. She also founded two more. In 1580, she became seriously ill with influenza and never fully recovered. She completed the Rule and Constitution for her order, every detail a model of charity and common sense: "Never punish until your anger has died down"; novices must have "good health and common sense"; the prioress is at the head of the list for sweeping duties.

In April 1582, she left in the pouring rain for Burgos to found yet another convent. On the way her cart tipped over in a stream and she was soaked. When she complained to the Lord, He responded, "Teresa, don't you know that this is the way I treat my friends?" reminding her that suffering is the mark of the friends of Christ.

Teresa, on very good terms indeed with Our Lord, responded: "If this is the way you treat your friends, then it's no wonder you have so few!"

At Burgos she had the usual difficulties in establishing the convent. She finally moved into two small rooms on the top floor of a hospital. The only reason she got them was that they had the reputation of being haunted. Finally the bishop gave in and let her have a house.

Teresa died on October 4, 1582, in Alba da Tormes. Her body remained incorrupt and regained its youthful beauty. She was canonized in 1622, and in the twentieth century declared a Doctor of the Church.

Teresa's life shows us many things. We learn that sanctity does not come easily, and that one must face and overcome many trials in the service of God. We learn that we must do God's will no matter what difficulties come to us, and that if we trust in Him the difficulties will be overcome. We learn above all that prayer and closeness to God must come first if any activity undertaken in God's name is to succeed. Prayer, then action, then more prayer, and always prayer: that is the lesson of St. Teresa of Avila, mystic, author, founder, reformer, Doctor, saint of God.

Chapter 6
Review Questions

1. When and where did Teresa of Avila live?

2. What did Teresa do when she was only seven?

3. What was the inner struggle Teresa had between the ages of 15 and 20?

4. What happened to Teresa at the Incarnation Convent?

5. Who was Don Pedro? What did he teach Teresa?

6. What did Our Lord do to pull Teresa back from her life of worldliness?

7. Why did Teresa decide to start her own convent? What was the name of her convent? What did her nuns vow to do?

8. Describe the way of life of the Discalced Carmelites of Teresa.

9. What made Teresa decide to start other convents?

10. Who was St. John of the Cross? How did he help Teresa?

11. Who arrested St. John, and why?

Briefly explain each of the seven mansions of The Interior Castle.

12. First Mansion: _____

13. Second Mansion: _____

14. Third Mansion: _____

15. Fourth Mansion: _____

16. Fifth Mansion: _____

17. Sixth Mansion: _____

18. Seventh Mansion: _____

19. How did St. John of the Cross escape from prison?
    _____
    _____

20. After Teresa died, what happened to her body?
    _____

21. When was Teresa canonized a saint?
    _____

22. What title was given St. Teresa by the Church?
    _____

What four things does St. Teresa's life teach us?

23. First: _____

24. Second: _____

25. Third: _____

26. Fourth: _____

St. Elizabeth, by Murillo

Chapter 7

Roses and Bread

The patron saint of Portugal, the other country on the Iberian Peninsula, is St. Elizabeth of Portugal (1271-1336). She was born in Zaragoza, the capital of Aragon, then still an independent country. (How long would it be before Aragon and Castile would be united under Isabel and Ferdinand?) The court of Aragon in which she grew up was very immoral, but Elizabeth maintained her virtue and her integrity. In 1283, when she was twelve, she was married to Denis of Portugal. The marriage was political, to bring about an alliance between Portugal and Aragon. In 1290 she gave birth to a daughter, Constance, and in 1291, a son, Alfonso.

Peacemaker Queen

Elizabeth is known as "The Peacemaker" because all her life she tried to reconcile warring factions. Her first peacemaking effort concerned a quarrel between her husband Denis and her brother Alfonso. Elizabeth summoned an arbitration council, but the two men angrily rejected the terms of reconciliation. Elizabeth refused to give up. To ease bad feelings, she made the personal sacrifice of giving over some of her own possessions to the niece of Alfonso. This gesture shamed the quarreling men into making peace.

As queen, Elizabeth set an example of justice and charity. For instance, she set up a college at Coimbra for orphan girls where they would be trained in farming so they could marry the sons of farmers. She gave them farms from her own estates as wedding gifts.

One of the noblemen in the court developed an intense hatred for Elizabeth because her purity and goodness were an affront to his own wickedness. He went to the king and told him that Elizabeth had been unfaithful to him with one of the pages in the court. Denis, who was not known for his self-control, flew into a rage. He summoned the overseer in charge of his lime-kiln and told him that he was sending to him a wicked man whom the overseer was to throw into the furnace. Then Denis summoned the page who had been slandered and sent him to the lime-kiln with a message, presuming that the overseer would throw him into the furnace and thus eliminate him from the court. On the way to the lime-kiln, the unsuspecting page heard the bells ringing for Mass. He decided to stop off at church for Mass before finishing his errand. The nobleman, meanwhile, waited impatiently for word that the page was dead. Finally he could wait no longer and went off to the lime-kiln to see for himself. He arrived at the lime-kiln. The overseer, assuming that the nobleman was the one he was supposed to execute, threw him into the furnace. Thus was the nobleman justly punished.

Elizabeth continued her peacemaking efforts, reconciling her brother, King James of Aragon, and Ferdinand of Castile who had married her daughter Constance.

Miraculous Charity

Elizabeth's charity was overflowing. She constantly gave out alms to all those who needed it, so much so that her husband objected. One day she was on her way to visit a poor family with her apron full of bread. Her husband intercepted her and demanded to know what she was carrying in her apron. She opened it up and he saw only roses, so he let her go on her way.

Another time, a miracle the reverse of

Bread and Roses

that one occurred. Elizabeth was sponsoring the building of a church in honor of the Holy Spirit. The workmen had run out of money. When they asked Elizabeth for money, she said she had nothing to give them but roses. When she gathered the roses, they miraculously changed to gold pieces.

Then Elizabeth began to know deep tragedy. Her husband was unfaithful and sent her away from the court. Her daughter and her son-in-law died in 1312. Her son was scheming to seize the throne and had no time to spare for his mother. Elizabeth never complained. She simply placed all of her trust in God.

The men of Coimbra came to her and offered to lead a rebellion in her name to restore to her the rights due her as queen. The Peacemaker Queen refused to do anything to cause suffering or bloodshed, saying, "Let us commit our ways to Providence. Let us trust in God alone." One of the noblemen on her side said of her, "She would rather bear poverty and endure all the injuries inflicted on her than consent that such a war should be waged. She expressly forbade these generals to begin a war for these reasons."

Her patience was rewarded when the king recalled her to court. For a time she was able to persuade her son to stop rebelling against his father, but war broke out again. Denis and Alfonso waged war against each other in a bloody battle at Alvalade. The fighting was at a high pitch when suddenly the lookout shouted that a stranger was riding onto the battlefield. It was Elizabeth, riding into the midst of the battle, risking death to persuade her husband and son to stop this terrible war. So impressed were they by her courage that they were reconciled.

Service to the Poor

In 1325, King Denis died. Elizabeth became a Poor Clare nun and devoted herself to the service of the poor. During Holy Week she always made a point to wash the feet of twelve poor persons in a gesture of humility and fraternal love. Once a sentinel found a lame leper. Angry that this man would dare show himself in spite of his loathsome disease, the sentinel struck the leper with a stick and seriously wounded him. Elizabeth came on the scene, reprimanded the sentinel and gently bound up the leper's wound. She gave him a warm place to spend the night. The next day,

Batalha (Battle) Monastery in Portugal

the man's wound and his leprosy had both disappeared, miraculously cured by Christ through the intercession of Elizabeth.

In the summer of 1336, her son went to war against the King of Castile. Elizabeth was in pain from a tumor and blood poisoning in her arm. Nevertheless, she left the convent in the intense heat to go to Estremez. She summoned the two kings into her presence. They did not dare refuse to come, so great was her prestige among the people. She emphasized to them the great evils brought upon the people by the continuing warfare and feelingly depicted to them their sufferings, especially of the poor. Once again, Elizabeth was a Peacemaker.

The next day she was too weak to leave her tent. The following day the priest was called to give her Viaticum. Her daughter-in-law Beatriz was at her side. Suddenly, Elizabeth said, "My child, bring a chair for this Lady."

Beatriz looked around the room, puzzled, asking, "Which lady?"

Elizabeth said gently, "She who is drawing near, smiling, in garments of white."

Her last words were, "Mary, Mother of Grace, Mother of Mercy, from the foe shield us, in the hour of death take us." She died on July 4, 1336.

Since St. Elizabeth's feast day is the same day as Independence Day in the United States, her feast is rarely celebrated in this country. It is fitting that we pray to Elizabeth on that day, though, asking her to intercede for our own country, that we may know peace, that we may never wage war unjustly, that we will always be concerned with the sufferings of the innocent.

Portugal is also important to Catholics because of the apparitions of Our Lady of Fatima, and our study of Portugal should remind us that Our Lady asked us to pray the Rosary for peace and for the conversion of Russia. Have we been heeding her requests?

Zaragoza - Birthplace of St. Elizabeth

Chapter 7
Review Questions

1. Where was Elizabeth born? Where did she live? Was the government, that is, the royal court, moral or immoral?

2. What happened to Elizabeth when she was only twelve?

3. Why would you assume that Elizabeth did not love her new husband?

4. How did Queen Elizabeth make peace between her husband and her brother?

5. How did Queen Elizabeth set an example for justice and charity?

6. An evil nobleman hated Queen Elizabeth because of which of her qualities?

7. What saved the page from being killed by the king?

8. What was the miracle that happened when the workmen building a church ran out of money?

9. How did Queen Elizabeth's husband make her very unhappy?

10. Why did Queen Elizabeth's son make her unhappy?

11. Why did Queen Elizabeth not allow a rebellion or war against the court?

12. Whom did Queen Elizabeth want to trust to take care of the problems of the court?

13. What did Queen Elizabeth do to stop the battle between her son and her husband?
    _____

14. After King Denis died, what did Queen Elizabeth do?
    _____

15. What did the queen do during Holy Week in a gesture of love?
    _____

16. What was the miracle that happened to a leper because of Elizabeth?
    _____

17. How did Queen Elizabeth prove she was still a peacemaker the day before she died?
    _____

18. Whom did Queen Elizabeth see on her deathbed?
    _____

19. For what causes should we ask St. Elizabeth for her intercession?
    _____

20. In what ways is St. Elizabeth of Portugal a model for rulers and others in authority?
    _____

Belem Tower in Lisbon Harbor

49

Chapter 8
Eldest Daughter of the Church

France is defined by the Pyrenees, the Alps, and the Rhine. In pre-Christian days it was populated by Celtic Gauls, whose Druid priests presided over a form of nature worship. Julius Caesar conquered Gaul in 52 B.C., and a temple to Jupiter was built on the site of a Druid altar in the city that came to be known as Paris, from the Latin word *par* meaning *boat*, because the island in the center of the Seine, which was the heart of the city, was shaped like a boat. (The Parisii were excellent boatmen and had a motto for their city: It may rock, but it never sinks.)

The first Christian diocese was Lyon, established by the martyr,-Saint Pothinus. St. Irenaeus, who had been taught by Polycarp, who in turn had been taught by the Apostle John, was one of its early bishops. Parisian merchants had spoken to Irenaeus and were impressed by him, but the city still was unconverted. Under Marcus Aurelius (161-180) persecution came to Lyon, and children as well as adults were tied in nets to be gored by wild bulls.

In 250 A.D., Rusticus, Eleutherius, and Dionysius (Denis) arrived at the city on the Seine, the first great missionary effort to convert Paris. They immediately began preaching in the square in front of the statue of Jupiter. The crowd ridiculed the missionaries. They were arrested, tortured, beheaded. Legend has it that St. Denis' head was being kicked around by irreverent bystanders. To save it from disrespect, he picked up his head and walked four miles before laying it down and his body beside it. The Church of Saint-Denis was built on that spot, and statues of him in France's great churches show him with his head tucked under his arm. The Parisians eventually grew to love him and carried his banner into battle.

In 312, came the conversion of Constantine, and in 363, the first Christian church was completed in Paris on the site of the old temple of Jupiter (it would one day be the site of the great Cathedral of Notre Dame). It was *St. Étienne*, St. Stephen's Church, built in basilica style; its fourth wall was the city wall and it used stones from Jupiter's temple.

Saint Genevieve

In 451, Paris found itself under attack from the savage Huns, the "Scourge of God." The city found its leader in a most unlikely person. Genevieve was a young orphan who tended sheep outside the city. The Bishop of Paris, St. Germain, brought her to Paris at the age of eight. She went to school, prayed and cared for the sick, crippled, and the poor. A

Julius Caesar

A painting of *The Baptism of Clovis* in Reims

stunningly beautiful young woman, she could have married royally, but she preferred to be a Bride of Christ. By the time she was twenty-five, she had built a hospital, the Hotel Dieu, near St. Étienne's. There is still a hospital near the site today. Two hundred years earlier, the site had been a small house by the river for storm-tossed travelers and invalids under the supervision of St. Julien le Pauvre, a ferryman who rowed pilgrims across the river in the worst of weather for no charge. Once, so the story goes, a pilgrim roused St. Julien out of bed on a stormy night. The wind extinguished his lantern, but somehow, as he rowed, the ship was bathed in a splendid glow from the garments of the passenger. When they reached the other side, the passenger blessed St. Julien and suddenly departed. Christ had come to Paris. Genevieve continued this tradition of service. She had no modern equipment, but made up for it by loving care, serving the sick until her death at the age of eighty-two.

As the Hunnish horde filled the hills around Paris, the people called upon Genevieve, because they knew that only God's grace could save them; and Genevieve, as a living saint, could beg that grace. (Only five times afterwards would enemies set foot in Paris: the Norse, the English during the Hundred Years War, the allies at Napoleon's fall, the Prussians in 1870, and the Nazis in 1940, though eighty or more other attempts were made. The people always prayed to St. Genevieve when enemies threatened Paris.) Four armies arrayed themselves against the Huns: Aetius from Rome, Merovee with the Franks, Theodoric and the Visigoths, and Genevieve's Parisians. A whole host of Huns covered the plains at Chalons. To the south rode the Visigoths and the Romans, to the north the Franks, while the Parisians held the center. Again and again the Huns attacked. Then in the evening the defenders launched a countercharge. The Huns were forced to flee. Genevieve and the Parisians returned to sing a *Te Deum*. Paris was saved.

Merovee, who would found the Merovingian line, then decided that he wanted to marry Genevieve as an easy way of taking over Paris. She refused to so much as open the city gates to him because he was not a Christian. After Merovee died, his son Childeric, in 476, again sought Genevieve's hand in marriage. Her answer was again no. He threatened to besiege the city. Again she said no. Childeric tried to bluff Genevieve into capitulation by conquering land around the city. She remained firm and he went off without attacking Paris.

Clotilde

Meanwhile, in 474, in the city of Lyon, a young Burgundian princess was born. Her mother was a Catholic and named her daughter Clotilde, raising her under the inspiration of the Martyrs of Lyon. When Clotilde's father died in 490, the family moved to Geneva. It was there that she was courted by the triumphant young King of the Franks, Clovis. He had many reasons for wanting to marry her: her beauty, his desire to have Burgundy as an ally, and though he was not himself a Christian, a belief that a Christian wife would bind his Roman subjects more closely to him. Her guardian eagerly accepted the marriage suit, because he wanted the protection of Clovis against the more powerful tribes. So at the age of seventeen, frightened, knowing little of her future husband, Clotilde left Geneva to become Queen of the Franks. They were married at Soissons; her wedding present was a magnificent alabaster castle to the north of the town.

During the first year of marriage a son was born, but he died immediately after baptism. Enraged, Clovis accused Clotilde: "It is your God who is the cause of our child's death. If it had been consecrated to mine, it would have been alive now." Her husband's wrath was a heavy cross for Clotilde to bear, but her faith and trust in God were unshaken.

"I give thanks to Almighty God that He has not considered me unworthy to be the mother of a child admitted into the celestial kingdom. Having quitted the world in the white robe of his innocence, he will rejoice in the presence of God through all eternity."

The next year a second son, Clodomir, was born. He too became ill shortly after his baptism, but this time God answered Clotilde's prayers by sending a recovery.

In 496, Clovis was at war against the fierce Allemani tribe. During the crucial battle, the Franks found themselves losing. Desperate, Clovis prayed: "Jesus Christ, Thou who art, according to Clotilde, the Son of the Living God, help me in my distress, and if Thou givest me victory, I will believe in Thee and will be baptized in Thy Name." Clovis' soldiers recovered and attacked so fiercely that the Allemani flung away their arms and begged for mercy. Clovis gave them mercy and then made ready to fulfill his promise.

Just as Constantine's conversion during a key battle had brought an end to the pagan Roman Empire, so Clovis' conversion in similar circumstances marked the beginning of Christian Europe. The baptismal ceremony took place on Christmas Day, 496, in the city of Reims. The whole city was decorated.

St. Genevieve, by Champaigne

Dressed in white garments, Clovis, along with his personal bodyguard and 3,000 Franks, marched in solemn procession to the cathedral to be baptized by the bishop, St. Remi. Clovis was baptized by triple immersion, symbolizing his acceptance of the Trinity. It was Clotilde's proudest moment.

The next year, 497, the Franks marched on Paris. Seeing Genevieve, white-haired and courageous, Clovis was ashamed of himself for trying to conquer the city. He withdrew his forces and sued for peace. Genevieve opened the gates and the Parisians and Franks embraced in brotherhood, singing a *Te Deum*. Clovis rode over the north bridge and into the city in armor and crown, with bells ringing.

Genevieve died not long after, with Parisians surrounding her. They called her the Daughter of Heaven, the mother of France, the patron of Paris. She was buried in the Church of St. Peter and St. Paul, which Clovis had built. The church was renamed in her honor. Later the French Revolutionaries would try to burn her relics, but one brave Parisian rescued them and they were later reburied in a golden shrine. On January 3, her feast day, her relics are carried around the city in a procession in which everyone, rich or poor, takes part.

With the addition of Paris, the Frankish kingdom was complete. Clotilde bore two more sons and one daughter: Childebert, Clothair, and Clotilde. Through her influence and the influence of Christ's teachings, Clovis practiced moderation in warfare. Clotilde founded convents and monasteries, which helped provide havens of peace in the midst of the Dark Ages.

Clovis died in 511, and his kingdom was divided among his sons according to custom. Clotilde had no further influence over the government and her great cross in her old age was the almost constant barbaric wars that her sons waged. Her son Clodomir was killed in battle. His widow married Clothair, but Clotilde was given charge of Clodomir's three children: Theobald, Gunther, and Clodoald, whom she raised with loving care.

Clothair and Childebert were jealous, worried that the three nephews would be given part of the kingdom. They hatched a plot. They sent a message to Clotilde: "Send us the children and we will make them kings." As soon as they had the boys, they killed the two older ones and sent the five-year old, Clodoald, to the cloister, as a monk. Clotilde, heartbroken, had the two boys buried in royal tombs, then took refuge in Paris at the tomb of St. Martin.

Her daughter Clotilde, who married the Visigothic King Amalric of Spain, also suffered. The Visigoths were Arians (a group that denied Christ was God), and life at the court soon became intolerable for Clotilde. She was bombarded with filth on the way to church and frequently beaten. Once, in a mute plea for help, she sent her brother a handkerchief stained with her own blood. Childebert attacked and defeated Amalric, but on the way home, young Clotilde died at the age of only thirty.

Then Childebert and Clothair declared war on each other. Clotilde prayed night and day before the tomb of St. Martin and the war ended. Just before the battle, a heavy hailstorm pelted the battlefield, but not a drop fell in Clothair's camp. The brothers saw it as a miracle and agreed to make peace.

Clotilde spent her last years in charity and pious foundations, dying on June 3, 545. Through her example and prayers, Clovis and the Franks had been converted, and France had earned the name "Eldest Daughter of the Church."

Notre Dame

Chapter 8
Review Questions

1. Which two mountains and which river set the borders of France?
   _____

2. Julius Caesar conquered Gaul in 52 BC where a temple to Jupiter was built in a city which came to be known as_____.

3. What was the first Christian diocese? Which martyr-saint established it?

4. St. Irenaeus was one of the early _____ of Lyon.

5. St. Denis made one of the first great missionary efforts to convert the city of _____

6. How was St. Denis killed? What is unusual about the statues of St. Denis?
   _____

7. In 363, the first Christian church was completed in Paris on the site of the old pagan temple of _____.

8. What were the Huns called?
   _____

9. Who was the Bishop of Paris who brought Genevieve to Paris when she was only eight?
   _____

10. Besides going to school and praying, how did Genevieve practice Christian charity?
    _____

11. What did Genevieve build by the time she was twenty-five?
    _____

12. How were the Huns defeated?
    _____

13. Why did Clovis want to marry Clotilde, a Burgundian princess?

    _____

14. Why did Clovis convert?

    _____

15. Clovis' conversion marked the beginning of Christian _____.

16. Clovis was baptized by which saint? _____

17. What happened when Clovis tried to conquer Paris?

    _____

    _____

18. How did Paris become the capital of the Frankish kingdom?

    _____

    _____

19. What were the titles that the Parisians called Genevieve after she died?

    _____

20. Through the influence of Clotilde, Clovis practiced what in warfare?

    _____

21. What did Clotilde found which provided havens of peace in the midst of warring factions?

    _____ and _____

22. Clovis died in 511, and his kingdom was divided among his _____.

23. Clotilde spent her last years doing works of _____.

24. Through her example and _____, Clovis and the Franks had been converted.

25. Because France had been converted to Christianity in the 500's, France earned the name

    _____

55

Chapter 9

Spires in the Sky

The thirteenth century, also known as the High Middle Ages, has been called "the greatest of centuries" by the historian James Walsh in *Thirteenth: Greatest of Centuries*. It has also been called the "Glory of Christendom" by historian Warren H. Carroll in his book of the same name. During that century, God was glorified in every aspect of life: art, music, literature, customs. Even the simplest daily routines reflected love of God.

The architecture of the High Middle Ages was no exception. The last part of the twelfth century and the entire thirteenth century saw the building of the great churches known as Gothic cathedrals. These magnificent structures, which still stand throughout Europe, show the desire of the people to give glory to God and bring souls to Him. The first Gothic church was the Church of St. Denis, completed in 1144 outside Paris. The abbot of St. Denis, Abbé Suger, said, "It is only through symbols of beauty that our poor spirits can raise themselves from things temporal to things eternal."

The Gothic architects wanted to make the cathedrals a *microcosm* of the universe. A microcosm is a copy of something but on a smaller scale. The universe is God's house, and everything in the universe can remind us of God if we look at it correctly. The Gothic cathedral, as a microcosm, was also God's house, and everything in it can remind us of God if we look at it correctly.

Characteristics of Gothic Cathedrals

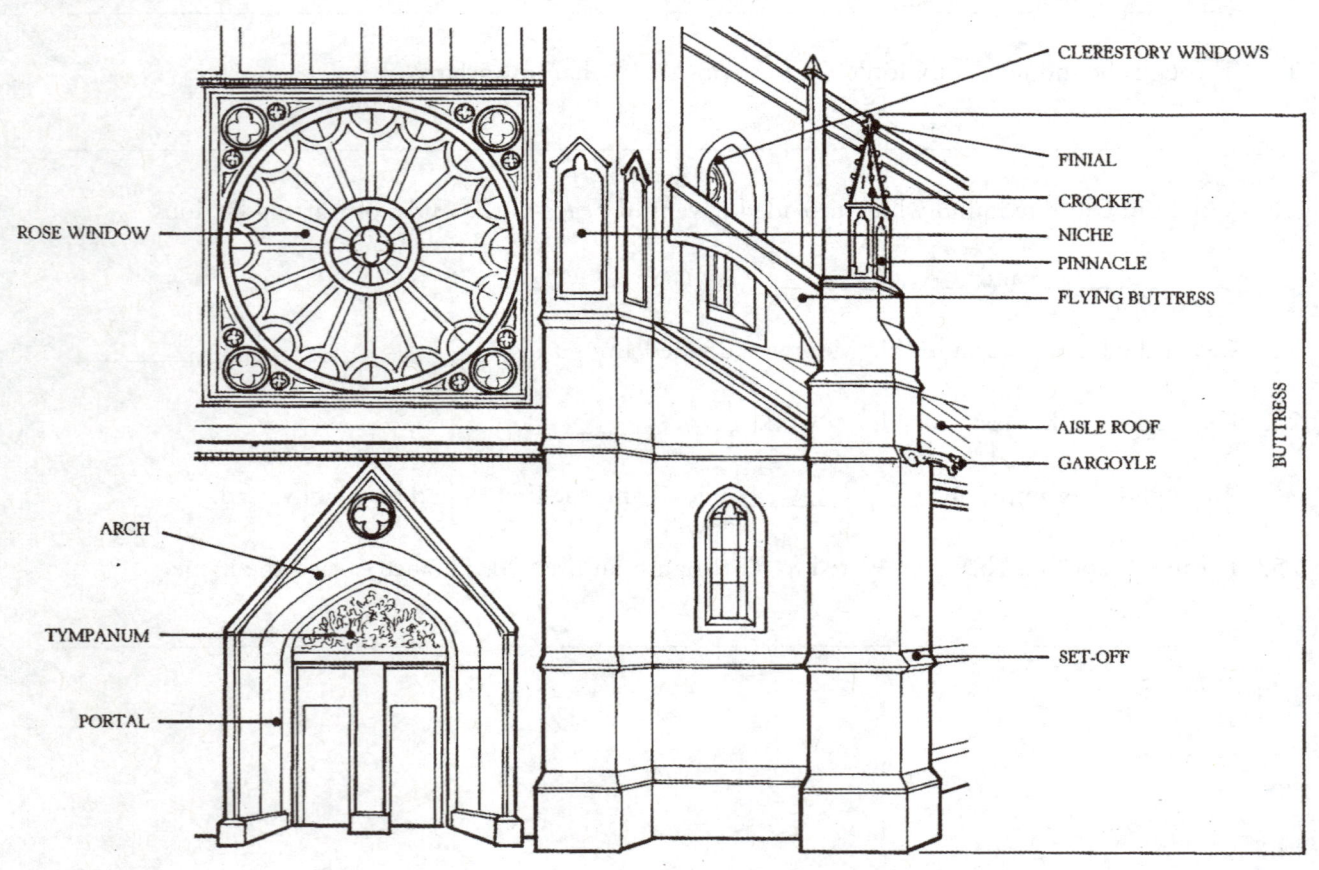

Probably the most notable characteristic of the Gothic cathedral, in comparison to earlier styles of church architecture, was its height. The gothic walls were higher than any other church walls. The arches in the church were pointed, not rounded. Rounded arches bring the eye of the viewer around from floor to floor. The pointed arch takes the eye straight up to Heaven. Most of the stained-glass windows were in the shape called *lancet*, because of their pointed tops. Thus the cathedral pointed the worshippers to Heaven, the dwelling place of God and their ultimate goal.

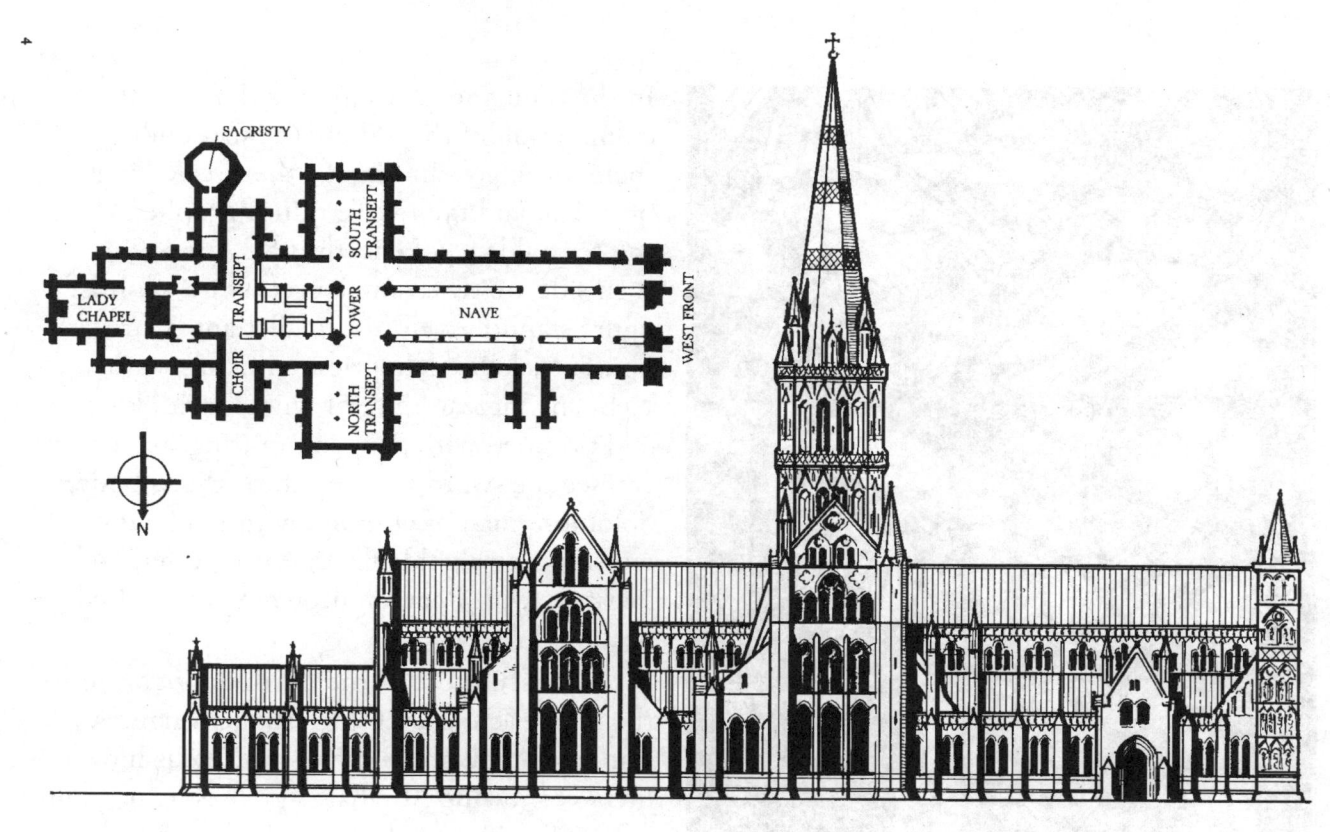

The Gothic architect used several techniques to make the higher walls possible: the pointed arch, the ribbed vaulted ceiling, and the flying buttress. The pointed arch reduced the outward pressure caused by the rounded arch. The ribbed vault reinforced the ceiling. The flying buttress, attached to the outer wall, carried stress away from the walls out to standing buttresses outside the walls, which in turn carried the stress down to the ground. The walls no longer had to bear all of the load of the ceiling.

Other characteristics of Gothic cathedrals are proportion and harmony. We know that the universe is orderly. In fact, many people have come to believe in God because they know that an orderly, harmonious universe could never have come about by chance. In the Old Testament, the Temple of Solomon, which was also regarded as a microcosm of the universe, was built according to strict laws of proportion. (Read Chapter 6 of the First Book of Kings to see the dimensions of Solomon's Temple.) The Gothic cathedrals also followed strict geometrical laws of proportion. The nave of the cathedral was divided into three parts: two side aisles and the main aisle. The sides of the cathedral were divided into three parts. The first was the arcade, closest to the floor with piers to hold up the next levels. Next came the triforium, often with a gallery or balcony. Finally came the clerestory with stained-glass windows. The vaults of the ceiling were divided into triangular structures. Not only do this order and harmony create a beautiful structure, but they remind us of the importance of living a life of order and harmony that is pleasing to God.

A third characteristic of the Gothic cathedrals is the stained-glass windows. Because the weight of the walls is carried outside by the buttresses and flying buttresses, the walls can be thinner and filled with glass.

19th century glass from Birmingham Cathedral

The glass lets in light, to remind us of the beginning of Creation, when God said, "Let there be light," and of Christ, Who is the Light of the World.

A fourth characteristic is the principle of totality. A walk through a Gothic cathedral takes the Christian through all of salvation history. We will use Chartres Cathedral outside Paris as an example. In the Good Samaritan window, the Creation and Fall of Man are depicted. Adam is the man set upon by robbers in the Good Samaritan parable and Christ is the Samaritan who will bind up his wounds. The detail of the window is exact. In the portion of the window showing God telling Adam and Eve not to eat the fruit, the viewer can count six apples on the tree. After the Fall, the viewer will see that there is not a single apple left. On the outer arch of the central north door, the story of Creation and the Fall is again told, this time in stone.

The north rose (round) window then gives a summary of Old Testament times. In the center are the Virgin and Child, the culmination of the old order. Surrounding them are angels and doves, the twelve kings of Judah, and the twelve minor prophets. In the central lancet beneath is St. Anne. On each side are two more lancets, with a Christ figure standing before a smaller anti-Christ figure: Melchizedek, priest and king, with Nebuchadnezzar, the evil king; David, king and prophet, with Saul committing suicide (we can see the sword running through his body); Solomon, man of wisdom, with Jeroboam worshipping a golden calf; Aaron, offerer of sacrifice, with Pharaoh drowning in the Red Sea.

The sculpture of the north door continues the theme. Here are Old Testament figures. The statue of Abraham and his son Isaac is movingly lifelike, showing Abraham's grief as he prepares to sacrifice his son. In the right tympanum (triangular-shaped area above the door) is a vivid scene of Job tormented by devils while his "comforters" look on. God the Father is above, showing that God was with Job, helping him to bear his sufferings. The most beautiful statue is that of the last and greatest of the prophets: St. John the Baptist. He holds a disk on which is the Agnus Dei and a cross. His face is alive, expressive, filled with love for his cousin and Savior, with sorrow for the sufferings he foresees for Him.

Old Testament history reaches its climax at the Incarnation, the pivotal point of all history, depicted in the three windows in the west front. One window depicts Christ's genealogy according to St. Matthew through the symbolism of the Jesse tree. The second portrays the Christmas story, and the third portrays Easter.

The artists of the windows were masters of detail. For example, in the episode of the scourging, the body of one of the soldiers is so real it almost appears to move. His face is contorted, he draws his arm back, and one foot is placed slightly outside the frame to provide a better brace. In the Emmaus scene, the artist captured expressions of great amazement on the faces of the disciples as they recognize Christ. In the Massacre of the Innocents we can see the swords bristling.

The side lancets develop other New Testament themes. For example, there is the Mary Magdalen window. In the section depicting the raising of Lazarus, we again see remarkable detail. When Lazarus is lying dead, his face is chalky white. When he is being raised up, it is flesh-colored.

After the Incarnation comes the working out of the Redemption in time — the story of Christ's Mystical Body, the Church. Many of the windows depict events from the lives of the saints, to inspire people to imitation. Throughout the windows and the sculptures there are reminders of daily life. The Good Samaritan window was donated by the *cobblers,* or shoemakers, and in the pane depicting the window's donors, the viewer can see the eyelet holes in the shoe on which the cobbler is working. The window donated by the *vintners* shows a poor horse straining to pull a wagon with a huge wine keg. These homely details show that religion is not to be separated into a compartment, but should be woven throughout every aspect of life.

Eventually the building up of the Body of Christ will be complete, and Christ will come again as King and Judge. In the west rose window, Christ the Supreme Judge sits in the center, the wounds by which He redeemed the world clearly visible. He is surrounded by the angels and the four beasts of the Apocalypse. Angels carry instruments of His Passion. The south rose window develops the same theme, which is completed in the sculpture of the south porch. In the center is a beautiful Christ, blessing mankind, as if to welcome them into His Kingdom. On either side are the twelve Apostles. Below, the dead rise from their tombs; St. Michael weighs a soul in a balance (the devil is trying to cheat on the side of the sins); the Blessed are led to Heaven and the damned to hell. On either side is the Church Triumphant: to the left are the martyrs, to the right are the confessors.

Thus the Chartres story of salvation is completed. The individual who reads and understands the story receives a powerful aid in working out his salvation. In the Gothic cathedrals, talent, skill and creativity were lavishly poured out to glorify God, to honor His Mother, and to help one's brothers and sisters in Christ to know, love and serve God.

Chartres Cathedral

Chapter 9
Review Questions

1. Why is the thirteenth century thought of as the "Glory of Christendom"?
   _____

2. What is the name of the architecture of the cathedrals during the thirteenth century?
   _____

3. These cathedrals were built to show the desire of the people to _____.

4. What was the first Gothic church built? _____

5. Abbé Suger said that it is only through symbols of beauty that our spirits can be raised from things in this world to things that are _____.

6. What is a microcosm? _____

7. The Gothic cathedral is a microcosm of the _____ because it reminds us of God.

8. The most notable feature of the Gothic cathedral is its _____.

9. The arches are _____, not round.

10. The stained-glass windows are in the shape called _____.

11. What carried stress away from the walls? _____

12. What Old Testament Temple showed the technique of proportion and harmony?
    _____

13. The _____ of the Gothic cathedral is divided into three parts, two side aisles and one main aisle.

14. The sides of the cathedral are divided into _____ parts.

15. What is the third characteristic of Gothic cathedrals? _____

16. A fourth characteristic is that the art takes the Christian on a visual trip through all of
    _____.

17. In the famous Chartres Cathedral outside of Paris, the rose window depicts a summary of _____ times.

18. The most beautiful statue in Chartres is of the last of the prophets, _____.

19. The three windows in the west front of Chartres Cathedral depict Christ's geneology according to Matthew, Christmas events, and the events of _____.

20. The artists of the stained glass windows were masters of _____.

21. Because of the homey background details in the stained-glass windows, we can see that the Gothic cathedral reflects the attitude that life and _____ are not separate.

22. In the west rose window of Chartres, we see Christ the Supreme _____, surrounded by angels.

23. In the south rose window, we see Christ blessing mankind, and surrounded by _____.

24. The stained glass windows and the sculptures serve as a wonderful catechism aid in helping someone work out his own _____.

25. In the Gothic cathedrals, talent, skill, and creativity were poured out to glorify God, to honor His mother, and to help others to _____.

Chartres Cathedral

Chapter 10

Saint in Armor

Besides Genevieve and Clotilde, France has had many other heroines, the most famous of whom is the peasant girl who led an army to victory — St. Joan of Arc.

Joan was born in January, 1412, in Domremy, a small village of the Meuse valley in the Lorraine province of France, the fourth child and second daughter of Jacques and Isabelle. She had an ordinary childhood, taking her turn caring for the communal herds of the village.

In 1424, at the age of twelve, she was in the garden when she heard voices and saw a strange light. The young girl trembled in fear but listened as the first voice identified himself as St. Michael the Archangel. He comforted her and told her to be a good girl. Soon, he said, God would send to her St. Catherine and St. Margaret. She must do what they told her, and she would help the king. Joan told no one of the voices.

At this time England and France were engaged in the Hundred Years' War. England had held large areas of France and was now trying to conquer the whole country. The rightful king of France was the Dauphin (Prince) Charles who was too cowardly to take his throne and assert his authority.

The Voices Direct

In May of 1428, the voices told Joan to find the Dauphin. She decided to go to Vaucouleurs, the nearest town held in the name of the dauphin, and seek aid from her cousin Durand Lassois. She told Durand her amazing story. Impressed by her sincerity, Durand did not laugh at her. He believed her and took her to the garrison to introduce her to the commander, Robert de Baudricourt. Baudricourt was not impressed. He laughed in her face and told Durand to take her home and give her a good smacking.

Joan of Arc, Heroine of France
by Jean Auguste Dominique Ingres

Joan returned home, but in January, 1429, she left Domremy forever. She returned to Durand, under pretext of helping his wife in childbirth. It was very hard for her to leave her family, but she knew she must obey her voices. She stayed in Vaucouleurs until mid-February. Then she met Bertrand de Poulengy and Jean de Metz, adventurous young soldiers who also believed her story. The two men went to Baudricourt to persuade him to give Joan help. Baudricourt had a priest brought into Joan's presence to see if she was possessed by the devil. Finally, he agreed to send Joan to the Dauphin. Since nothing else was working,

Joan of Arc in Prayer, by Stilke

Baudricourt reasoned, he might as well try Joan's crazy idea.

Metz, Poulengy, and Joan left on February 23. For the first time, she dressed in men's clothing. During the 350-mile ride to Chinon, her goodness inspired everyone who saw her, and the little group had no difficulty even when passing through enemy territory, just as Joan had predicted, since her voices had assured her they would be safe. They arrived in Chinon on March 6, 1429, the fourth Sunday of Lent. The Dauphin Charles was spoiled and soft, weak-willed and uncertain the exact opposite of Joan, but he was the king. Joan had a double responsibility, given her by her heavenly voices, to raise the siege of Orleans and to lead Charles to Reims to be crowned.

Charles delayed for two days before finally agreeing to give Joan an audience. On her way into the castle, a coarse soldier ridiculed her, blaspheming. Joan warned him that he should watch his tongue since he was so near death. An hour later he fell into the moat and was drowned.

Joan, in her rough traveling clothes, passed into a splendid room. The king was in disguise off in a corner, thinking to trick the uneducated peasant girl. Joan went to him immediately and curtsied, saying, "Your Majesty, I am Jeanne la Pucelle (Joan the Maid). The King of Heaven sends me to you with the message that you shall be anointed and crowned in the city of Reims, and that you shall be the light of the King of Heaven, Who is the King of France."

Charles, still trying to trick her, pointed to a richly dressed nobleman and said, "There is the king."

Joan replied, "In God's name, noble prince, it is you and none other." She then took him aside privately and told him three things that he had prayed for the last All Saints Day, none of which he had mentioned to a single person. Now Charles knew that Joan was who she claimed to be, but still he hesitated because of the improbability that this little girl could succeed where experienced generals had failed.

He sent her away and she waited impatiently. Charles had her spied upon and then interrogated. The interrogators tried to trick or upset her but failed. Finally, they gave Charles their decision: "We decided that, in view of the imminent necessity and of the danger of Orleans, the King might allow the girl to help him and might send her to Orleans."

By the end of six weeks in Chinon, she had won everyone's heart. She received a suit of armor, horse, flag, lance, pennon, small battle ax, and sword. She carried a white flag fringed with silk. On it was the world supported by two angels with a portrait of Our Lady, the words "Jesus, Maria," and the fleur-de-lis (the lily symbol of France).

By April 29, 1429, Orleans had been besieged for six months. Before departing for the city, Joan required the entire 4,000-men army under her command to go to confession. Upon her arrival at Orleans on April 30, Joan went onto the bridge and shouted to one of the English commanders to surrender and thus save lives. He called her a "cow-girl" and threatened to burn her if ever he caught her. Unfrightened, she said they were all liars and then went back into the city. Though she had been within bowshot and the English could easily have killed her, she escaped unharmed because they did not take her seriously.

On May 6, Joan led the French in their first major attack since her arrival. Joan inspired the men, and they captured two forts, though she was wounded in the foot. That evening the French council wanted to wait before attacking again. Joan would not hear of delays, declaring, "You have been with your council and I have been with mine. Believe me, my council will hold good and will be accomplished. Yours will come to naught." Joan's council, of course, was her saintly voices.

May 7 became known as the Day of the Tourelles (Towers). Joan, supported by the people, began attacking the main English fort at 7 A.M. She assaulted the walls again and again, but was always repulsed. Around noon she was hit by an arrow in her chest, which sank in about six inches. She pulled it out, had the wound dressed, then rested. She came back with a new attack in the afternoon. By 8 P.M., when the French General Dunois decided to withdraw, she begged him to wait a few minutes before sounding the retreat. She went out and prayed for about fifteen minutes. She returned, seized her flag, and rallied the men for one last attack. This one was successful. The enemy was routed and the siege raised. She rode into Orleans with bells ringing and sang the *Te Deum* in thanksgiving.

She returned to Chinon to tell Charles that the way was clear for him to be crowned in Reims, but Charles still procrastinated. Finally he said he would go to Reims if she would capture the other towns held by the British along the Loire. From June 10-18, Joan led the army almost daily in a series of victories. Her victories followed a regular pattern. On the night before she attacked, she would ask the garrison to surrender. They would refuse. Her advisers would try to dissuade her from attacking. She would attack the next day anyway and win. Her soldiers loved her and would follow her anywhere.

Dauphin Charles Crowned King

On Saturday, July 16, she and Charles entered Reims. The city was in confusion because they had not known for sure until the last minute whether the king would actually come. The townspeople had to spend all night getting ready for the coronation. Charles was crowned Charles VII of France on July 17, 1429, with Joan standing at his side holding her flag.

The next step was to march to Paris. The English asked Charles for a truce. He was glad for an excuse to stop fighting and unwisely agreed to the truce, thereby allowing the English army a chance to get to Paris first. Joan, who had opposed the truce, led the attack to regain the city on September 8. Joan was as courageous as ever, but the French lost, and she was wounded in the leg. Charles ordered the abandonment of Paris. In sorrow, Joan left her armor lying before the statue of Our Lady at the Church of St. Denis.

Finally Charles told her to defend Compiegne. She rode out to reconnoiter. A force attacked and the French were driven back. Joan commanded the rear guard and gave time for the main French force to get back to Compiegne. When she reached the city walls, though, the drawbridge was up and she was captured by Burgundians, allies of the English. Charles made no attempt to rescue or even ransom Joan. The Burgundians then sold her to the English.

Very upset, she wanted to escape. Her voices told her not to make the attempt, but she would not listen. She jumped from the top of the tower where she was imprisoned (60-70 feet above the ground). She suffered only a mild concussion but was immediately recaptured. St. Catherine told her to ask forgiveness for her rash act.

A Powerful Enemy

The Bishop of Beauvais was Pierre Cauchon, who supported the English. He wanted to get vengeance on Joan for her leadership and inspiration of the French and urged that she be tried as a witch. She was taken to Rouen, arriving in December of 1430. Thrown into irons in a tiny cell, she was denied even a visit from a priest.

Bishop Cauchon dominated the legal proceedings. The English wanted a guilty verdict, and Joan never had a chance. A trial was necessary because of her standing with the French people.

Her enemies tried every sort of trick on her. In spite of her weakness and exhaustion, she eluded all their traps. For example, they asked her, "Do you consider yourself to be in a state of grace?"

If she answered yes, they would accuse her of pride and presumption; if no, she would have condemned herself. Though exhausted and ill, Joan kept her wits about her. Her answer, "If I am not, may God put me there; if I am, may He keep me in it."

Once she caught a judge in an inaccuracy over one of her answers, given eight days earlier, though he had it written down and she could neither read nor write. She said, "If you make such a mistake again, I will pull your ears!" She warned Bishop Cauchon: "You say you are my judge; I do not know if you are or not; but be very careful not to judge me wrongly, for you would be putting yourself in grave danger. I am warning you of it now, so that if Our Lord punishes you for it, I shall have done my duty in telling you."

Joan had no friend, no lawyer, no one on her side. Her enemies dodged from one subject to another, to see if she would contradict herself. Their questions came back to the voices, again and again. She never denied that she heard them and did what they told her. They wanted her to give details. She said she would sooner have her throat cut than say all she knew. Once they asked her if St. Catherine and St. Margaret hated the English. She replied, "They love what God loves and hate what God hates." Her enemies also condemned her for dressing in men's clothes. She was exasperated and regarded her dress as unimportant.

Charles VII, King of France

They read off the Act of Accusation: that Joan "shall be denounced and declared as a sorceress, diviner, pseudo-prophetess, invoker of evil spirits, conspirator, superstitious, implicated in and given to the practice of magic, wrongheaded as to our Catholic Faith, schismatic, and in several other articles of our Faith skeptical and astray, sacrilegious, idolatrous, apostate, accursed, and mischievous." They told her she would be burnt if she did not recant. She said: "I will say no more about that. Were I to see the fire, I would still say all that I have said, and would not do otherwise."

The first public sitting of the trial was February 21, in the royal chapel of the castle at Rouen. From February 24–27, Joan was violently ill. On March 27, in the large hall of the castle, they began to read the seventy articles against her. They did not finish until the following day. Again they tried to get her to confess. She refused. Then they wrote reports until April 12. They took the final report to her on April 18, and again she refused to confess. She had been alone for months, suffering mentally, spiritually, emotionally, and physically. She asked to be buried in consecrated ground, but they told her that if she did not recant, she would be treated as a pagan. She said: "I am a good Christian; I have been properly baptized. As a good Christian I will die."

By May 2, she had regained her strength, and they dragged her back to the main hall. Cauchon rose with his sheaf of papers. Joan said: "Read your book, and I can respond to you. I acted for God, my Creator, in everything. I love Him with all my heart." They gave her another week to think it over. She said: "Even if you were to tear my limbs asunder and drive my soul out of my body, I could not speak otherwise; and if I did say anything, I should always say afterwards that you had forced me to say it."

They finally decided that torture would not do any good. They went to Paris for more deliberations, a journey very hard on Joan. On May 24, they set up two stands. One had all the dignitaries and judges; the other had Joan and William Erard, who gave a very long sermon, again calling on her to recant. She said, "I will answer you. As for my submission to the Church, I have already given them my answer. Let all my words and deeds be sent to Rome, to our Holy Father the Pope, to whom, after God, I will refer myself. As to what I have said and done, I have done it through God. I charge no one, neither my king nor any other; if there is any fault, it is mine alone." They ignored her noble words, reading more accusations and condemnations.

Joan's Martyrdom

The strain on Joan for the past year had been enormous. After imprisonment, torture, endless interrogations, her strength was exhausted. She broke down, saying, "I will follow everything my judges say." She signed a confession and received a sentence of life imprisonment on bread and water in an English prison.

Her accusers exulted. They had won out over the woman they called the witch. The day after their triumph, May 28, they returned to her cell to savor their victory. Wanting to hear her deny her mission one more time, they asked her again if she heard the voices. Yes, she cried, they had spoken to her again that very night: "They told me that, through them, God sent me His pity of the betrayal to which I consented in making the abjuration and revocation to save my life." Joan was her old self again. Furious, her judges condemned her to be burned at the stake.

On May 30, 1431, they took her from her cell. A big crowd had gathered in the square in Rouen, where two platforms and a stake had been set up. A sign proclaimed Joan's crimes: "Joan, liar, pernicious, deceiver of people, sorceress, superstitious, blasphemer. . . ."

She knelt and prayed and forgave all her enemies. An English soldier made her a cross out of two pieces of wood after she had begged, "A cross, a cross, give me a cross." They tied her to the stake and lit the fire. She prayed, "St. Catherine, St. Margaret, St. Michael." She repeated the name of Jesus, the last word she spoke. Her ashes were thrown into the Seine so that the people could not have any relics to honor.

After her death, the French united in love of her and began working together. Gradually they drove out the English. In 1436, the French entered Paris in triumph. Charles, weak as he was, ruled over a united France, thanks to Joan. He has gone down in history as "Charles, the Well-Served," because he owed his throne to the young peasant girl who won his battles for him.

Chapter 10
Review Questions

1. In which year was Joan of Arc born? In which city? In which country?

2. What kind of work did Joan do as a child?

3. What did Joan hear when she was twelve?

4. Who were the three saints who spoke to Joan?

5. What was the name of the war going on between England and France?

6. Who was the rightful king of France?

7. Why had he not taken his rightful throne?

8. How old was Joan when the voices told her to find the dauphin?

9. What was the name of the commander of the French forces?

10. What kind of people were the two men who went to the commander for Joan?

11. During the 350-mile ride to see the dauphin, what inspired the French people along the way?

12. What did the voices tell Joan to do regarding Charles?

13. How was the king dressed when Joan went to meet him?
    _____

14. What was the message that Joan gave the king from the King of Heaven?
    _____

15. How did Joan prove to Charles that she had a message from heaven?
    _____

16. Describe the white flag that Joan of Arc carried into battle?
    _____

17. What was the first thing that Joan demanded that her 4000 men in the army do?
    _____

18. Before Joan and her soldiers went into battle, what did Joan ask the English to do, and why?
    _____

19. On May 7th, 1429, at 7 A.M., Joan and her soldiers began attacking the main English fort in which city? _____

20. In July, 1429, Charles was crowned as Charles VII of France in the city of _____ with Joan standing by his side.

21. What major city was lost to the English? _____

22. Who captured Joan and sold her to the English? _____

23. Which French bishop supported the British enemies and urged that Joan be tried as a witch?
    _____

24. In which city of France was Joan burned at the stake by the English?_____

25. After her death, the French united in defeating the British; how many years after Joan's death did the French march triumphantly into the city of Paris?

    _____
    _____

Chapter 11

Martyrs and Miracles

The Netherlands, which is now about thirty percent Catholic, has had a stormy religious history. At the time of the Protestant Revolt in the sixteenth century, the Netherlands was part of Spain. A few rebels wanted to break away from Spain. They decided to bring about the separation by breaking away from the Catholic Church first. At the beginning of the rebellion (1568), most of the people were loyally Catholic. Gradually, though, many were persuaded that they could not be independent in government unless they had a different religion. Those who remained loyal to the Church were persecuted. The most famous of the martyrs of this time are the Nineteen Holy Martyrs of Gorkum.

The Martyrs of Gorkum

Of the nineteen holy martyrs who died in the night of the ninth of July in 1572, several were well known as excellent preachers who had done their best to combat the false doctrines. The youngest of the martyrs (and their leader) was St. Nicholas Pieck, aged thirty-eight. The oldest (and the only one who had been born outside of Holland) was St. Antony van Willehad, aged ninety. He had been born in Denmark, where he became a Franciscan. The heretics there had chased him to England. From England he had then been chased to Scotland, and from there to Holland where he found refuge in a monastery, only to become a martyr at the age of ninety. There were ten other Franciscans in the group, four secular priests, two Premonstratensians, one Dominican, and one Canon Regular of St. Augustine.

When the town of Gorkum was captured by *Watergeuzen* (Calvinist pirates), under the command of the cruel Lumey (a sworn enemy of the Catholics who had in his service an apostate priest), the Franciscans knew what was in store for them; but all of them, except two, refused to flee. They wished to give a good example and remained with the faithful in the hour of peril. The secular priests and the Augustinian did the same. They were all captured in the dungeon of the town's castle, to which they had fled to escape being murdered by the invading soldiers and mob.

The Prince of Orange had forbidden the detention of priests and religious solely for their religious convictions, but the hatred of his commander, Lumey, was more powerful

Nineteen Holy Martyrs

than the wishes of the prince. The nineteen were maltreated and tortured. During the interrogations they had to endure from their captors, they were commanded to make public denial of the Catholic truth concerning the Eucharist and the Sacrifice of the Mass, and to reject the authority of the Pope. In their struggle against the Church, Luther and the other leaders of the Protestant Revolt used to call the successor of St. Peter the "Antichrist." The hatred of the heretics was directed in quite a special way against the fundamental Catholic doctrine of papal primacy.

The martyrs indignantly refused to comply with the wishes of their enemies and preferred to die. Originally, the number of those captured was twenty-three. Four of them were weak and apostatized. Of these, two later repented, and one of them, after three months, was hanged by Lumey.

William of Orange

Among the martyrs was one who, during his previous priestly life, had given a very bad example to his flock: Andreas Wouters, vicar of Heinoudenaarden. Another, James Lacops of Oudenaarden, had previously denied the Faith and joined the heretics. Both of them, however, later repented and made heroic amends by their martyrdom.

After cruel sufferings and tortures which for most of them lasted more than two weeks, the nineteen were hanged in a barn, on two beams. The hanging was done in such a cruel way that some of them died only after many hours. They were beatified in 1675 and canonized in 1867.

Worshipping in Secret

Amsterdam, the largest city in Holland, outlawed Catholic Masses in 1578. Catholics had to attend Mass in private houses and in other secret places. They would use code names for these secret hideaways. A Catholic could whisper to a Catholic neighbor that he was on the way to "The Parrot," "The Tree," "The Mail Bugle," or "Chalk Mountain."

Gradually, the persecutions were relaxed but laws against Catholics remained. Catholics, for example, were not permitted to have processions in the streets without permission, which, of course, was rarely given. The anti-procession law prevented a procession that began in the fourteenth century, when a sick man, after receiving Communion at his home, accidentally spit out the Host in a fit of coughing. A woman in the house, fearing germs from his disease, placed the Host in the kitchen fire. At once she saw an image of the Holy Spirit in the flames, and the Host was not burned. She rushed to the church and told the priest what had happened. He told her to burn the Host the next day. Again she saw the Holy Spirit in the fire. The priest decided to bring the miraculous Host to the church in a procession. When processions were outlawed, the people developed the tradition of the "silent walk." They walked though the streets quietly, without singing or praying out loud, thus keeping the tradition alive.

One of the secret places for Mass was the attic of the five-story home of businessman Jan Harman. Its code name was "The Deer." When Harman wrote his will, he asked his heirs not to sell the building. The family needed money, however, and a few years after his death sold the building to a non-Catholic. Catholics feared that they would have no place for Mass, but the new owner of the building rented the attic to them. Catholics got into the habit of saying that they were going to "Our Dear Lord in the Attic." The attic church is still called that today. It is now a museum, but on the first Sunday of each month, a special Mass is held, with about 200 persons crowded in. Weddings and baptisms are also held in the little church.

Another old tradition is in the town of Den Bosch, where the people honor an ancient wooden statue of Our Lady known as the Sweet Mother. The statue was found by a workingman early one morning in a shop near the cathedral. It was a cold morning, and he thought of using it to make a fire. The master of the shop ordered him not to do this, and the statue was given to Brother Wouter who intended to put it in his room. On the way the statue became so heavy that he could not carry it, so he placed it in the cathedral. When the Protestants seized Den Bosch, the statue was taken to Belgium for safekeeping. It remained there until 1853 when a Catholic bishop was allowed to reside in the city. On the Sunday nearest July 7, the feast of the Sweet Mother, the statue is carried in procession through the streets of Den Bosch, following the route of its return to the city, which in turn followed the route of a procession during the Middle Ages which had prayed for help against the plague. For the procession, the statue is dressed in a fur cloak and a jeweled crown.

The silent walking, the procession with the Sweet Mother, and the Masses in the Church in the Attic are Catholic traditions loved and honored even in a Protestant country.

"The Parrot." This Catholic Church is located in Amsterdam. Note how it is built in between two other buildings. The building on the right is an apartment building and the building on the left is a tire store! Also, look closely at the two statues on the front of the church. The statue on the right is of St. Joseph, but the statue on the left is a parrot. You can see not only the parrot but his perch and what appears to be a feeding dish in front.

Chapter 11
Review Questions

1. In the sixteenth century, the Netherlands were part of which country? _____

2. The beginning of the rebellion to break away from the Catholic Church and Spain began in which year? _____

3. The most famous martyrs of this time in the Netherlands were the _____

4. These martyrs were killed in the year _____ .

5. The oldest of these martyrs was St. _____ .

6. The town of Gorkum in the Netherlands was captured by "Watergeuzen", who were _____ .

7. What was the name of the cruel commander of the Watergeuzen? _____

8. Who was Nicholas Pieck? _____

9. What was the name of the ruler who forbade persecution of priests and religious for their religious convictions? _____

10. The enemies of the Church wanted the Catholics to deny the Sacrament of the _____, and the Sacrifice of the _____ .

11. The enemies of the Church wanted them to reject the authority of _____ .

12. How did the Martyrs of Gorkum come to be martyred? _____

13. What happened to the martyrs who at first did not hold fast to their Faith? _____

14. Another name for the Netherlands is Holland; the people are called Dutch. What is the largest city called? _____

15. Since Catholic Masses were outlawed in 1578, how did people know where Mass was being held during the days of persecution?

16. Even after the persecutions and torture stopped, what still remained in effect against Catholics?

17. Tell the story of the miraculous Host. What did the priest and people do in honor of this miracle?

18. When processions were outlawed, what kind of "procession" did Catholics have?

19. What is the story of "Our Dear Lord in the Attic" church?

20. In which town did the story of the statue of the Sweet Mother take place?

21. What was the name of the religious who put the statue in the cathedral?

22. What happens in the Attic Church today?

23. In what year was a Catholic bishop finally allowed to reside in the city of Den Bosch?

24. The route of the annual procession in Den Bosch is the same route taken during the Middle Ages by people praying for help against what?

25. What lessons can we learn for our own life from the facts of the persecutions of the Catholics in Holland?

Chapter 12
Portraits that Breathe

Although the great Dutch painter Rembrandt (1606 -1669) was not a Catholic, his works are quite often deeply spiritual.

Rembrandt Harmenszoon van Rijn was born in Leiden on July 15, 1606, the eighth of nine children. His father was a miller and fairly well off.

In 1609, seven provinces of the Low Countries with the name United Provinces achieved independence from Spain. (The name Netherlands means "Low Lands.") Holland was the biggest of the provinces, so its name was used to refer to the whole area, much to the disgust of the other six provinces. The new government was Calvinist. Catholics were forced to worship in private; churches were stripped of their altars and taken over by the Protestants. Hence, the Church was no longer commissioning paintings, and the Calvinists did not want any religious art. Rembrandt was thus the last of the great religious painters of the Netherlands.

There was a great demand for paintings among the ordinary people at this time. The Netherlands was a wealthy area and people spent their money on art. Artists fulfilled the demand. One artist painted 10,000 paintings, approximately three each week. Another did so much painting that he became bored, so to get variety he painted with his toes.

Rembrandt attended Latin School in Leiden from the ages of seven to fourteen to prepare for a learned profession. He went to the University of Leiden for a couple of months, then dropped out to become an artist.

Rembrandt passed a three-year apprenticeship with an untalented painter who specialized in architecture and scenes of hell. Never afterwards did Rembrandt paint these things. When he was seventeen or eighteen he went to Amsterdam, where he learned the chiaroscuro technique, which he was to develop to a high degree. When he was eighteen or nineteen, Rembrandt went home to Leiden as an independent master. His earliest regular painting was the *Stoning of St. Stephen*. Notable features of it are the lighting, detail, and multi-figured excitement. Rembrandt painted in his own face on one of the onlookers. The painting was completed in 1625.

In 1627, he did the *Money-Changer*. This painting shows an interest in costume and hidden lighting, with an unknown light source illuminating the money changer. He also did miniatures and early self-portraits. Probably no other artist has done as many self-portraits as Rembrandt (ninety altogether).

Rembrandt began doing etchings. Here is the technique. A plate would be covered with

Rembrandt Self-Portrait

resin. The artist would scratch the design with a needle. The plate would be dipped in acid which would bite into the scratches, making the imprint. The plate would be inked and the etching printed. Rembrandt did detailed, realistic etchings. Today a Rembrandt print may sell for as much as $84,000.

In 1632, Rembrandt went to Amsterdam under the patronage of Constantin Huygens, a leader and statesman. Amsterdam was the leading seaport of Northern Europe, busy and bustling. The city had originally been built on a swamp, and a popular jingle went: "The great town of Amsterdam/ is built on piles, until/ the day the whole place tumbles down/ then who will pay the bill?" The main buildings were on piles sunk down to solid earth. The easiest way of getting about the city was by the canals.

In 1632 Rembrandt rose high in public esteem by painting the *Anatomy Lesson of Dr. Tulp*. The group portrait was a popular type of painting in Holland because of the number of guilds, charitable societies, militia companies, and the like. The officers and members of these groups wanted to be immortalized. Each person would pay the artist individually and want to be in a prominent position in the finished painting. So artists usually solved that problem by painting the figures in a monotonous row or crescent. Rembrandt's *Dr. Tulp* broke with tradition by using a triangular composition, with the figures attentively observing Dr. Tulp's dissection. Unity was achieved by the focusing of the subjects' attention and by the use of monochrome colors. Rembrandt realistically portrayed personality by depicting some of the onlookers as quite interested in the operation and others as slightly ill at the sight.

In 1633, Rembrandt became engaged to Saskia and then married her in 1634. In

Presentation in the Temple (Detail)

1633 he painted the *Descent from the Cross*, in which the limp body of the crucified Christ emphasizes the horror of crucifixion.

After his marriage, Rembrandt used Saskia as a model. His paintings of her poignantly display her wasting illness. Between the years 1635 and 1642, Rembrandt suffered many personal tragedies. He lost three infants, his mother, his sister-in-law, and finally in 1642 his beloved Saskia, who was not yet thirty. He was left with one surviving son, Titus. He made an etching of Saskia just before death, a painfully objective portrait showing the ravages of her illness. The next year he did a beautiful idealized portrait of Saskia on the most costly surface he could find, a rare mahogany panel.

His year of tragedy, 1642, was also the year of one of Rembrandt's best-known and greatest works, the painting known as the *Nightwatch*. The official title was *The Company of Captain Frans Banning Cocq and Lt. Willem van Ruytenburch*. The work was a painting of an Amsterdam militia company assembling for a social or sporting event or a parade. They were not going on watch, so that part of the title was inaccurate. The "night" was added to the title because during the eighteenth century, the painting became darkened by dirt and varnish. When the painting was cleaned in modern times, it was jokingly referred to as the "Day Watch."

Most of Rembrandt's major works were covered with varnish to protect their bold colors, passages of broken color, and textured surface caused by his use of the palette knife, his fingers and rough brush strokes. In 1911 an unemployed ship's cook tried to slash

The Night-Watch

the *Nightwatch* with a knife but the varnish protected it.

The *Nightwatch* is thirteen feet by sixteen feet. Not only did Rembrandt paint the eighteen members of the militia company, but he added sixteen extra figures. The painting is characterized by light, color, a baroque splendor, and a sense of movement. The painting was moved to the town hall where it had to be cut to fit the space set aside for it. The greatest loss was on the left where a two-foot strip with three figures was removed.

Though the painting was well received, Rembrandt began to fall from popularity. A new taste for elegance had emerged to the detriment of Rembrandt's profound, religious works. Rembrandt did not change his style to meet fashions. In 1648, he painted the *Meeting at Emmaus*, showing Christ, bathed in light from a window, breaking bread with his surprised disciples.

In 1654, Rembrandt did one of his greatest portraits, a portrait of Burgomaster (an official like a mayor) Jan Six. Novelist Henry Fielding once wrote, "It hath been though a vast commendation of a painter to say his figures appear to breathe; but surely it is a much greater and nobler applause, that they appear to think." Rembrandt's earlier portraits breathe. The later portraits, such as *Jan Six*, appear to think.

Rembrandt seemed to spend more money than he received from his paintings, and in 1658 he was forced to declare bankruptcy. All of his pictures and prints were sold. He had to move to a less expensive house on the outskirts of town.

In 1661, he did the greatest of his group portraits, *The Syndics of the Drapers' Guild*. In it, the Drapers have been disturbed by the entrance of the spectator, who is not shown, giving the viewer the feeling of being part of the painting. This event adds animation to the group, some of whom are rising and seeming to question the intrusion of the spectator.

In 1661-62 Rembrandt painted *The Conspiracy of Julius Civilis*. The painting is of the beginning of a barbarian rebellion in 69 A.D. against the Romans. The barbarians were the Batavians, supposed ancestors of the Dutch. Rembrandt depicted the barbarian king, Julius Civilis, in barbaric majesty, brutally realistic. The patrons were displeased. Their supposed ancestors were too barbaric and not noble enough for their tastes. They refused to purchase the painting.

While he was working on these other projects, Rembrandt did a series of Biblical scenes. In 1656 he did *Jacob Blessing the Sons of Joseph*, in 1658 *Saul and David*, and in 1669 *The Prodigal Son*. Each of these paintings depicts a moving emotional scene with the rich, warm colors characteristic of Rembrandt.

Though brought up in a Calvinist background, Rembrandt had no Calvinist hatred for material creation and saw goodness and beauty in all things.

Rembrandt self portrait

Chapter 12
Review Questions

1. When did the great Dutch painter, Rembrandt, live? _____

2. At the time Rembrandt lived, the Dutch government was of which religion? _____

3. Catholics were forced to worship in private, altars were taken out of churches, and churches were taken over by _____.

4. Because the people in the Netherlands were wealthy, they wanted to buy _____.

5. When Rembrandt was seventeen or eighteen, to which great city did he go to learn painting techniques?
   _____

6. What were the notable features of the painting *Stoning of St. Stephen*?
   _____

7. What were two noteworthy features of the painting *Money-Changer*?
   _____

8. Rembrandt began printing from an ink-covered plate on which he had scratched a design. What is this technique called?
   _____

9. How did Rembrandt arrange the people in *Anatomy Lesson of Dr. Tulp* which was different from previous group portraits?
   _____

10. In *Anatomy*, how did Rembrandt portray the personalities differently from previous paintings?
    _____

11. What is emphasized in the painting *Descent From the Cross*?
    _____

12. *Nightwatch* is a huge thirteen by sixteen foot painting, characterized by light, color, splendor, and a sense of _____.

13. Rembrandt's religious painting, *Meeting at Emmaus*, shows what? From where does the light come?
    _____

14. When Rembrandt painted *Jan Six*, it was pointed out that the portrait showed not only that Jan Six appeared to breathe, but also that he appeared to _____

15. In the group portraits in *Syndics of the Draper's Guild*, not only did the people appear to have personality, but Rembrandt added animation to the group, showing some of the people _____ and questioning.

16. Rembrandt painted the Old Testament Biblical story of Saul and _____.

17. What is the name of the painting depicting the famous story of the parable told by Jesus of a father and son?
    _____

18. What kind of scenes were depicted in the Biblical paintings?
    _____

19. The colors in the Biblical scenes are _____ colors, typical of Rembrandt's paintings.

20. Rembrandt saw _____ and goodness in all things and did not hate material creation.

Belshazzar's Feast

79

Chapter 13
Kings and Crowns

The first great hero of England is King Arthur. To this day, his grave is pointed out at the ruined monastery of Glastonbury. For centuries, the Arthurian stories have fascinated nearly everyone who hears them. The legends are enchanting, but the real Arthur, the historical figure who actually existed, is little known.

King Arthur: More Fact then Fiction

The earliest known historical record referring to King Arthur is the *Annals of Wales*, an ancient document which makes two references to Arthur. The first reference is as follows:

> *The Battle of Badon in which Arthur bore the cross of our Lord Jesus Christ on his shoulders for three days and three nights, and the Britons were the victors.*

From this we learn that Arthur was a great military commander. From other sources we know that the Battle of Mt. Badon was crucial to the Britons in defeating the pagan Saxon barbarians who were trying to wipe out all that remained of Roman Christian civilization in Britain.

We also see that he was a committed Christian, though we do not know exactly what is meant by the phrase "the cross of Our Lord Jesus Christ on his shoulders." Perhaps he wore an image of the cross, or had a relic of the True Cross with him at the battle.

The second reference to Arthur from the *Annals of Wales* is this one:

> *Battle of Camlann in which Arthur and Medraut perished; and there was plague in Britain...*

Here we learn of the death of Arthur. Since the source mentions Medraut in the same breath as Arthur, he is obviously a crucial figure. The legends identify him as a traitor who was responsible for Arthur's death.

The reference to plague throughout the land emphasizes how the nation suffered after Arthur died.

Both of these references date to the 500s, so it is probable that the real Arthur lived in the sixth century.

The Knights of the Round Table are Summoned to a Quest.

The departure of the Knights

Another early historical source referring to Arthur is *The History of the Britons*, which refers to the Battle of Mt. Badon, and also lists several other battles that Arthur won. In describing the battle of Castellum Guinnion, the author says that it was at this battle "where Arthur carried the portrait of Saint Mary, ever Virgin, on his shoulders; and the pagans were routed on that day, and there was a great slaughter of them through the power of Our Lord Jesus Christ and the strength of the holy Virgin Mary, His Mother." Again we see confirmation that Arthur was a Christian hero, who had a great devotion to the Blessed Mother.

From these few brief historical references, we can already see the beginnings of some of the King Arthur legends. He took the lead in holding back the pagan Saxons from their drive to wipe out Roman civilization in Britain during the declining days of the Roman Empire. Rome had brought civilization and Christianity to Britain, but now Britain could expect no help from Rome, which was corrupt and collapsing. During his lifetime, Arthur held the Saxons at bay, winning his greatest victory at the Battle of Mt. Badon. His heroism and the gigantic deeds he performed almost single-handedly to preserve civilization during his lifetime sparked the many legends.

History and legend become mingled in the book *History of the Kings of Britain*, written in the tenth century by Geoffrey of Monmouth. The book describes Arthur's battles and his devotion to Christ and the Blessed Mother. The book tells us that Arthur rebuilt churches destroyed by the Saxons and established convents and monasteries.

The descriptions of some battles seem somewhat exaggerated, as the years that had passed since the battles actually took place had caused the memories to expand and to make Arthur seem even greater than he actually was.

The book also introduces us to Arthur's wife Guinevere, who is described as the most beautiful woman in all of Britain, to Arthur's friend Bedivere, and to his sword Excalibur.

Medraut is now Mordred, the traitor, who allied with the Saxons against Arthur. Arthur slew Mordred in battle but was himself mortally wounded and carried off to the island of Avalon.

With the Norman conquest (a Frenchman from Normandy, William the Conqueror, conquered England), King Arthur became known in France. The history was elaborated and enlarged on and soon became more legend than fact. The Arthurian stories were set in the medieval time of knight, chivalry, castles, and lovely ladies. Sir Lancelot, a Frenchman, comes to play a major role in the story. Arthur remains a Christian hero fighting evil. Now it is no longer evil Saxons he fights, but all the greed, pride and violence of human nature, including his own human weaknesses. Camelot becomes the symbol of a dream, a dream of justice and peace which can unfortunately never be fully realized in this fallen world.

The main legends were pulled together into a connected narrative by Sir Thomas Malory in the fifteenth century. He called his work *Le Morte D'Arthur* (*The Death of Arthur*). Even though Malory devotes most of his book to the life of Arthur, he wants the reader to be aware always of the death of Arthur and the death of his dream of Camelot. Yet there is hope at the end of the book that the dream will live on.

From that time until the present day, authors have been taking the Malory story and writing their own versions of it. Some of the most famous are "Idylls of the King" by Alfred Lord Tennyson, *The Once and Future King* by T. H. White, and *Camelot* by Lerner and Lowe.

Excerpts of the Legend

Here are some brief selections from a variety of authors, to give you an idea of how various writers have approached the King Arthur legends.

First from Malory, describing the death of Arthur:

> Then Sir Bedivere took the King on his back, and so went with him to that water side. And when they were there, even fast by that bank hoved a little barge with many fair ladies in it, and among them all was a queen, and they all had black hoods. And all they wept and shrieked when they saw King Arthur. Now put me

Galahad Sees the Grail

into the barge, said the king. And so he did softly; and there received him three queens with great mourning; and so they set them down, and in one of their laps King Arthur laid his head. And then that queen said: Ah dear brother, why have ye tarried so long from me? alas, this wound on your head hath caught over-much cold. And so then they rowed from the land, and Sir Bedivere beheld all those ladies go from him. Then Sir Bedivere cried: Ah, my Lord Arthur, what shall become of me, now ye go from me and leave me here alone among mine enemies? Comfort thyself, said the king, and do as well as thou mayest, for in me is no trust for to trust in; for I will into the vale of Avalon to heal me of my grievous wound: and if thou hear never more of me, pray for my soul.

But ever the queens and ladies wept and shrieked, that it was a pity to hear. And as soon as Sir Bedivere had lost sight of the barge, he wept and wailed. . . .

Yet some men say in many parts of England that Arthur is not dead, but had by the will of Our Lord Jesus into another place; and men say that he shall come again, and he shall win the Holy Cross. Yet I will not say that it shall be so, but rather I would say: here in this world he changed his life. And many men say that there is written upon the tomb this: *Hic jacet Arthurus, Rex quondam Rexque futurus.* [Here lies Arthur, the Once and Future King.]

The next passage is from Tennyson, the introduction to the poem about Elaine, the Lily Maid of Astolat, who fell in love with Lancelot and died for love of him:

> Elaine the fair, Elaine the lovable,
> Elaine, the lily maid of Astolat,
> High in a chamber up in a tower to the east
> Guarded the sacred shield of Lancelot;
> When first she placed where morning's earliest ray
> Might strike it and awake her with the gleam;
> Then fearing rust or soilure fashioned for it
> A case of silk, and braided thereupon
> All the devices blazon'd on the shield
> In their own tinct, and added, of her wit,
> A border fantasy of branch and flower,
> And yellow throated nestling in the nest.
> Nor rested thus content, but day by day,
> Leaving her household and good father, climb'd
> That eastern tower, and entering barr'd her door,
> Stripped off the case and read the naked shield,
> Now guessed a hidden meaning in his arms,
> Now made a pretty history to herself
> Of every dint a sword had beaten in it,
> And every scratch a lance had made upon it,
> Conjecturing when and where: this cut is fresh;
> That ten years back; this dealt him at Caerlyle;
> That at Caerleon; this at Camelot;
> And ah God's mercy, what a stroke was there!
> And here a stroke that might have kill'd, but God
> Broke the strong lance, and rolled his enemy down,
>
> And saved him: so she lived in fantasy.

T.H. White, in *Once and Future King* took a humorous approach and especially enjoyed writing about Merlin's upbringing of the young Arthur, who did not even know he was the heir to the throne. In the passage below, Merlin is trying to show Arthur that jousting is just a mindless sport and that Arthur would be better off spending his time in studies. King Pellinore and Sir Grummore Grummorson are having a joust, sort of:

> They met in the middle, breast to breast, with a noise of shipwreck and great bells tolling, and both bouncing off, fell breathless on their backs. They lay thus for a few minutes, panting. Then they slowly began to heave themselves to their feet, and it was obvious that they had lost their tempers once again.
>
> King Pellinore had not only lost his temper but he seemed to have been a bit astonished by the impact. He got up facing the wrong way, and could not find Sir Grummore. There was some excuse for this since he had only a slit to peep through — and that was three inches away from his eye owing to the padding of straw — but he looked muddled as well. Perhaps he had broken his spectacles. Sir Grummore was quick to seize his advantage.
>
> 'Take that!' cried Sir Grummore, giving the unfortunate monarch a two-handed swipe on the nob as he was slowly turning his head from side to side peering in the opposite direction.
>
> King Pellinore turned round morosely, but his opponent was too quick for him. He ambled round so that he was still behind the King and gave him another terrific blow in the same place.
>
> 'Where are you?' asked King Pellinore.
>
> 'Here,' cried Sir Grummore, giving him another.
>
> The poor king turned himself round as nimbly as possible, but Sir Grummore had given him the slip again.

Finally, here is a brief passage from a modern book, *Sword at Sunset*, by Rosemary Sutcliffe, which attempts to recreate the historical Arthur from the legends. Arthur's mission is described in his own words speaking of the growth of a friendship between the son of one of his Companions (his cavalry troops) and the son of a Saxon Warrior.

> They walked around each other on stiff legs at first, like young hounds, and then they went away, and no man saw them again until evening. They came back at suppertime, being hungry, and told no one what they had done with their day, and no one asked, but they looked as if they had spent part of the day fighting and the rest eating blackberries. They shared the same broth bowl, and spent the evening among the hounds by the fire, picking bramble thorn out of each other's feet. And suddenly I knew, watching them...that the longer we can hold off the Saxons...the more time there will be for other boys to pick thorns out of each other's feet and learn the words for hearth and hound and honey cake in each other's tongues. Every year that we can hold the Saxons back may well mean that the darkness will engulf us less completely in the end, that more of what we fight for will survive until the light comes again.

Sir Galahad

Chapter 13
Review Questions

1. King Arthur was the first great Christian hero of which country? _____

2. Though we don't know the date for sure, when did King Arthur probably live?
   _____

3. What is the title of the first known historical record of King Arthur? _____

4. What did King Arthur carry on his shoulders for three days and three nights during an important battle? _____

5. The Battle of Mt. Badon was vital to the Britons in defeating the pagan _____ barbarians.

6. In *The History of the Britons*, the author wrote that King Arthur carried the portrait of whom on his shoulders? _____

7. In this history, we see that King Arthur took the lead in holding back the barbarians as they tried to wipe out which civilization?
   _____

8. What devotion by King Arthur is emphasized in the book *History of the Kings of Britain*?
   _____

9. In the *History of the Kings of Britain*, we learn that King Arthur rebuilt churches and established convents and _____.

10. King Arthur's wife was named _____.

11. King Arthur's sword was called _____.

12. What is the name of the Frenchman who played a major part in the stories of King Arthur?
    _____

13. What is the name of the author of the narrative about King Arthur, written in the fifteenth century, which was primarily about the death of King Arthur?
    _____

85

14. Who is the author of the famous narrative poem about King Arthur, called *Idylls of the King*? _____

15. In *Idylls of the King*, we learn about _____, the Lily Maid of Astolat.

16. Who is the author of the book *Once and Future King*? _____

17. In *Once and Future King*, who is trying to convince the young Arthur that jousting is a mindless sport? _____

18. What is the name of the symbol of the dream of justice and peace? _____

19. Why should it be important for us to know that King Arthur was a Christian hero? _____

20. In the last sentence of the quote from *Sword at Sunset*, how can the message at the end help us in our current cultural battle for Catholic values in our own country? What is the "light" for which we look to return?

_____

_____

The Death of Arthur

86

Chapter 14
Prayers and Penance

Ireland became Catholic in the fifth century when their patron Saint Patrick brought Christ to the island. Patrick established the Faith so firmly that the most vicious persecutions have not shaken it. The first enemy that tried to destroy the Faith in Ireland was the pagan Vikings who came in the 900s. The Vikings burned churches and killed innocent people. Eventually they were defeated by the great Irish leader, Brian Boru, when he led his men into battle with a crucifix in one hand and a sword in the other. Then the English conquered Ireland. When England left the Church, English soldiers tried to force Ireland out of the Church as well. Henry VIII and Elizabeth persecuted Irish as well as English Catholics. When a man named Oliver Cromwell killed the king of England and took over the government, he ruthlessly persecuted the Irish. He massacred whole towns of Irish Catholics. His soldiers broke into churches and smashed statues and stained-glass windows.

Oliver Plunkett

Cromwell was followed by King Charles II who became a Catholic on his deathbed and had a Catholic wife. At first he did not enforce all of the anti-Catholic laws, but in the early 1670s the English again began hating the Catholics. The leader of Irish Catholics at this time was Archbishop Oliver Plunkett. His life is an example of steadfastness in the Faith, the great gift of Ireland to the Church.

When the new persecutions broke out, Catholics were forced to worship in secret. Their leaders had to go into hiding. Archbishop Plunkett went with them. For the remainder of his life he was an outlaw in the hills, hedges, and hovels of Ireland. Never did he neglect his people to protect his own life. Instead he went wherever he was needed to encourage the people not to give up, to bring them Mass and the Sacraments, to pray the Rosary with them.

In 1679, Plunkett received word that his relative, Patrick Plunkett, the Bishop of Ardagh, was dying. Longing to see Patrick before he died, he came out of hiding. British soldiers caught him and threw him into prison. The Archbishop was put on trial in Ireland. The British made up all sorts of false crimes and false evidence. The jury was Protestant, but they were Irish, too, and they refused to convict their fellow countryman on

St. Patrick

a false charge. The British were furious so they dragged Oliver out of Ireland and carried him off to London. There he was convicted and hanged. His last words to his fellow Irish were, "And being first among the Irish, I will teach others, with the grace of God, by example, not to fear death."

Simplicity and Willingness to do Penance

The Irish learned their lesson well. The threat of death could not drive them from the practice of their Faith. When King William III came to the throne in England, he enforced the Penal Laws, which prohibited the Irish Catholics from owning land, from going to school, and from practicing their religion. King William thought that by making the Irish poor and ignorant, he would drive them from their Church. He could not have been more wrong. Following the example of Oliver Plunkett, they held fast to their Faith and still hold fast to it today. Their main weapons have been the Mass said in secret, the Rosary, and the willingness to accept any sufferings sent their way. Masses were said on Mass rocks, small ledges deep in the woods where the British would never think to look for them. To say the Rosary undetected, they developed penal rosaries, small one-decade rosaries which could be easily hidden. They would carve crucifixes out of peat, the turf used in their fireplaces to heat their homes and cook their meals. These penal crosses could be quickly hidden in the peat baskets if any British soldiers should come to search their homes.

Two of the reasons why the Irish Catholics have held fast to the Faith are their simplicity and willingness to do penance. Since they did not feel the need for huge churches, richly decorated, to worship God, they did not miss them when they were forced to go out into the hills and worship God in the open air. Since they always practiced penance, they were not afraid of suffering. One of the best examples of the simplicity and penance of the Irish is Lough Derg.

Pilgrimage at Lough Derg

Lough Derg is a lake near the border of Ulster (the northernmost province of Ireland). Offshore is a small island called Station Island. Every year hundreds of Irish Catholics come to Station Island for a three-day pilgrimage of penance and fasting. The Irish call it the toughest pilgrimage in Ireland which means that it is probably the toughest pilgrimage in the world.

The pilgrimage goes back to the time of St. Patrick. Patrick had fought against paganism. The devils or spirits who had inhabited the pagan gods were said to have gone into a cave on Station Island and the local people were petrified. Patrick bravely rowed alone across the few hundred yards to the island because no local boatman would dare go near the place. Patrick entered the cave. For forty days no one saw him. At the end of that time, he staggered from the cave, exhausted. He had driven the spirits not only from the cave but from all of Ireland as well. He told the people that he had been granted a vision of Purgatory, so the cave was given the name Patrick's Purgatory.

About 1150, a knight named Owen came to the island. Owen said that he had lived a sinful life but now intended to do penance. As he prayed in the cave, he saw first a vision of Purgatory, then of Hell and finally of Heaven. He was so overwhelmed that he could not walk, and his friends had to carry him from the cave. Soon hundreds of pilgrims were coming to Lough Derg.

Then the British ordered that all religious buildings on the island be torn down and the cave filled in. It was against the law to go out to the island. That did not stop the Irish. They would gather on the shore and pray and fast as if they were on the island. Gradually they began making their way out to the island. Queen Anne passed a law that anyone going to the island would be fined or whipped. So many people went anyway that she could not enforce the law. One summer after the Catholics were finally given some legal rights, more than 30,000 persons made their way to Station Island.

If a person wants to go to Lough Derg, now he must begin to fast (eat nothing) at midnight of the day he is coming. He comes to the boat landing and is rowed to the island where he is assigned to a small cubicle. He leaves his shoes and socks at the cubicle because he must spend his three-day pilgrimage going barefoot, as a sign of penance. Then he is ready to begin the first of the nine stations (rounds) of prayer. To make a station, the person spends forty-five minutes outdoors, praying special prayers given him in a little booklet. On the first day he must complete three stations before 9:30 P.M.

Anytime after he has finished his first station, he is allowed his first and only meal of the day, with black tea, dry toast and/or oatmeal biscuits. The pilgrim can have all he wants, and take as much time as he likes for finishing the meal. Once he gets up from the table, though, he cannot eat or drink anything except plain water until the following afternoon.

The vigil (staying awake all night to pray) begins with religious services in the basilica at 10 P.M. During the night the pilgrims recite together the prayers for the fourth, fifth, sixth, and seventh stations, a total of 1,200 individual prayers.

Pilgrims agree that the second day is the hardest. They must remain awake all day after having been up all night. Mass and Confession start the day. During the morning the pilgrim makes the eighth station. There is another Mass at noon and a set of evening services. He can pick his own time during the afternoon for the second meal allowed him on the island. At last, at 10 P.M., he can go to bed for his first sleep in more than thirty-six hours.

The next day, the last of the pilgrimage, he is awakened for 6 A.M. Mass. The pilgrim completes the last of the nine stations. No meal is served. Once the pilgrim has left the island, he can have a tea-and-toast meal similar to what he ate on the island, but nothing else until midnight.

It's a tough three days, going barefoot on the rough ground, fasting, keeping vigils and making the stations. Yet hundreds of people do it every year, many of them coming back year after year. They want to show sorrow for their sins, to share a little of the sufferings Christ felt. We will not know until Heaven how many souls have been saved because of sufferings cheerfully offered up by Irish Catholics.

St. Patrick wrote this beautiful poem, a masterpiece of Irish literature:

St. Finbar's Cathedral, Cork, Ireland

ST. PATRICK'S BREASTPLATE

I arise today
through the strength of Christ with His Baptism
through the strength of His Resurrection with His Ascension
through the strength of His descent for the Judgment of Doom.

I arise today
through the strength of the love of Cherubim,
in obedience of Angels,
in the service of the Archangels,
in hope of resurrection to meet with reward,
in prayers of Patriarchs,
in predictions of Prophets,
in preachings of Apostles,
in faiths of Confessors,
in innocence of Holy Virgins,
in deeds of righteous men.

I arise today
through the strength of Heaven:
light of Sun,
brilliance of Moon,
splendor of Fire,
speed of Lightning,
swiftness of Wind,
depth of Sea,
stability of Earth,
firmness of Rock.

I arise today
through God's strength to pilot me:
God's might to uphold me,
God's wisdom to guide me,
God's eye to look before me,
God's ear to hear me,
God's word to speak for me,
God's hand to guard me,
God's way to lie before me,
God's shield to protect me,
God's host to secure me
against snares of devils,
against temptations of vices,
against inclinations of nature,
against everyone who shall wish me ill,
afar and anear,
alone and in a crowd...

Christ to protect me today
against poison,
against burning,
against drowning,
against wounding,
so that there may come abundance of reward.

Christ with me,
Christ before me,
Christ behind me,
Christ in me,
Christ beneath me,
Christ above me,
Christ on my right,
Christ on my left,
Christ where I lie,
Christ where I sit,
Christ where I arise,
Christ in the heart of every man who thinks of me,
Christ in the mouth of every man who speaks of me,
Christ in every eye that sees me,
Christ in every ear that hears me.

I arise today
through a mighty strength,
the invocation of the Trinity,
through belief in the Threeness,
through confession of the Oneness toward the Creator.
Salvation is of the Lord.
Salvation is of the Lord.
Salvation is of Christ.
May Thy salvation, O Lord, be ever with us.

Chapter 14
Review Questions

1. When and where did St. Patrick live?
   _____

2. When did the pagan Vikings arrive in Ireland? What did they do in Ireland?
   _____

3. Who defeated the Vikings? How did he defeat them?
   _____

4. Which king and which queen of England persecuted the English Catholics as well as the Irish Catholics?
   _____

5. What did the English soldiers do in Ireland under the government of Oliver Cromwell?
   _____

6. In the 1670's, new persecutions began; Catholics had to worship in _____ and leaders had to go into hiding.

7. Archbishop Plunkett was forced to live as an outlaw but he still encouraged the Irish; he brought them _____ and the sacraments.

8. When Archbishop Plunkett was put on trial in Ireland, he was not convicted, so the British took him to England where they convicted him and _____ him.

9. Which king of England enforced the Penal Laws? _____

10. What were the Penal Laws which England forced on the Irish?
    _____

11. Where did the Irish say Mass under the Penal Laws?
    _____

12. What were penal rosaries? _____
    _____

91

13. What were the penal crosses? _____
_____

14. What are two reasons why the Irish held on to their Catholic Faith in spite of persecution?
_____

15. Lough Derg is a lake in northern Ireland. What is the name of the small island in the lake?
_____

16. Why was the cave that St. Patrick lived in for forty days called Patrick's Purgatory?
_____

17. When did a knight named Owen pray in the cave? What happened to Owen which caused hundreds of people to start visiting the cave?
_____

18. What did the British do on the Island to keep the Irish from going there?
_____

19. How did the English punish the Irish for going to St. Patrick's cave? Who was the British queen who ordered the punishments?
_____

20. What did the Irish do when they could not visit the cave?
_____

21. What are some of the details of the current pilgrimage to Lough Derg?
_____

22. What are five lines of St. Patrick's Breastplate that you like the most?
_____

23. Why do you think that simplicity and penance are so important to a people undergoing persecution? To what extent are these virtues present in our own lives?
_____

Chapter 15
Wife, Mother, Foundress

St. Bridget of Sweden

The great saint of Sweden, St. Bridget, was born June 14, 1303. Her father's name was Birger, her mother's Ingeborg. Her family was one of Sweden's noble families and related to the king. When she was seven, Bridget saw a vision of an altar opposite her bed. By it stood a beautiful lady holding a crown. The lady said, "Bridget, come. Will you have this crown?" Bridget replied, "Yes." This was her first known supernatural experience. When she was ten, she saw a vision of Christ crucified. From then until the day she died, she had a deep devotion to the Passion. When she was eleven, her mother died, and Bridget was sent to live with her Aunt Katherine. Her aunt later told the story that once she gave Bridget some very difficult embroidery to do. She looked into the room and saw a beautiful lady bending over the embroidery frame. When the aunt returned, the embroidery was done perfectly, and she was convinced that Mary had helped Bridget with her work.

In 1316, Bridget was thirteen, of an age to marry. Her father arranged a double marriage between eighteen-year-old Ulf and Bridget, and Ulf's brother Magnus and Bridget's sister, Katherine. At first Bridget did not want to marry, but after prayer decided that it was God's will.

On her wedding day, Bridget was led out by her father, wearing the bridal crown set with precious stones. Ulf sent a bridal train of his brothers-in-arms and many bridesmaids, all on horseback, to escort Bridget to his home. The trumpets announced the approach of the bride, and Ulf came out to meet her. Bridget's father presented his daughter to Ulf with the words: "I give her to you to honor and marry; to share your bed, your locks and keys, every third penny and all legal right. In the name of the Father and of the Son, and of the Holy Ghost. Amen."

After the marriage ceremony in the private chapel, the many guests sat down to the wedding banquet. The wedding festivities went on for several days, with tournaments, dancing, music and banquets, along with food and alms for the poor of the neighborhood.

Bridget and Ulf were very happy, helping each other to grow spiritually. They lived frugally and shared with the poor. Once they purchased a luxurious bed. Then Bridget saw a vision of Christ who criticized her for buying such a fine bed when He had only a cross on which to rest. Bridget immediately sent the bed away. She and Ulf had strict fasts. They built a hospital on their estates in which Bridget herself cared for the sick. They gave dowries to poor girls.

The couple had four sons and four daughters: Charles, Birger, Benedict (who died young), Gudmar, Merita, Katherine, Ingborg (who became a Cistercian nun) and Cecilia. Bridget took her children with her on errands of mercy. Her children were high-spirited, and Charles especially gave her anxiety. Bridget already had the gift of reading consciences, and one day she said to her eldest son, "Go and confess that mortal sin you have committed." Charles at first denied having committed the sin, but then he had to admit it.

In 1335, Bridget and Ulf became part of King Magnus II's traveling court when she was appointed lady-in-waiting for the new queen, Blanche of Flanders. Magnus was extravagant and cruel; later he would kill his own son. Bridget's uncompromising condemnations of his immorality often angered him. She exhorted him to be better. Magnus and Blanche were awed by Bridget and had fits of trying to be better; then they would relapse. Bridget and Ulf were in the court six years, then resigned because they could see no noticeable improvement in the king's behavior.

Devoted to Pilgrimages

Bridget and Ulf were greatly devoted to the pious medieval practice of pilgrimages. The most famous pilgrimage sites were Jerusalem, Rome, and Santiago de Compostela (the shrine of St. James the Greater) in Spain. For each destination, the pilgrim had a special sign which protected him from assault and enabled him to pass through enemy lines. If he wore two crossed palms, he was going to Jerusalem; two crossed keys signified Rome; a scallop shell signified Compostela. A pilgrim, no matter how rich or noble, would dress in a simple smock, with hood, cape and broad-brimmed hat. He would carry food and money in a wallet hung from a broad strap hung across his chest, and he must make the entire journey on foot.

Bridget and Ulf visited all the major Scandinavian shrines. Then in 1341, they made a vow to visit the shrine of St. James at Compostela. The journey was long and arduous, and on the way back, Ulf became ill. He recovered briefly, only to fall into his final illness after reaching Sweden. He died in February 1344, in the monastery at Alvastra. His death was a great blow to Bridget, for she had deeply loved her husband. She had to accept God's will and purify herself from this earthly attachment.

After Ulf's death, Bridget felt torn between two vocations. On the one hand she felt drawn to the cloister. On the other hand, her pilgrimage to Santiago had widened her horizons and made her more aware of the problems of the world. It seemed to her as if God wanted her to take some hand in the great affairs of the Church. She prayed for

Santiago de Compostela

guidance, receiving a vision that she was to obey her confessor, Mathias. Mathias was not sure what to do either, but sent her to the Alvastra monastery, where she lived for two years in a small house, devoting herself to prayer, penance, sewing and study.

Peter of Alvastra

Her wealthy friends ridiculed her for putting aside worldly riches and honors, and it was not easy for her, but Bridget fortified herself with prayer and obeyed. At Alvastra she met Peter of Alvastra, a Cistercian monk. In a vision Christ told Bridget that Peter was to record and translate her visions. Peter received this message with surprise. That evening, while praying in the chapel, he became convinced that he was unworthy to record these divine revelations. Suddenly he felt a violent blow on his cheek, knocking him to the ground. There he lay unable to move, until he was found by some monks and carried to his cell where he remained unconscious. Suddenly a thought came to him that Christ had sent the blow because of his refusal to accept the commission. Then from his heart he said, "Oh, Lord God, if it be this, spare me, for I am ready to obey and write all the words she will say to me from Thee." Immediately he was cured and hastened to Bridget to offer to write anything she wished. He was to record her many visions for the next thirty years.

In 1346 Bridget returned to court, again trying to influence Magnus, especially regarding unjust taxation. He made some changes, but then he slipped back into his old ways. The noblemen of the court ridiculed her. One nobleman poured water out of a window on her head. Another "accidentally" shoved her and made her trip. Another pretended to be drunk and called out insults. She accepted all without complaining.

She began to have visions of a new order to be founded, with strict enclosure and special devotion to Mary. The nuns would wear a white crown of linen covering the head with five red spots in the shape of a cross in honor of the five wounds of Christ. The foundation would have sixty nuns and twenty-five monks, who would also live in the enclosure. Christ was giving her a monumental task because it was no easy thing to start a new order. Bridget told Magnus that she had a vision that he was to help her in this foundation to expiate his sins. He gave her land at Vadstena, on which the foundation would eventually be built, as well as other gifts. Bridget returned to Alvastra.

She was commanded by Christ to go to Rome and decided to go in 1350, a jubilee year. Christ also commanded her to send a letter to the Pope in France (this was the time of the Babylonian Captivity), chastising him for his worldliness.

Christ warned Bridget that a chastisement was coming to the world for its sins. When the Black Death broke out, Bridget believed that this was the punishment. So many died that they had to be buried in rivers or great pits. Then a fire and attack by invaders destroyed everything that had been built at Vadstena. Bridget had to accept these setbacks with equanimity.

When she arrived in Rome, she found it in a state of chaos because of the Pope's absence. Rival families had turned the city into two armed camps. Buildings had collapsed, and the streets became quagmires after rainstorms. The weather was unusually cold and the Tiber flooded. Pilgrims had to make their way as best they could. In the midst of the chaos, Bridget's visions continued. The special Office of Our Lady, known as the "Angelic Discourse" which her nuns would later say, was dictated to Bridget by an angel each day after Mass.

Christ commanded Bridget to reform a monastery in Bologna. While she and her companions were there, Peter had a sudden, urgent desire to go to Rome. Bridget let him go. When he came back, he was accompanied by Bridget's daughter Katherine. Katherine had married at twelve to Edgar von Kyren (who was twenty-two). They had lived a happy life similar to Bridget's and Ulf's. They were devoted to each other and the poor whom they served. However, Edgar was sickly. Katherine felt that Christ was calling her to come to Rome. Edgar gave her permission, and she made the long journey. When she arrived at her mother's house in Rome, she found no one there. She searched the city unsuccessfully. One day while she was praying in St. Peter's, she looked up and saw Peter, who had been sent by God to find her. Bridget received a vision that Edgar had died on Good Friday. She asked Katherine if she would stay and be her helper. Katherine was homesick and had to renounce the comforts and freedoms of her past life. Finally, after much prayer, Katherine made a vow of obedience to Peter, gaining peace and strength.

Katherine was a strikingly beautiful blonde who stood out among the darker Italians. When eligible young men of Rome found out that she was a widow, offers of marriage began to pour in. Count Latino Orsini was so smitten that he twice tried to ambush and kidnap Katherine. The first time, a stag raced by and his men chased it, forgetting their assigned task. Bridget saw it all in a vision; when Katherine returned home, her mother said, "Blessed be that stag that saved you." The second attempt was made at night. The servants saw Katherine coming and awaited Orsini's word, but Orsini was struck with blindness and saw only the darkness. Orsini recognized this blindness as a punishment. He went to Bridget and Katherine and confessed. Their prayers led to his cure and he became their faithful friend and supporter. Later, after he had married, his young son was dying. Bridget spread her cloak over the boy and prayed. Then she said, "Sleep, my child, sleep. The child is not dead but sleeping."

When the child awoke he said, "Mother, what has happened? When Lady Bridget spread her cloak over me, I did not feel ill anymore." The boy got up and went out to play.

In Rome, Bridget lived according to the rule which the convent she later founded was to follow. She practiced strict penances. Many visitors called. Those in a state of sin would be detected by Bridget because of an intolerable odor and a bitter taste in her mouth. Once she told a man that he was possessed by a devil. At first he was furious, but then he repented of his sins. The next time he came, he was surrounded by a good fragrance. Bridget cared for the sick in her home. In her prayer life she reached the seventh mansion (mystical marriage) and she had detailed revelations of the life of Christ and Mary.

Thanks partially to Bridget's urging, the Pope, Urban V, returned to Rome, but he stayed only three years. As he prepared to return to Avignon, Bridget gave him a paper in which she transcribed a revelation from the Blessed Mother: "Now I will speak of Urban. It was through my prayer that he received the inpouring of the Holy Spirit which prompted him to go to Rome... It was I who gained for the Pope the grace of the Holy Ghost to leave Avignon for Rome and who brought him in safety. And what has he done to me? He turns his back on me and it is the Evil Spirit who leads him. He is weary of the divine labor and seeks only bodily comfort.... If he ever reaches the land in which he was elected pope, he will shortly after have a stroke which will make his teeth chatter, his eyes grow dim and all his limbs tremble." The Pope ignored the warning, returning to Avignon. When he arrived, he was worn and ill. Mary's prophecy came true, and he died on December 30, 1370.

The new Pope was Gregory XI. Bridget now bent her efforts to persuade him to return to Rome. She did not live to see him return, but her efforts were one of the reasons that he did leave Avignon.

Now Christ commanded Bridget to go to the Holy Land. She pleaded her feebleness and her old age, not wanting to make the arduous journey. Christ assured her that He would be her strength and that all but one of her party would return to Italy safely.

A Prayer for Death

Bridget was accompanied on this pilgrimage by Charles and Birger. On a stopover in Naples, Charles fell in love with Queen Joanna of Naples and proceeded to make a fool of himself. Bridget was greatly distressed because both Joanna and Charles were already married. In February, Charles became very ill. Bridget felt that the illness was an answer to her prayers that Charles would die rather than persist in mortal sin. In two weeks he was dead. Afterwards the Blessed Mother spoke to her:

I stood by your son Charles just before he died, that he might lose all memory of carnal love, might not think or speak anything contrary to God. . . . I helped him in that strait passage when the soul leaves the body. . . . And when his soul left the body I took him under my protection and the devils fled. . . . But just how the soul of Charles was judged after death I will tell you when it seems good to me."

The pilgrims left Naples and went on to the Holy Land. At the shrine of the Holy Sepulchre, Bridget saw in a vision the soul of her son standing at the Seat of Judgment. The devil accused him of his sins and the Virgin Mary pleaded for his soul. The devil asked why he was driven away from Charles at the time of death. Mary answered, "This I did because of the ardent love he had for me and because of the joy he always felt that I am the Mother of God." The devil replied that Charles was lacking in virtue. His angel answered that Bridget's prayers and works of piety had knocked at the door of mercy for more than thirty years, and therefore, God had granted him the grace of final perseverance and would usher him into eternal life.

After the pilgrimage, during which Bridget had visions of the Crucifixion and the Nativity, the party returned to Rome. Bridget, now seventy, was beset with temptations to discouragement regarding the founding of her order. But on July 18, 1373, Christ appeared to her and gave her consolations. He told her that she would die in five days and that she would be mystically clothed as a nun. Christ promised that her foundation would be realized. All came true as Christ had told her. Bridget died on July 23, her last words being, "Into thy hands, O Lord, I commend my spirit."

Katherine took her mother's body back to Sweden and completed the work of founding the Order of the Most Holy Saviour, which is popularly known as the Bridgettines. Katherine returned to Rome to work for the canonization of her mother and the ratification of her Rule. Pope Gregory returned to Rome but died soon after. Pope Urban VI's election was soon followed by the Great Schism. Katherine of Sweden and Catherine of Siena became friends and supported the valid Pope.

Katherine died on March 24, 1381. Her mother was canonized in 1391, and the Bridgettines spread throughout Europe. The English Bridgettines at Syon is the only English pre-Reformation community that has survived unbroken to the present day. Gustavus Vasa drove the Bridgettines out of Sweden in the sixteenth century. Now the great church in Vadstena is a museum. But Bridget's influence lives on, as Swedes of all faiths pray before her tomb in Vadstena.

Chapter 15
Review Questions

1. When and where did St. Bridget live? In what kind of a family was Bridget born?

2. Describe the vision of Bridget when she was seven years old.

3. Describe the vision of Bridget when she was ten years old.

4. Though the wedding of Bridget to Ulf seemed materialistic, what words did Bridget's father use to indicate they were good Christians?

5. Did Bridget and her husband live as most royalty live? What word in the book tells you they did not?

6. How do you know that Bridget and her husband did not indulge in overeating?

7. What kind of charitable things did Bridget and her husband do for the poor and the sick?

8. Why did Bridget and her husband resign from the court of King Magnus II?

9. How many children did Bridget and her husband have?

10. Bridget and her husband went on pilgrimages to all the major shrines in which area?

11. After Bridget's husband died, she was not sure of her vocation. Where did she go to pray and do penance to discover her vocation?

12. Who was Peter of Alvastra? How did he come to be Bridget's spiritual director?

13. What were the characteristics of the religious order that St. Bridget wanted to found?

14. Where was the land that King Magnus gave her to establish her order?

15. What showed Bridget that Rome was in a state of chaos?
    _____

16. What did Bridget do to get the pope to return to Rome?
    _____

17. What spiritual experience did Bridget have while she was in Rome?
    _____

18. Why did Christ send the Black Death? What was the result of the Black Death?
    _____

19. Who was Katherine? What vow did Katherine make after her husband died?
    _____

20. Who was Count Orsini? What did he try to do? What made him change his life? What was the final result?
    _____

21. Bridget lived according to the rule of life she wanted for her convent. Besides practicing strict penances, what did she do in charitable works for others?
    _____

22. How could Bridget detect that someone was in a state of sin?
    _____

23. What message did Bridget give to Pope Urban V when he wanted to leave Rome and live in Avignon, France?
    _____

24. Who was the pope that Bridget finally convinced to return to Rome? _____

25. How did Bridget's son Charles die? What were the visions she had of his judgment? What were the reasons his soul was saved?
    _____

26. While Bridget was in the Holy Land, she had visions regarding two aspects of the life of Jesus, the Crucifixion and the _____.

27. Describe the death of St. Bridget. _____

28. Katherine finished the establishment of which Order? What is the popular name? _____

29. Gustavus Vasa, the King of Sweden in the sixteenth century, made himself the head of the church in Sweden, and made Sweden a Protestant country. What did he do to the Bridgettine Order?
    _____

Chapter 16
Trading Crowns

In November 1632, King Gustavus II Adolphus of Sweden was killed in the Battle of Lutzen, one of the important battles of the Thirty Years' War. After the king's death, the Swedes and Lutherans rallied to defeat the forces of the Holy Roman Empire. After this Protestant victory, it was clear that Emperor Ferdinand could never restore the unity of Christendom or even the unity of the Holy Roman Empire. In winning the many victories prior to the Battle of Lutzen, Gustavus Adolphus had struck a deadly blow at the heart of Christendom. One of the great ironies of history was that the only child of this Lutheran general and king, who waged war successfully against Catholics, was herself to become a convert to the Catholic Church.

When Gustavus Adolphus was killed in battle, the male line of the Vasa dynasty of Sweden was extinct. His only child was six-year-old Christiana, the heir to the throne, who had been born December 8, 1626. Axel Oxenstierna served as regent for the little girl, who was brought up as if she were a prince, being trained in all aspects of ruling. Christiana was intelligent and curious. Her brilliant mind was constantly searching for intellectual fulfillment.

Christiana was brought up a Lutheran in a very intolerant country. In 1617, laws had been passed decreeing exile and property confiscation for anyone who converted to the Catholic Church. Anyone teaching Catholic doctrine risked banishment as a traitor. Christiana did not share this hostility to Catholicism. When she was only twenty she faced down the Council on an issue of religious intolerance, namely a law prohibiting Catholic foreigners to have Mass in their homes. But since her only understanding of Catholic doctrine had come from Lutheran preachers, she was at first not able to accept Catholicism either, so she devised a Christianity of her own and worshipped God according to what seemed best to her. She remained a firm believer in God, Christ, and the Bible.

King Gustavus II

Christiana and Charles Gustavus

As the time came for Christiana to assume the full exercise of royal authority, the country asked one major question: whom would Christiana marry? She had received various proposals, but in her teenage years she was in love with her cousin Charles Gustavus, and the two had become secretly engaged. In a letter from Charles in 1644, when Christiana was seventeen, he swore his undying love. She advised him to keep their engagement a secret for a year or two until she could be crowned and then no one could prevent their marriage.

Charles served in the army in Germany from 1642-1645. When he returned to Sweden, he found Christiana a reigning sovereign, no longer an infatuated young girl. She was preoccupied with her responsibilities and enthusiastic about ruling. Though he was still infatuated with her, she no longer loved him.

Queen Christiana of Sweden by Sebastien Bourdon

In the meantime, Oxenstierna, while regent, had put more power into the hands of the nobility at the expense of the crown. Christiana did not like this unbalanced situation and wanted to reassert the royal authority. But she could not really establish her position firmly until the question of the succession could be solved. A serious illness and an attempted assassination in 1647 emphasized the importance of securing the succession to the throne.

Everyone tried to push Christiana into marriage, but she had no intention of marrying except for love, and at this point, she was not in love. Her plan for the succession was to make Charles Gustavus commander-in-chief of the armies, successor to the throne and hereditary prince. She had to handle this plan carefully because the council would not like it and neither would Charles. Charles guessed what she was doing and sent frantic letters to persuade her to marry him, all in vain. When he referred to himself as "the most wretched man on earth," Christiana pointed out that he was going to succeed to the throne. She WENT ahead with her plan to appoint him commander-in-chief and sent him off to the army. He said, "I leave with a pain in my heart which scarcely permits me to breathe."

Christiana finally brought her plan out into the open. The noblemen of the council were angry because they did not want Charles to be given royal honors. If he had married Christiana, he would have had no special privileges because all rights of succession would have descended upon the children. But if he were appointed hereditary prince and successor, he would receive authority over the nobility. There was a terrific clash in the Council, and Christiana and the nobility were at an impasse. She played clever politics by going to the Estates, the assembly of the commoners, and getting them on her side. When the Council saw that Christiana was starting to give some of their powers to the commoners, they were forced to go along with her plan. By 1650, she was in firm control of the country. Charles, meanwhile, withdrew to his estates and sulked.

Accepting Catholicism through Descartes

Christiana's intellectual interests continued after she became queen. She was especially intrigued by philosophy, science and mathematics. In 1649 the great philosopher-mathematician Descartes came to Stockholm at her invitation. Two or three times a week they met at 5 A.M. (she had little free time otherwise) to study together. Descartes died in Stockholm on February 11, 1650. During the time he was working with Christiana, she had come to realize that Catholicism could be the true religion. She had found through Descartes that nothing in the Catholic religion was contrary to reason, unlike what her Lutheran teachers had led her to believe. That this brilliant man, whom she had so much admired, could also be a dedicated and convinced Catholic, persuaded her that Catholicism was the true religion.

In the summer of 1650, a new ambassador from Portugal arrived in

Stockholm. His regular interpreter fell ill, and a substitute was found from among his suite. It turned out that the substitute was the ambassador's chaplain, a Jesuit priest in disguise. Christiana soon realized the situation and in the midst of diplomatic discussions with the ambassador asked the interpreter questions about religion. The ambassador, not understanding Swedish, could not figure out why his interpreter took so long to translate what he had said. The priest, Father Macedo, was finally given the mission by Christiana of carrying a letter to the Jesuit general in Rome, asking for two Jesuits to come secretly to Stockholm to instruct her in Catholic doctrine and to receive her into the Church. Father Macedo knew that he would not get permission from the ambassador, who was fearful of diplomatic repercussions, to carry out his mission, so he had to flee secretly. This was in August, 1651.

Signor Teofilo

The mission was completed, and two Jesuits, Francesco Malines and Paolo Casati, came to Stockholm disguised as laymen. They carried instructions in code, referring to Christiana as Signor Teofilo. When they arrived in Stockholm, Christiana was immediately curious at the presence of these two Italians in her city, suspecting that they might be the Jesuits she had requested. At an opportune moment she asked, "Have you a letter for me?"

Without turning his head, Casati murmured, "Yes." The next day she received them in private audience and her instructions began.

Demanding an intellectually satisfying religion, Christiana had many questions and insisted on rational explanations for each disputed point. Some of her questions were: Was there such a thing as Providence?; Was the human soul immortal?; Was there any difference between good and evil or did everything depend on effects? She hungrily absorbed all that the Jesuits had to tell her and knew that her conscience would permit her to do nothing else but to become a Catholic.

Having committed herself to the Catholic Church, she now faced a serious dilemma. The anti-Catholic laws in Sweden were fierce, and the government was intimately bound up with the Lutheran Church. Christiana could not see how she could remain as queen and still be faithful to her new religion. Therefore, she resolved to abdicate. This abdication would be a great sacrifice. Sweden was one of the strongest nations in Europe, and Christiana possessed every conceivable royal privilege. By abdicating she would surrender her position and all guarantee of security for the rest of her life.

She risked even more than material loss. If her secret conversion were revealed prematurely, a revolt might break out. Christiana could be imprisoned, even killed.

Abdicating an Earthly throne for the Kingdom of God

On June 6, 1654, she formally abdicated in favor of Charles, who was crowned King Charles X Gustavus. The real reason for her abdication was her conversion, but that was a well-kept secret. The publicly announced reasons were that the abdication would be in the best interests of the country, of Charles, and of herself. She stated that her country would be in a stronger position in Europe with a male ruler, that Charles would no longer be in a position of uncertainty, and that she would have time to devote to the arts and sciences and other intellectual pursuits.

There was much opposition but no one could prevent her abdication. She left Stockholm and went to Halmsted. Christiana sent part of her suite home, including her Lutheran chaplain. She had her hair cut and dressed in male clothes. Under the name of Count Dohnas, she went to Hamburg (Germany) and then to Antwerp (the Low Countries, ruled by Spain). There, she wrote to Charles that she would never return to

Sweden. She made this secret journey because she feared that she might be forcibly detained in Sweden to prevent her conversion. She had lived under great strain for three years, afraid that her conversion would be found out and that she would therefore face all the heavy legal penalties. Even though she had been queen, she knew that anti-Catholic feeling in Sweden was so strong that it would not have exempted her from the full force of the penalties. Fearful that at the last minute she had been found out, she had chosen to escape in disguise.

Now on friendly soil, she formally but secretly embraced the Catholic Faith on Christmas Eve, 1654. Christiana still did not publicly reveal her conversion because she had to get her assets out of Sweden, so that she would not be a pauper the rest of her life.

On October 31, 1655, she entered Innsbruck, Austria, territory ruled by the men her father had defeated in the Thirty Years' War. On November 3, before the high altar of the Innsbruck royal chapel and in the presence of Pope Alexander VII's personal representative, Christiana made her public profession of faith. The ceremony was moving and beautiful with all the pageantry of the Church and of royalty brought out to celebrate the occasion.

As Christiana had known, she was immediately vilified by anti-Catholics. They said her conversion was a whim, that no one as intelligent and educated as she could seriously embrace Catholicism. But Christiana did not care about the criticism; she had found her true spiritual home.

On December 23, 1655, she entered Rome, met by a royal reception. Bernini redesigned the Porta del Popolo in her honor, and to this day it bears the inscription welcoming her. She spent most of the rest of her life in Rome, occasionally involving herself in diplomatic negotiations with Spain and France. She died April 19, 1687, and was

Monument of Queen Christiana of Sweden

buried in St. Peter's Basilica, where a beautiful monument celebrates her conversion, honoring the queen who gave up an earthly throne for the Kingdom of God.

Chapter 16
Review Questions

1. When and where did Christiana live?

2. Who joined with the Swedes to defeat the Catholic Holy Roman Empire?

3. Why did Christiana ascend to the throne at such an early age? How was she trained? What characteristics did Christiana show at an early age?

4. Sweden was a Lutheran country. What were some of the laws against Catholics?

5. Christiana was tolerant of Catholics. Which law did she abolish?

6. Christiana was to marry her cousin Charles Gustavus. Why did she want to wait? Why did Christiana change her mind?

7. Why was Christiana unhappy with the regent?

8. What was the appointment that Christiana gave Charles Gustavus?

9. Why did the Council of nobles not want Charles to be the successor and hereditary prince?

10. Why did Christiana want Charles Gustavus to be successor to the throne?

11. How did Christiana get control of Sweden?

12. What were the three areas of study that interested Christiana?

13. Who came to help Christiana in her studies? What did she come to realize?
    _____

14. Who was Portugal's ambassador's chaplain? _____

15. What did the chaplain do at the request of Christiana?
    _____

16. What were some of the questions that Christiana asked the Jesuit priests?
    _____

17. What was the state religion of Sweden? What was the dilemma for Christiana?
    _____

18. If Christiana decided to abdicate, what were some of the effects that might happen?
    _____

19. Why did Christiana decide to abdicate, that is, to give up being the queen of Sweden?
    _____

20. What were the public reasons given by Christiana for abdicating the throne to Charles?
    _____

21. How did Christiana escape from Sweden?
    _____

22. Where and when was Christiana received into the Church?
    _____

23. When did Christiana enter Rome? How was she received?
    _____

24. What did Christiana do in Rome for more than thirty years?
    _____

25. Where is Christiana buried?
    _____

Chapter 17
Conversions in the North

The countries of Norway, Sweden, Denmark, Iceland, and Finland are often grouped together and called Scandinavia. Scandinavia has some of the most beautiful scenery in the world. It is an exciting place to visit during the summer because it is daylight for almost twenty-four hours, since Scandinavia is so far north. It is "the land of the midnight sun." Scandinavia was Catholic during the time of Christendom, but during the Protestant Revolt became almost totally Lutheran. For a time Catholics were persecuted. The Catholic Church is now legal, but few Scandinavians are Catholic. These few Catholics, however, can be inspired by the stories of the conversions of their countries.

When Charlemagne became Holy Roman Emperor in 800, one of his goals was the conversion of the barbarians. He was successful in converting the Saxons and the Avars, but the Danes from Scandinavia continued their pagan ways and their raids on the rest of Europe. The opportunity for conversion came during the reign of Charlemagne's son, Louis the Pious. Harold Klak, a *pretender* (one who has a claim) to the throne, was expelled from Denmark four times. After his second expulsion, he asked Louis the Pious for help in regaining the throne. In exchange, he offered to take a priest with him. The person Louis sent was St. Anskar.

St. Anskar: Sowing seeds in Scandinavia

St. Anskar was a Frank born in 801 in northwest France. His mother died when he was five, so his father sent him to be brought up in the Abbey of Corbie. This was a deeply disturbing experience for the young boy, to lose his mother and be uprooted from his home. It was hard for him to settle down to study. One evening he dreamed that he was stumbling through a muddy field, trying unsuccessfully

St. Henry Catholic Cathedral in Helsinki

to reach a fence. On the other side of the fence was a broad and pleasant path. A lady radiant in face and clothing stood on the other side. With her were many women dressed in white, including Anskar's mother. Anskar tried to reach her but was held back by the mud. The lady said to him, "Son, do you want your mother? Some day you will have her again, if you work as hard as we do here. We who dwell here have no time to be lazy." Afterwards Anskar worked very hard in his studies.

When he was thirteen, he had another dream, of a place of light, joy, color, and gladness. He heard a voice rich and resonant, "Go forth to thy labor and return here to Me with a martyr's crown." Anskar was sure that he had been granted a vision of Heaven.

Anskar became a teacher, then head of the school at Corbie. When he was only twenty-one, he was transferred to be head of a new school and was ordained. In 826, came the plea of Harold Klak. No one wanted to answer the call to the barbarian lands. The abbot asked Anskar if he would go and Anskar agreed. His friends thought him conceited or a fool; others begged him to change his mind. He spent many hours wondering if he could really go through with it. One day, he was sitting in the orchard thinking over his decision. His friend Autbert came to sit beside him, asking him if he was sure he wanted to go. When Anskar said that he was, Autbert said he would go with him.

Anskar and Autbert spent two years in Denmark. They set up a school for twelve boys but accomplished little else. Harold was again expelled, and Autbert fell ill and died. Anskar came home to get advice on how best to convert the Danes, but no one could help him.

In 829, delegates from Sweden petitioned the Frankish king to send men to Sweden to teach Christianity to the king. Louis sent a message to Anskar, "Tarry not, not even to shave." Anskar was delighted with this new missionary opportunity. With his friend Witmar, he boarded a boat for Sweden. The boat was attacked by pirates. Anskar and his companion jumped overboard and swam for shore. They barely made it with their lives and lost everything else, including forty books. Finally, another boat brought them to Sweden. They met King Bjorn. Anskar stayed in Sweden for a year and a half but made little progress. The Vikings were strongly resistant to Christianity. In 831 he returned home.

Louis decided to try missionary efforts in Denmark again. Anskar was consecrated an archbishop and returned to Denmark in 832, where he stayed for thirteen years. Anskar bought slaves, instructed them, baptized them, and trained them for Christian work. He lived an austere life, suffering from cold and hunger.

In 845 Viking pirates attacked Hamburg, which was then in Danish territory. The attack was sudden and fierce. It fell to Anskar to help save the people. He organized the escape from the town, but he did not have time to bring out any of the precious altar vessels or sacred books. He did not even have time to get his cloak. The Vikings destroyed the city, even burning down the cathedral Anskar had built. The people were left homeless. When the Vikings finally withdrew, Anskar had to rebuild the city from the ashes. He made friends with Horik the Elder, the Danish king, and received permission to carry on his work. He built a new church and a school. Out of the destruction, Christianity was being reborn.

He then received a call from Sweden, which had not had a priest at all between the years 845 and 851. When he arrived, he found pagan belief and custom stronger than ever. The pagan priests were afraid that Anskar would take the people out from under their control. Anskar went to see King Olaf to get his support for his mission. Olaf had no strong feelings about Christianity, so he asked Anskar: "What will you give me to protect you?"

Anskar said, "I won't give bribes even to save my life." The king said that he would have to wait until the assembly could meet and cast lots on the subject. Anskar could not budge the king so he had to wait patiently. One day while he was saying Mass, Anskar had a feeling that all would go well. The assembly met, the lots were cast, and the result was favorable to Christianity. Anskar began his Swedish mission. By 854, things were going well enough that he returned to Hamburg, where he spent the remaining eleven years of his life until his death in 865.

Anskar lived an ascetic life with constant traveling and concern for the poor. He practiced strict tithing, giving one-tenth of all the revenues the diocese received to the poor. Each Lent he would feed two poor men

Sweyn Forkbeard's death and that of his elder son brought Canute the Great to power. Canute had accompanied his father on the invasion of England, and after his victory in 1017, began to profess Christianity. He quickly perceived the need of an understanding with the English bishops if he were to hold England as well as his dominions in Denmark and Norway. As he grew older, he became an ardent champion of Christian religion and culture. He made Christianity the dominant religion in Denmark and used his influence to secure for it toleration in other Scandinavian lands. Canute's wife, Queen Emma, assisted in the foundation of many monasteries. At Canute's death in 1035, though isolated Danish districts were still pagan, there could be little doubt of the Christian victory. The seeds sown by Anskar had at last borne fruit.

Patron Saint of Norway

Norway's patron saint is St. Olaf, who lived from 995-1030. When he was young, Olaf lived a wild life. When he was fourteen, he joined in a raid on England that brutally murdered St. Alphage, the Archbishop of Canterbury. Olaf apparently enjoyed the bloodthirsty life. Then something happened to him. At the age of eighteen, he was baptized a Catholic. We do not know what changed him. Perhaps Olaf met a Catholic who showed him that violence could never bring happiness. Perhaps he became sickened at the continuing bloodshed. Perhaps he had a narrow escape, almost losing his life, and became frightened about the future life. Whatever the reason, Olaf turned to God.

Though Olaf had now dedicated his life to Christ, he was still a good fighter. His country was controlled by Denmark and he wanted Norway to be free. Fighting his battles under the Sign of the Cross, he became king. Norway had two enemies: the Danes and the pagans. Olaf fought the pagans with all of his strength. He brought in missionaries and

King St. Olaf

and two poor women each day. He redeemed prisoners with his own money. He bore up well under the almost constant sorrow and failure he had to face, realizing that he would sow the seed which others would harvest. The final conversion of Scandinavia had to wait until the tenth and eleventh centuries. In Denmark, the daughter of Harold Klak, Thyra, married Gorm, who became king and was known as Gorm the Old because he lived eighty-five years. His son Harold Bluetooth was the first reigning king to be converted to Christianity. Though Harold's son, Sweyn Forkbeard, also went through the baptismal rite at the same time (965), after he became king in 985 he quickly revealed himself as a pagan. The missionaries had to go underground while an active persecution raged.

teachers from England. He built churches. He declared that Christianity was the official religion of Norway. The powerful leaders of paganism hated Olaf. They refused to support him in his struggles with the Danes for the freedom of Norway.

His enemies pursued him, and for a time Olaf had to hide in Russia. He could not stay long from his beautiful homeland, with its tall mountains snowcapped even in the middle of summer, its rushing waterfalls, its icy glaciers, its deep blue fjords carved into the coastline. He returned to Norway as the defender of Norwegian independence and the Catholic Church. On August 31, 1030, he led his men into battle. The sky turned dark; there was a total eclipse of the sun. In the darkness swords clashed and arrows whizzed through the air. The enemies fell upon Olaf and killed him.

He was buried in the new cathedral at Trondheim. So many miracles occurred at his tomb that he was soon canonized a saint.

Iceland Accepts Christianity

The first known explorers to reach Iceland were Irish monks, probably led by St. Brendan. The first settlers were Vikings from Norway in the late 800s. The Vikings fled Norway because they did not like the government of King Harold Fairhair.

The first known missionary was the Saxon priest, Friedrich, who arrived in 981. Despite his ignorance of the language, he had some success. Olaf I of Norway sent Norse-speaking missionaries at the end of the century. The missionaries impressed the people greatly and thus had a great influence on society. The pagan leaders even threatened war in defense of their customs. Finally, the matter was submitted to the *Althing*, or Parliament, and by majority vote Christianity was adopted and the idols ordered destroyed. In 1056, Isleif became the first native bishop, with his diocese at Skaholt.

Iceland came under Danish rule. When Denmark joined the Protestant Revolt and embraced Lutheranism, the new Protestants attempted to enforce it on the Icelanders as well. The people rejected Lutheranism, under the leadership of Bishop Jon Aresson. Finally, the Lutheran leaders seized Bishop Aresson and put him to death at Skaholt in 1551. Catholicism was declared illegal. With no Catholic priest left in the country, the people were unable to hold on to their faith. Iceland became totally Protestant. Not until 1896 did Iceland have resident priests once again. In 1942, the native Icelander Johan Gunnarson became bishop. The Catholics built Christ the King Cathedral which sits atop a hill in Reykjavik, the country's capital city. In 1944, Iceland became an independent country and remains so today. In Iceland, as in the rest of the Scandinavian countries, Catholics are few. Many prayers are needed for the conversion of these countries.

Christ the King Cathedral

Chapter 17
Review Questions

1. What are the countries of Scandinavia?

2. Scandinavia was Catholic, but what happened during the Protestant Revolt?

3. When Charlemagne became the Holy Roman Emperor in 800, he was unable to convert the Danes. What did the Danes do?

4. Who did Charlemagne's son, Louis the Pious, send to Denmark? _____

5. Describe the childhood of St. Anskar. When did he live? Where did he live?

6. What was the vision of St. Anskar when he was a boy? How did it affect him?

7. Was St. Anskar successful with the Danes when he went there for two years? Was he successful in converting the Swedes when he went there for less than two years?

8. What happened when the Vikings attacked Hamburg in Denmark?

9. After the attack, what happened to help St. Anskar to help convert the Danes?

10. What happened when St. Anskar went to visit King Olaf in Sweden?

11. After being in Sweden for four years, St. Anskar went back to Denmark. How long did St. Anskar continue his missionary work in Hamburg in Denmark?
   _____

12. What kind of a life did St. Anskar live? What specifically did he do to help the poor?
   _____
   _____

13. Who was the first king of Denmark to be converted to Christianity? _____

14. Who was Sweyn Forkbeard? What happened when he was king?
   _____

15. Tell the story of the king of Denmark, Canute the Great.
   _____
   _____
   _____

16. What did Queen Emma do?
   _____

17. What was it that kept St. Anskar to keep up his courage and continue to labor for converts in Denmark even though he did not see success in his lifetime?
   _____

18. Who was St. Olaf? When and where did he live?
   _____
   _____

19. At what age did St. Olaf convert to Catholicism? _____

20. How did Olaf become king of Norway?
   _____

21. What did Olaf do to promote Catholicism in Norway?
   _____
   _____

22. The leaders of paganism hated King Olaf. Where did he need to hide for a time?

    _____

23. Olaf returned to Norway to fight for independence and for the Catholic Church. What happened in August of 1030?

    _____

24. What made the Church declare King Olaf a saint?

    _____

    _____

25. Who were the first missionaries in Iceland?

    _____

26. Who was the first known missionary in Iceland? When did he arrive?

    _____

    _____

27. St. Olaf sent Norse-speaking missionaries to Iceland. What happened when Iceland's parliament met? Who was the first native bishop in Iceland?

    _____

    _____

28. When Denmark became Protestant during the Protestant Revolt and conquered Iceland, what did they do in 1551?

    _____

29. Today, there are only about 6 priests in Iceland in four parishes; about 5000 people are Catholic, less than two percent of the population. In Denmark, less than one percent are Catholic, about 35,000 people in 50 parishes with 40 priests. In Sweden, less than two percent are Catholic, about 144,000 Catholics with 75 priests. In Norway, there are about 29 priests, about 52,000 Catholics representing about one percent of the population. What can we do to help the Scandinavian people to convert to Catholicism?

    _____

    _____

    _____

    _____

    _____

Chapter 18
Switzerland's Heroes

A close rival with Norway for Europe's most beautiful scenery is Switzerland. The snow and glacier covered Alps tower above the meadows bright with flowers, deep blue-green lakes, and rushing rivers. The Swiss are fiercely independent. The country has stayed neutral in two world wars, protected by rugged mountains and well-trained citizen-soldiers. Switzerland is slightly more than half Protestant, but it has a rich Catholic heritage.

Early in the 800s, a young Benedictine monk named Meinrad became a hermit and lived alone, except for two pet crows, for twenty-six years. Then one night two wandering men clubbed him to death and fled. The crows followed them, shrieking loudly until the two murderers, on arriving in Zurich thirty miles away, were captured by suspicious residents. Other monks were sent out to live at Meinrad's hermitage, which was given the name *Einsiedeln*, from the German word which means hermit. In 934, a Benedictine monastery was organized there.

Einsiedeln now has 13,000 residents, not counting the many pilgrims. The townsfolk have an ancient tradition of cheerfully greeting every stranger in the streets, to let pilgrims know that they are welcome in the town. The monastery has a basilica with two bell towers, nearly 170 feet high. There are also workshops, barns for the milk cows and stables for the thoroughbred horses that are sold to the Swiss army. At the top of the basilica is a statue of the Blessed Mother with an angel on either side.

A miracle occurred the day the church was consecrated, September 14, 948. A vigil and a fast were held the evening before the scheduled consecration day. Two bishops were present: Conrad and Ulrich. As they knelt in prayer, they all at once observed Christ standing at the altar with angels and saints beside Him. When Bishop Conrad began to consecrate the church the following morning, an angel held him back. The angel announced that Christ had consecrated the church the night before. The anniversary of the consecration has been a festival day at Einsiedeln ever since.

When Meinrad arrived at the spot, he brought with him a wooden statue of Mary. The statue was destroyed by fire in 1464,

The Matterhorn, Switzerland

and a new statue put in its place. Centuries of candles lit by millions of pilgrims have darkened the once flesh-colored features of the Virgin and the Child she holds in her left arm, so pilgrims refer to her as the Black Madonna.

The four-foot statue is dressed in a robe of red and gold brocade. There are special robes for feast days and a collection of crowns.

When Napoleon's troops invaded Einsiedeln, they attacked the church. The stone church was too sturdy for them, so they tore down Our Lady's chapel. Before they arrived, the monks hastily buried the statue in the hills, then after three weeks carried it to Austria. Napoleon's men seemed to be following the statue. Every time they moved it to a new spot, the French army would soon arrive. For three years, the Black Madonna traveled from one place to another. Finally, an Austrian villager carried the statue over the Alps to Trieste. There the villager turned the statue over to a friend who promised to keep it safe in his house. The friendly protector happened to be a Protestant.

On September 29, 1803, the statue made a triumphal return to Einsiedeln. Each year on the anniversary, a High Mass is celebrated in the chapel and the statue is dressed in the same gold-embroidered white robe it was wearing when it made its safe return.

While the real statue was on its travels, another statue was substituted for the Black Madonna in the church. When Napoleon's troops reached the basilica they seized the substitute statue and, thinking it was the miraculous image, took it with them. A few years before his defeat at Waterloo, Napoleon sent a message to the monks at Einsiedeln offering to return the miraculous statue. The humble monks informed the lofty emperor that the real Black Madonna was safely home.

Our Lady of Einsiedeln

Patron Saint of Switzerland

Another of Switzerland's heroes is its patron saint, St. Nicholas. Nicholas Von Flue was born March 21, 1417, in Obwalden, not far from Lucerne. He came from a peasant family and lived in a forest *canton* (a political division of Switzerland). The canton was a direct democracy with all men over fourteen eligible to vote. As a young man, Nicholas was elected a councilor and a judge.

From the age of sixteen, a male citizen was liable for military service. Nicholas fought in two wars. The first was against Austria, in which he was promoted to captain. In 1446, he fought in a battle in which 1,100 Swiss defeated 5,000 Austrians.

Nicholas fought in his second war by papal invitation against Duke Sigismund, who had been excommunicated for aggression against the Bishop of Brixen. The enemy had occupied a nuns' convent. The Swiss proposed to storm the convent and destroy it and the church. After praying before a crucifix, Nicholas persuaded his compatriots to change their plans. He promised that the enemy would evacuate in three days. They did, and Nicholas' moral authority was established.

Nicholas held the traditional Church attitude toward war and taught the just war doctrine: that war is justified if attacked or if it is waged to defend the innocent or to correct some great moral evil. The war must have some chance of success, the good to be done must outweigh the harm, the war must be proclaimed by just authority, and moral means must be used in waging war (for example, no attacking of innocents and no use of force beyond that which is necessary).

Nicholas was cheerful, hardworking and popular. At the same time, he practiced mental prayer and mortification, as well as contemplation. His rosary was his constant companion.

Nicholas fasted four days a week and all of Lent. He would eat only a piece of bread or a few dried peas. All the while, he would work in the fields, tend to his official duties, and fulfill his military obligations.

St. Gallen Cathedral, one of the most important Baroque buildings in Switzerland

Nicholas experienced mystical prayer and symbolic visions. One evening he saw a tower rising to the clouds. He understood it as God's invitation to a more perfect life.

He married Dorothy Wiss in 1447, and lived with his wife and family on a farm. He was the father of ten children: five boys and five girls. His children had successful lives; one became a priest and two held political office.

One case he decided as a judge offers an excellent example of his principles. A poor man mortgaged his garden. When the mortgage came due, he was barely able to pay. The rich man who had loaned him the money claimed to have bought the garden. The other judges, except Nicholas, sided with the rich man. Nicholas resigned in disgust from the court in 1465.

The divine call to a higher vocation became more insistent. He had a vision of three noblemen representing the Trinity. They asked, "Nicholas, will you give yourself body and soul into Our power?"

He answered, "I give myself to none save God Almighty whom I would serve with body and soul." The Three said that if he would loyally persevere in God's service, he would bear in eternity the banner of Heaven's victorious army.

Once, his eldest son left him clearing ground on a mountainside. Suddenly the son heard a cry and found his father rolling in a thicket of thorns, unconscious. When he regained consciousness, Nicholas said, "The devil has played a dirty trick on me, but it was the will of God."

A Life of Asceticism

Nicholas felt called to be a hermit. He did not want to leave his family, though they were well provided for. But he realized that he had to do God's will no matter how painful. On October 16, 1467, four months after the birth of his tenth child, he gave his family a blessing and departed, with his wife's consent. Though this seems cruel on his part, God had a special vocation for him to save his country. If he had not gone to live as a hermit in the special way that he did, he would have been unable to fulfill his vocation because he would not have acquired the moral authority that he needed.

Benedictine Abbey of Engelberg, Switzerland

A comparison can be made with a husband who goes to fight in a just war, knowing that he may leave his wife a widow and his children fatherless, but knowing also that his country needs him.

At first Nicholas was ridiculed by his neighbors. He decided to leave Switzerland and enter a community of monks in Alsace. When he was within sight of the Alsatian township of Liechthal, lightning flashes seemed to wrap the town in flames. As Nicholas slept in the open fields, a ray of brilliant light flashed from Heaven and pierced his body. This miracle convinced him to stay in Switzerland. It also left him unable to eat or drink.

When he returned home, he saw four rays of light with the appearance of burning tapers shining in Ranft. He understood that it was God's will that he build his hermitage there.

He would sleep for two or three hours, rising at midnight to pray. He had no table or chair. His bed was a log of wood. He went barefoot and bareheaded even in winter.

Because of his asceticism, hostility changed to veneration. His ability to go without food was seen as a mark of God's favor. For an entire month, sworn agents of the government kept strict watch around his hermitage to make sure that he took no food.

The Bishop of Constance wanted to test Nicholas. He asked Nicholas what was the most important virtue of a Christian life. Nicholas replied: obedience. So the bishop commanded Nicholas to eat a bit of bread soaked in wine. Nicholas complied, but suffered agonies. He was never again asked to eat. His only nourishment was the Blessed Sacrament. He put off the questions of the curious with "God knows."

Visitors flocked to Ranft for help and advice. Others came out of curiosity or hostility. Nicholas talked to all of them, and pilgrims from many countries found him cheerful and friendly. He was often visited by his wife and children.

Nicholas had telepathic knowledge. He told a farmer he did wrong to suspect a woman of bewitching cattle, and a jealous wife that her suspicions were unfounded. A German abbot asked a definition of avarice from Nicholas. He replied, "You know better than I; you were planning to sell twenty-seven barrels of wine for profit, but unfortunately for you, your bishop has seized them."

Preserving the Swiss Confederation

The cantons sent deputations to ask his advice. After a successful war against Burgundy, the cantons were quarreling over booty, and the federation was in danger of destruction. The parish priest of Stans, Heini Amgrund, hurried to Nicholas with the problem. Nicholas gave him detailed terms for a settlement. Amgrund rushed back to Stans where the delegates were about to separate. He persuaded them to listen out of respect for Nicholas. They accepted his sensible compromise, which united them into a strong federation. Each canton retained its individual values but they would work together when threatened from outside. The federation continued to seek Nicholas' advice. His statue now stands in the building which houses the federal assembly.

In 1487, Nicholas became ill and his body wasted away to bones and sinews. He was unable to lie comfortably and suffered mental pains of fear as well. He died on his seventieth birthday, March 21, 1487, in the presence of his wife and children. Although popular devotion and miracles attributed to his intervention were instantaneous, he was not canonized until 1947.

St. Nicholas had fulfilled his vocation to save the Swiss confederation from imminent danger of dissolution. Because of St. Nicholas' efforts, Switzerland remained an oasis of peace and humane living through two world wars.

Chapter 18
Review Questions

1. Who was Meinrad? Where and when did he live? How did he die?
   _____

2. What was Einsiedeln? What does it mean? What was organized there?
   _____

3. Describe Einsiedeln today.
   _____
   _____

4. What was the miracle at Einsiedeln? When did it occur?
   _____

5. Describe the Black Madonna and her early history.
   _____

6. What happened to the statue when Napoleon's soldiers attacked the church?
   _____

7. Where and when did Nicholas von Flue live? _____

8. What were some of the events in the life of young Nicholas?
   _____
   _____

9. What is the just war doctrine taught by the Catholic Church?
   _____
   _____

10. Describe the spiritual life of Nicholas as a young man.
    _____

11. Describe the family of St. Nicholas.
    _____

12. Why did Nicholas resign as a judge?

13. What was the vision of Nicholas?

14. What was the miracle which prevented Nicholas from joining the monks?

15. Where did Nicholas build his hermitage? _____

16. Describe the life of Nicholas as a hermit.

17. Who came to observe Nicholas? Who came to test Nicholas?

18. Who came to visit Nicholas for help?

19. What was the only nourishment Nicholas had as a hermit? _____

20. What kind of knowledge did Nicholas have? Give an example.

21. Various leaders in Switzerland were having an argument. What was the recommendation that Nicholas gave them?

22. When did Nicholas die? _____

23. How can we see today the respect that the country has for Nicholas?

Chapter 19

Master of Music

Ludwig van Beethoven

Ludwig van Beethoven was the second child of Johann and Maria Beethoven; their first child lived only six days. The couple had five more children after Ludwig, but only two survived infancy. Ludwig was baptized December 17, 1770, in Bonn, Germany. He went to school when he was six, but had a terrible time with math and never did learn his multiplication tables.

Though the family was not wealthy, Ludwig's father, a musician himself, saw to it that Ludwig had music lessons. At the age of eight, Ludwig gave his first recital. The ad for the recital, however, said that he was only six. Apparently, being a genius at eight was not a sufficient drawing card.

At the age of thirteen, Ludwig played the organ at a 6 A.M. Mass as a substitute for his teacher. He was so good that the regular organist's salary was cut in half and Beethoven hired in his place. That same year, his first compositions, three sonatas for klavier, were published. At fourteen, he became a piano teacher in the Breuning family. For the first time, Beethoven was introduced to the world of culture and society, and the Breuning house became his second home.

At the age of seventeen, he went to Vienna to study music but was soon called home because his mother died. Because his father was often drunk and in trouble with the police, Ludwig had to be the head of the family. It was not until late 1792 that he was able to return to Vienna.

Vienna, Austria was a beautiful city then at the height of its glory. Vienna was to music what Renaissance Florence had been to art. Ludwig received a small stipend from Maximilian Franz, an elector of the Holy Roman Empire. He kept careful accounts, which still exist. From them we learn of his meals "with wine," his cleaning woman, a piano rental and the purchase of a wig and of good clothes so he could go out into society. He began to study under Haydn, a famous composer of the time. He worked hard, though Ludwig later said that he did not learn much from Haydn.

In 1795, a rich man named Lichnowsky became his patron. Beethoven was ill-mannered but so talented that the people of fine society put up with him. He would be invited to parties where the only place available to sit was the piano bench, so that he would have to play for the company. He began to be well known, selling his compositions and giving concerts.

Bridging the Classical and Romantic Movements

Music in the late eighteenth and early nineteenth century was written in the *classical* style, complicated and intellectual, without emotional depth. Soon after the disruption caused by the French Revolution and Napoleon, it would become obvious that the human intellect was not the sole solution to the problems of man. Instead of turning to God, Who is the solution, many people came to glorify the emotions. In music, this new emphasis on emotional content was the *romantic movement.* Beethoven was the bridge between the classical and romantic movements, and he was able, especially later in his life, to use his music specifically to the glory of God.

Beethoven was not always easy to get along with. He once wrote to another composer, "Do not come to me any more! You are a false dog, and may the hangman do away with all false dogs." The next day he repented and wrote, "You are an honest fellow and I now realize that you were right."

Creativity was a painful process for him. Once on a walk with a friend, Beethoven was said to have "muttered and howled." His friend asked what he was doing. He replied, "A theme for the last allegro of the sonata has occurred to me." He ran into his house; without taking off his hat, he sat at the piano, ignoring his friend. At last he got up, surprised to see his friend still there. He told the friend, "I can't give you a lesson today. I must go on working."

Beethoven was a procrastinator and disorganized. He would pile up manuscripts and then throw them around the room when trying to find one. He was awkward, always cutting himself when shaving. He was absent-minded. Once in a restaurant he walked in, sat down, waited awhile, then called for the bill without having ordered anything. He could also, however, be quite generous to his friends and relatives.

In 1800, Beethoven published his First Symphony, still in the classical style. Around this time, he would have periods when words became a babble, conversation unintelligible, and a ringing filled his ears. In 1801 he wrote, "Let me tell you that my most prized possession, my hearing, has greatly deteriorated." Doctors were no help; one applied an ointment to his arms. His reaction, "I will seize Fate by the throat. It shall certainly not bend and crush me completely." Though the hearing loss was never total, it is still the great tragedy of Beethoven's life that he was never really able to hear his greatest works. But nothing could stop his creativity. In 1802 he wrote the *Heiligenstadt Testament,* an essay in which his courage shines through. That same year also saw the publication of the joyous and optimistic Second Symphony.

The Third Symphony, also known as the *Eroica,* was published in 1804. He originally intended to dedicate it to Napoleon, but when he heard that Napoleon had become a dictator, he tore up the title page. The *Eroica* has grandeur and majesty. It is frightening in its innovations. He began with two hammer blows, startling and attention-getting. The horn player in the first *allegro* (a faster passage) sounds as if he is coming in at the wrong time. The funeral march in the middle is probably the most famous movement. Beethoven had definitely begun the romantic movement in music with the *Eroica.*

In 1805, he wrote the opera, *Fidelio.* The main character, Florestan, is a prisoner. His wife Leonore is warm and faithful. The opera communicates the pain of imprisonment and the eventual joy of liberation. Napoleon's armies marched into Vienna one week before *Fidelio* was performed.

In 1807, Beethoven published the Fourth Symphony, a lighter work than his other symphonies. In the same year he published the Fifth Symphony, probably his best-known work. In 1808, he published his Sixth Symphony, known as the *Pastoral.* Between 1804 and 1810, he wrote four symphonies, an opera, four sonatas, three concertos, and six other major works. He knew what he wanted to say and poured it out in an outburst of creativity.

On May 25, 1806, Beethoven's brother Carl married Joanna Reiss. Later Joanna gave birth to a son Karl, an event which would have great consequences for Beethoven.

In May 1809, Napoleon was attacking Vienna again, and Beethoven's house was under shellfire. Vienna surrendered March 30. Most of Beethoven's friends left the city, and Beethoven had to live in a cellar. Yet he worked continuously on what was to be the last of his piano concertos, *The Emperor Concerto*. (A *concerto* is a musical composition for one or occasionally more solo instruments accompanied by an orchestra.)

Beethoven's life was fatiguing. His creativity decreased somewhat, though he was able to complete the Seventh and Eighth Symphonies by 1821. He was forced to live in poverty. In 1812, he wrote a beautiful letter addressed to the Immortal Beloved. To this day, no one is sure to whom he was writing.

In 1815, his brother Carl died. Beethoven was made co-guardian of nine-year-old Karl with Joanna. Beethoven could not stand his sister-in-law, thinking she was morally depraved. She was not especially admirable but was not as bad as he thought. Beethoven filed a lawsuit for total custody of the child. The court ruled in Beethoven's favor, but Joanna fought back. Each thought the worst of the other; each made mistakes out of love for the boy. Beethoven was totally preoccupied with his nephew. His motives were noble but he was too possessive.

Karl finally ran away to his mother. Beethoven was able to bring him back and put him into a boarding school. Finally in September 1819, the court sent him to Joanna. Beethoven appealed the ruling. On April 5, 1820, Karl was sent back to Beethoven. Karl then ran away again. He was brought back to school forcibly. As Karl grew up, he wanted more independence than Beethoven would allow. Finally, in desperation the boy attempted suicide, which made Beethoven utterly

Vienna

miserable. In September 1826, he moved to the country with Karl to get away from bad publicity regarding the suicide attempt. Karl finally entered into a military career and had a fairly peaceful later life. But the emotional strain on Beethoven was great, and it must have affected his work.

Hymn to Joy

In 1823, Beethoven published the Ninth Symphony and the *Missa Solemnis* (Solemn Mass). The Ninth included choral parts as well as the well-known *Hymn to Joy*. His theme was "arrival at joy through suffering," which was a theme of his entire life. The rehearsals of the Ninth were very difficult. The notes for the sopranos were extremely high, but Beethoven would not change them. So the sopranos simply left them out. The basses had a solo and a melody, an unusual innovation. Beethoven helped conduct the first performance. At the end, the audience cheered wildly. Beethoven could not hear them. He stood exhausted at the podium, until an assistant gently turned him around to acknowledge the cheers he could not hear.

Missa Solemnis

Beethoven spent years working on the *Missa Solemnis*. One place in the manuscript was erased so many times that a hole wore through. The paper was the climax of his spiritual development. The *Kyrie* (Lord have mercy) expresses human hopes and fears. The *Gloria* (Glory to God) hymns the praises of the Creator. The *Agnus Dei* (Lamb of God) had a two-fold message. The *Miserere* (Have mercy on us) expresses human pain and sorrow. The *Dona nobis pacem* (Grant us peace) is a prayer for inner and outer peace. The *Missa* was moving and profound.

Beethoven seemed to have reached a peak with the publication of the *Missa*. He became even more uncaring about outward appearances. Once he was arrested as a tramp in a small town near Vienna because of his unkempt appearance. He would go for long walks composing in his mind, flailing his arms and muttering. He was working on the quartets, and he was getting on his brother Johann's nerves. (He and Karl were staying with Johann in his country home.) Finally, he stormed out of the house and went back to Vienna in December 1826.

The weather was extremely cold and he became ill with pneumonia. He scribbled out a will leaving everything to Karl. He received the Last Rites of the Church and died in the midst of a thunderstorm on March 26, 1827, as the elements provided a fitting closing theme to the life of this great composer.

Cathedral of Saint Stephen
Vienna, Austria

Chapter 19
Review Questions

1. When and where was Ludwig van Beethoven born?

2. Describe what happened to Ludwig van Beethoven when he was six? When he was eight? When he was thirteen? When he was fourteen?

3. Where did Beethoven go to study music at seventeen?

4. Who was the famous composer of the time under whom Beethoven studied?

5. What was the difference between the classical style of music and the romantic movement?

6. What were some of Beethoven's personality character traits?

7. What was the *Heiligenstadt Testament*?

8. What was the *Eroica*?

9. Describe the opera *Fidelio*.

10. Why did Beethoven have to live in his cellar for a time?

11. What was the theme of Beethoven's Ninth Symphony?
    _____

12. In the *Missa Solemnis*, what does the music for the *Kyrie* express?
    _____

13. What does the music for the *Gloria* express?
    _____

14. What does the music for the *Miserere* express?
    _____

15. What does the music for the *Dona nobis pacem* express?
    _____

16. How did Beethoven die? In what year did he die?
    _____

Beethoven's Tomb in Vienna

Chapter 20

Earthly and Heavenly Loves

Hungary became a Catholic nation with the conversion of King Stephen in the tenth century. Several centuries later, the nation's most famous woman saint was born. Although she spent most of her life in Germany, she is nevertheless known as St. Elizabeth of Hungary.

Elizabeth (1207-1231) was the daughter of King Andrew and Queen Gertrude of Hungary. When she was still a toddler, Elizabeth was betrothed to Louis, the son of *Landgrave* (a title of nobility) Hermann of Thuringia, a German state converted by St. Boniface. At the age of four, she was brought to live in the Thuringian capital, Wartburg. Elizabeth was sent with a sumptuous dowry, as her mother wanted to show off Hungarian wealth. Wartburg was an impressive castle, rising out of a rock on top of a mountain.

Louis was Elizabeth's senior by seven years. Elizabeth was very well educated in domestic arts, academic subjects, and horsemanship. She was an intelligent child and very pious. To train her will, she would deny herself something every day.

The marriage was scheduled for 1221, but by this time Hermann had died, Gertrude had been murdered, and Hungary had suffered many setbacks. The noblemen wanted the engagement broken. But Louis and Elizabeth were very much in love. However, Louis told them, "Do you see that mountain before us? If it were full of red gold and belonged to me, I would more willingly renounce it than I would my dear friend Elizabeth. Let people talk. I tell you that I love her and I own nothing in this world that is dearer to me." So the marriage took place. Louis was an excellent king, with great concern for the poor and those unjustly treated. He had a high sense of honor. He took care to respect God's laws, even to the extent that anyone who used God's name in vain in his presence had to wear a dunce cap.

On March 28, 1222, their first child, a son named Hermann, was born. Louis had to be away frequently on long journeys to fulfill his duties as king. While he was gone, Elizabeth was lonely. She would dress plainly and live quietly. When he returned, she would dress in her most beautiful gowns. Her religious fervor was unabated. She continued her life of prayer. Once at Mass, she had a vision of Christ crucified as the priest elevated the Host after the Consecration. She had a spirit of poverty. When the time came for the church ceremony after the birth of her child, she imitated Mary by dressing in simple clothes, walking barefoot, and carrying her own child. She was especially attracted by the simple piety and poverty of the Franciscans.

Elizabeth's charities were extensive. She assisted poor women in labor, cared for the sick in the worst conditions, paid the debts of the poor, spun wool for the poor, and made

Elizabeth caring for the poor

baptismal robes for poor children. On Holy Thursday, she washed the feet of lepers. Once, a leper came to the castle with a sore on his head; Elizabeth dressed the wound herself.

On another occasion, a leper came to the castle asking for charity. To care for him adequately, Elizabeth put him into Louis' own bed. Her mother-in-law, Sophia, was furious and complained to Louis. When Louis went up to check on his mother's complaint, he saw in his bed not a leper, but the image of the suffering Christ.

On March 20, 1224, Elizabeth bore a daughter, Sophia. The winter of 1225 was very rigorous, lasting until the end of April. Plague and famine were rife. Elizabeth distributed the food of the court and housed the sick in a building at the foot of the Wartburg. She visited the sick several times a day, tending and consoling them. She sold her own possessions to buy food and medicine and distributed food from her own table. When Louis returned after a long absence, the noblemen complained to him about Elizabeth's habit of giving so much away. Louis refused even to listen to their complaints.

In 1227, Louis left on Crusade, knowing that he might never return. Elizabeth, pregnant with their third child, rode with him for the first two days of the journey. At their leavetaking, she gave him a sapphire ring engraved with the Lamb of God and his flag. He said he would use it to seal his messages to her so she would know they were authentic.

The Renunciation of St. Elizabeth of Hungary by James Collinson

His farewell words, "May the God of Heaven bless you and keep you, my beloved. May God bless also the child you bear." Elizabeth returned home and put on a widow's dress.

In Italy, a fever epidemic broke out. Thousands fell ill, including Louis. He received the Last Rites, saying, "Do you not see those white doves? I shall leave here when they do." This just and noble king died September 11, at age twenty-seven. Elizabeth's daughter Gertrude was born September 29. When Elizabeth heard of her husband's death she said, "Death, death. . . . All happiness and worldly honor are henceforth past for me." She was deeply anguished and had to crush her own will to accept Louis' death as God's will.

Charity and Humility Ceaseless

During Louis' life she had been able to dispose of the revenues of her dowry. Now Henry Raspe, her brother-in-law, took these. She could have lived off what her brother-in-law gave her, but she knew that he was unjust, and her spiritual director, Conrad of Marburg, had forbidden her to eat or use anything not justly obtained. So she deliberately accepted poverty and obedience over the temptation to comfort. She gave up the security of a home to put herself totally in God's care.

She left the Wartburg on a cold November night and took shelter in a pigsty. The next day she sought lodging at the homes of the rich with her children. They refused because they did not want to be on the wrong side of Henry. Finally a rich official let her stay at a hovel behind his large house. Elizabeth's humiliation was increased when she was pushed into the water by an old lady she had once helped. Elizabeth just laughed. She became ill from the cold, lack of shelter, and poor food, but she never complained, knowing that she was called to a vocation of poverty and service to the poor. On Good Friday, 1228, she went to the Franciscan monastery at Eisenach, where she took a vow of poverty.

Elizabeth went to live in Marburg, Germany, where she made her profession as a member of the Franciscan Third Order. She wore simple clothes, abstained from meat four times a week, fasted on Friday and from All Saints Day to Easter, said the Divine Office, and assisted the poor. She established a hospital, keeping the worst cases for her personal treatment, especially children. Supernatural happenings occurred. Once a woman and her child were cared for by Elizabeth. The next day the woman sneaked off, abandoning her child. Suddenly she was unable to go any farther, no matter how hard she tried. She returned and, contrite, took her child. Another time a young man with worldly vanities visited Elizabeth. She said, "Why do you not serve your Creator?"

He replied, "I beg you to pray that God may give me the grace to serve Him." She prayed. The next year he joined the Franciscans.

Elizabeth died shortly after midnight on November 17, 1231. Her body remained supple and gave off the scent of roses. Miracles were worked at her tomb. The majority of the cures were of children. After five years, her body was still incorrupt. Elizabeth was canonized in 1235, an example of holiness as a wife, queen, and mother, and as a devoted servant to Christ's poor.

Chapter 20
Review Questions

1. When did Hungary become a Catholic nation? Who was the king at the time?

2. When was Elizabeth of Hungary born? Who were her parents?

3. How old was Elizabeth when she was sent to Thuringia, a German state?

4. Who converted Germany to Catholicism?

5. What kind of an education did the Germans give Elizabeth?

6. When did Elizabeth and Louis marry?

7. Why was Louis an excellent king?

8. How did Elizabeth show a spirit of poverty?

9. What was the vision Elizabeth had?

10. What were some of the examples which show Elizabeth's charity while she was still young?

11. What did Elizabeth do to help the sick during the plague of the winter of 1225?

12. How old was King Louis when he died? Of what did he die?
    _____

13. Who was Elizabeth's spiritual director? _____

14. What did Elizabeth's brother-in-law do that was a sin?
    _____

15. What happened to Elizabeth after she left her own castle home?
    _____
    _____

16. After Elizabeth joined the Franciscan Third Order, what kind of a life did she lead? Be specific.
    _____
    _____

17. What did Elizabeth establish to help the poor?
    _____

18. When did Elizabeth die?
    _____

19. What miracles happened with the body of Elizabeth?
    _____
    _____

20. When was St. Elizabeth of Hungary canonized a saint?
    _____

21. In which four vocations was St. Elizabeth of Hungary an example of holiness?
    _____
    _____
    _____
    _____

Chapter 21
Captive Cardinal

The Church in the captive nations is persecuted, sometimes to a greater degree, sometimes to a lesser, but always persecuted. Yet many of the Christians in these lands still hold fast to the Faith.

To understand how the Communists took over these countries, how they have persecuted the Church and how Christians have remained true to the Faith, we will tell in detail the story of one courageous man, Cardinal Joseph Mindszenty of Hungary.

Joseph was born on March 29, 1892, in Mindszent, Hungary. His last name, Pehm, was originally German, but when the Nazis ordered Hungarians to change their Hungarian names to German names, he deliberately changed his German name to Mindszenty, after his birthplace, to show his loyalty to his Hungarian heritage. Joseph was ordained a priest in 1915 and became the pastor at a parish in Zalaegerszeg in 1919 at the age of twenty-seven. His first direct conflict with the Communists came in 1919. During the confusing days after World War I, the Communists came briefly into power in Hungary. Father Mindszenty refused to cooperate in any way with the Communists.

Cardinal Joseph Mindszenty

For example, once a Communist leader was giving a speech in a city square. The city's workers were being forced to listen. As Father Mindszenty passed by, the noon Angelus bell began to ring. Mindszenty began loudly to pray the Angelus. The workers joined in. At the end of the prayer, he made the Sign of the

Hungarian Parliament, Budapest

Esztergom Basilica

Cross, turned around and left. The workers followed him and that was the end of the Communist meeting.

Another time, Father Mindszenty was taken into custody and ordered not to return to Zalaegerszeg. As soon as he was released, he immediately boarded a train for Zalaegerszeg. The Communist government collapsed soon after, but Father Mindszenty had made it clear that he would never cooperate with this enemy of the Catholic Church.

In March 1944, Mindszenty was appointed Bishop of Veszprem. The Nazis had just forced Hungary to enter the war, resulting in bombings of Hungarian towns by British and American planes and the deportation of Jews by the Nazis. Mindszenty was active in the resistance to Hitler and vigorously protested the deportation of the Jews. He turned every religious house under his jurisdiction into a sanctuary for Jews hiding from the Gestapo.

Because of his opposition to the Nazis, Mindszenty was arrested on November 27, 1944, with twenty-six other priests. Under Mindszenty's guidance, they celebrated Mass and said their prayers in prison. Among the priests were professors of theology from the seminary. Mindszenty directed them to continue their classes and give final exams. When the seminarians passed their exams, Mindszenty secretly ordained ten priests in prison, though they had only one candle, one cassock, and one surplice among them.

On March 31, 1945, Mindszenty was released. His diocese was in ruins. The Communist army terrorized the people. There were no trains. The roads were impassable. Mindszenty had to travel in a one-horse carriage to bring consolation to the people.

On December 21, 1944, the Communists had organized a provisional National Assembly in the Hungarian territory that they occupied. They organized several political parties and appointed members of the Assembly from these parties. Three of the parties and the labor unions were totally dominated by the Communists. They permitted one small party to exist without direct Communist control in order to create an illusion of free political activity. The Assembly was ordered to arrange

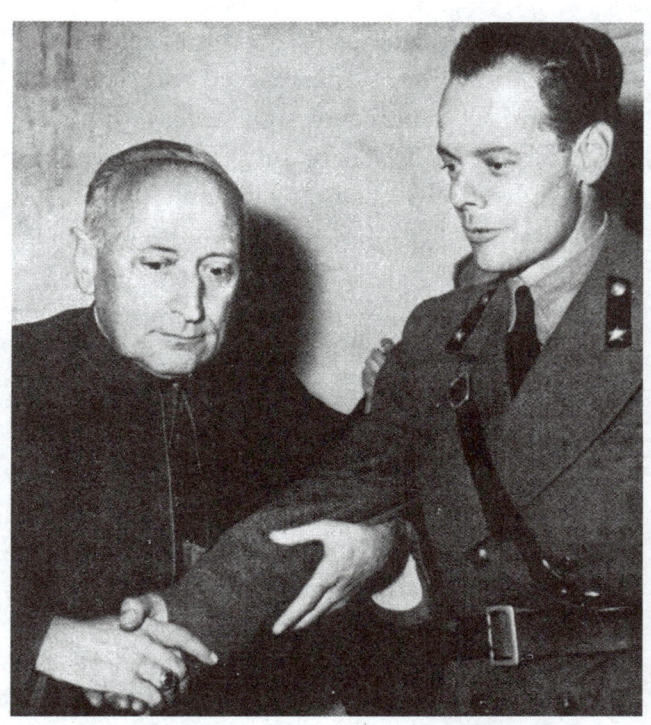

Cardinal Mindszenty with the officer who headed the Freedom Fighters who freed him from prison. Major Pallavicini, right, was later captured and executed by the Communists.

a parliamentary election for the fall of 1945. The Communists boasted that these elections would be totally free and would allow the people a full voice in the government. Many Catholic organizations were suspicious of the Communist promises and did not want to participate, but the Communists threatened to outlaw the organizations if they did not cooperate.

Strengthening the Faith of His People

On October 7, 1945, Mindszenty became Archbishop of Esztergom. Esztergom was the oldest diocese in Hungary. Therefore, Mindszenty was now the Primate of Hungary. A primate is the bishop in the oldest diocese, and he is regarded as the leader of the bishops of his country. Mindszenty's country was devastated. The new primate worked tirelessly to organize relief. He appealed for charity to other nations, especially the United States. He inaugurated a movement of prayer and penance in reparation for the sins committed during and after the war. He set an example of prayer and fasting, so much so that his priests often secretly mixed vitamins in his soup to prevent his becoming ill from so much fasting. In February 1946, Pope Pius XII made Mindszenty a cardinal.

Wherever Mindszenty went on his apostolic travels, huge crowds turned out to see him. On May 5, 1946, he personally led 100,000 men on a ten-mile walking pilgrimage from Budapest to the Shrine of Mariaremete in honor of the Blessed Mother. Under Mindszenty's leadership, Hungary began to experience a great religious revival.

Mindful of the great devotion to Mary throughout Hungary's history, Mindszenty proclaimed that August 15, 1947, through August 15, 1948, would be a Marian Year. The year of devotion to Our Lady was a huge success with rallies, pilgrimages, and other special observances. The people were so enthusiastic for the Marian Year that the Communists did not dare prohibit it altogether. So they tried to hinder the celebration in every way possible. They refused to issue railroad tickets to Marian celebrations. Traffic in entire counties would be prohibited on the pretense of fictitious epidemics. "Accidental" power failures prevented the use of public address systems. Tractors with noisy engines were operated near the churches during Mass and sermons. Nevertheless, four and a half million people participated in the observances.

Communists Hinder Catholic Activity

At first, the Communists held back on persecuting the Church because they did not want to antagonize the people. However, they did hinder Catholic activity in three ways: 1) no government financial support was given to any religious institution, organization, or school; 2) Church magazines and newspapers were refused permission to be published; 3) political parties were restricted so that no Christian political party could exist.

When the time came for the parliamentary elections of November 1945, only those parties in the Provisional National Assembly, which the

Cardinal Mindszenty with Pope Paul VI.

Communists had set up, were allowed to run candidates. The only non-Marxist party among them was the Smallholders Party. So Catholics voted for the Smallholders, which received 57.7 percent of the vote. But its weak leaders were pressured into giving the Communists 50 percent of the Cabinet positions. The government, now dominated by Communists (who claimed that they were in power by democratic elections), banned Catholic youth organizations and ordered nuns and brothers out of the Catholic schools. In the fall of 1947, the Communists increased their power in the government by fraudulent elections and persecution of opposition parties. On June 16, 1948, all Catholic schools were seized by the government, and courses in Marxism were required in all schools.

Faced with this increasing persecution of the Church, Mindszenty spoke out even more firmly. He gave information on the persecution to Western newspapermen, thereby making it more difficult for the Communists to pretend to the world that their regime was responsive to the people. So the Communists turned to personal attacks against Mindszenty, calling him an enemy of the people. They sent out teams of spies to uncover scandals in his past. Of course they found nothing. They forced some pro-Communist Catholics to sign statements condemning Mindszenty, but the majority of the people still loved their cardinal.

Then the Communists arrested a priest named Andrew Zakar. They brainwashed and drugged him. Brainwashing is a Communist technique whereby they put a man through such physical and mental stress that he can no longer think clearly. They repeat over and over to him Communist doctrines until the man can think of nothing else. The Communists brought Father Zakar to Mindszenty's residence to try to frighten Mindszenty into thinking that the same things were going to happen to him. After the Communists left with Father Zakar, Mindszenty wrote and sealed a letter to be opened only on his arrest. In it he said:

> I have never participated in any kind of conspiracy. I will not resign my office as Archbishop. I have nothing to confess and I won't sign anything. If you should ever read that I have confessed or resigned, and even see it authenticated with my signature, remember that it will have been only the result of human frailty. In advance, I declare all such actions null and void.

An Unbroken Will

Some priests urged Cardinal Mindszenty to escape to Rome, but he refused. He wanted to stay in Hungary and support his people.

On December 6, 1948, the day for which Cardinal Mindszenty had prepared, came. He was arrested. The Communists questioned him day and night. He had to stand with his arms raised for days at a time under blinding lights. On January 11, 1949, he signed a "confession" when he was on the verge of a complete breakdown and hoped to get rid of his interrogators for a few hours. Under his signature, he placed the letters *c.f.,* which stood for the Latin words *coatus feci* which means "I signed under force." The interrogators were jubilant that Mindszenty had confessed at last, until police experts deciphered the meaning of the Latin letters.

Then the Communists, realizing that they could never break Mindszenty's will, resorted to drugs. After forty days of brainwashing and drugs, a public trial was held on February 3-8, 1949. During the trial Mindszenty was obviously not responsible for what he said. He could barely stand. Deep circles ringed his eyes. His voice shook and could barely be heard. He recited a memorized confession. If he forgot a line, the judge finished it for him. He was convicted of treason and sentenced to life imprisonment. Mindszenty's sufferings shocked the civilized world, and newspapers in many countries condemned the Communist action.

Mindszenty was locked up in Central Prison in Budapest, the capital of Hungary, where his mother was allowed to visit only once a month. He became extremely ill with a thyroid condition. His mother informed Archbishop Grosz of Mindszenty's illness and the archbishop delivered a formal note to the government on October 16, 1949, requesting adequate medical care for Mindszenty. Immediately afterwards, Mindszenty disappeared.

His mother tried her hardest to find out where he was and to be allowed to see him, but the Communist government never gave her a straight answer. She then put her total trust in God. Although extremely poor, she scraped together enough money to buy a statue of the Sacred Heart which she donated to her village. The village then held a ceremony of consecration to the Sacred Heart. As she was leaving the church after the ceremony, on June 16, 1950, Mother Mindszenty was handed a telegram giving her permission to visit her son.

Accompanied by two friends, Sister Adelaide and Father Joseph Vecsey, she went to Budapest. Secret police followed the trio all the way to Budapest. But at last she was allowed to see her son for about half an hour. He had recovered from his illness, but Mother Mindszenty was unable to find out anything about his treatment since guards standing by listened carefully to every word spoken.

Religious Persecutions Increase

The Communists stepped up their attacks on the Church in June of 1950, with raids on monasteries and convents. On both June 9 and June 18, raids sent 1,000 religious to concentration camps. Then the government passed a regulation abolishing the teaching of religion in all schools unless the parents requested it. When 95 percent of the parents made such a request, the Communists fired many religion teachers, warned students that those who attended religion classes would not be allowed to attend college, and visited parents at home to pressure them to withdraw their children from the classes. Textbooks were rewritten to preach Communism. All non-Communist youth organizations were disbanded, including the Boy Scouts. Religious were expelled from hospitals, orphanages, and homes for the aged. Finally, the religious orders themselves were dissolved and all members of the orders forced to go into secular life. The Communists then set up the Bureau for Church Affairs so that priests sympathetic to Communism, or at least so afraid that they would do what the Communists told them, were running the Church.

Cardinal Mindszenty came down with tuberculosis during the winter of 1954. His weight dropped to ninety pounds, half his normal weight, as he received no medical care.

During 1955, a conference was scheduled in Geneva, Switzerland, between the Communists and the leaders of the U.S. and Great Britain. In order to convince the other nations that the Communists were not so evil as they had been pictured, the government moved Mindszenty out of prison to house arrest in the country. There he received better treatment, and his health improved.

Short-lived Freedom

Then in October and November of 1956, the Hungarian Revolution broke out in Budapest, led mainly by young Hungarian people. The Communist government was temporarily overthrown and a free Hungary was proclaimed. Mindszenty was freed and brought to Budapest, where he was greeted by cheering crowds.

Hungary's freedom was short-lived. The Soviet Union sent tanks into the streets of Budapest to crush the Freedom Fighters. Though the Hungarians appealed for help to the Free World, no help came. The Soviets killed thousands of brave Hungarians, and the Communists were once more in power.

When Soviet troops entered Budapest, Mindszenty took refuge in the American legation. There he remained for fifteen years as Communist police kept watch around the clock to arrest him immediately if he left the building.

In November, 1971, negotiations between the Vatican and the Hungarian government resulted in permission for Mindszenty to leave Hungary. Mindszenty did not want to leave Hungary, but in obedience to the Pope he put his own wishes aside, saying, "I have decided, as a proof of my unlimited love for the Church, to leave the United States embassy. I would like to spend the rest of my life in Hungary among my people, whom I love so much. But as this has become impossible, I will accept what is probably the heaviest cross of my life." Mindszenty went to Rome where Pope Paul VI embraced him warmly, putting his own pectoral cross around the cardinal's neck.

Cardinal Mindszenty lived in Vienna, Austria, until his death in 1975. Today he is buried in the Basilica of Esztergom. The inscription on his tomb reads as follows:

> Life humiliated him – Death has exalted him. Here rests in peace, Joseph Mindszenty, Cardinal Priest of the Holy Roman Church of the Titutlus (title) of Saint Stephen on the Caelian Hill, The last Prince-Primate of Hungary, Archbishop of Strigonia, a most faithful pastor in tribulation, who was born on March 29th, 1892 and died on May 6th, 1975. He was strong under the attack of war, tortured by a tyrannical power, condemned to prison, an exile from the Fatherland he remained until death the obedient son of (his) Mother, the Holy Roman Church and an honest worker for his beloved Fatherland. His relics were translated (brought here) sixteen years after his death and were buried in the Crypt of Mary.

Cardinal Mindszenty represents all the brave Christians who, though they live under oppressive governments, remain true to Christ no matter what Our Lord's enemies do.

Tomb of Cardinal Mindszenty

Chapter 21
Review Questions

1. When and where did Cardinal Joseph Mindszenty live?

2. Write two examples that show that Father Mindszenty defied the Communists in 1919.

3. How did Bishop Mindszenty defy the Nazis in 1944?

4. How did Bishop Mindszenty continue to be a bishop while he was in prison in 1944 and 1945?

5. What did the Communists do in 1944 and 1945 to impose their rule on Hungary?

6. In 1945, Bishop Mindszenty became the Archbishop of Esztergom. What did he do as Archbishop?

7. In 1946, the Pope made Mindszenty a cardinal. What were some of the things that Cardinal Mindszenty did to strengthen the faith of the Hungarian people?

8. What did the Communists do to stop the religious activities for the Marian Year?

9. In what three ways did the Communists hinder the Catholic Church?

10. How did the Communists gain control of the Hungarian government in 1945?

11. What did the Communist government do to persecute the Church in 1947 and 1948?

12. What is brainwashing?

13. Describe the arrest and brainwashing of Cardinal Mindszenty.

14. What did the Communists do to persecute the Catholic Church from 1950 to 1956?

15. Describe the Hungarian Revolution of 1956.

16. What happened to Cardinal Mindszenty in 1971?

17. Which pope welcomed Cardinal Mindszenty in Rome?

18. Who were the people who freed Cardinal Mindszenty from prison in 1956?

19. According to the message on the cardinal's tombstone, for what did he stand in his life?

20. What must we do to help Catholics wherever they are persecuted?

Chapter 22
Christ in Ukraine and Russia

Legend has it that Christianity first arrived in Rus (currently Ukraine) at the time of the Apostles, when St. Andrew came as a missionary to the Slavic and Scythian population along the Dnipro (Dnieper) River. Upon seeing the hills of Kyiv (Kiev), he raised a cross and predicted that a great city, filled with many churches, would rise there some day.

But is was not until nine centuries later that the early Ukrainian state, with all its far-flung principalities and dominions—known then as "Kyivan-Rus"—formally adopted Christianity. The people of that region were mostly pagans, worshipping idols and gods of the sun, thunder, and lightning. By the 900s, a few had been baptized, but Christianity was not making much progress.

One of the first sparks contributing to the conversion of Kyiv-Rus was Princess Olha (Olga), wife of Prince Ihor (Igor). Despite her early life as a pagan, she traveled to Constantinople (now Istanbul, Turkey) in 958 to be baptized and to receive the baptismal name of Helen from her godfather, the Emperor Constantine.

Although Princess Olha tried to convert Sviatoslav, her son and heir to the throne, this ferocious warrior refused, declaring: "My men would laugh at me if I took up with a strange religion." Olha died in 969 and is venerated as a saint, but she had not succeeded in converting her lands.

This distinction fell on her grandson, Volodymyr (Vladmir), who was born about the time of Olha's baptism. In 980, while still a dedicated pagan with five wives and many slaves, he ascended the throne of the Kyiv-Rus state. Eight years into Volodymyr's reign, the Byzantine Emperor urgently appealed to him for help against attackers. Volodymyr agreed to help, but on condition that the emperor give his sister, Anna, to him in marriage. The emperor, desperate, agreed, though he did not really mean it. After the battle was won, Volodymyr was ready to claim his reward, but Princess Anna dissolved into tears at the thought of marrying a pagan with five other wives. The emperor supported his sister, and Volodymyr sought to apply pressure by capturing the Byzantine city of Kherson.

After some negotiation, the two agreed that Volodymyr could marry Anna if he became a Christian. Although we cannot know his motives, Baptism may have seemed like a small price to pay for an alliance with a wealthy and powerful Byzantium.

St. Basil's Cathedral, Moscow

139

Upon his return to Kyiv in 988 with his new wife, Volodymyr decided that he would not be a Christian in name only. He reformed his life and put away his former wives. He ordered the destruction of all idols, pronounced Christianity as the state religion, and ordered all residents of Kyiv to be baptized. The broad street Khreshchatik ("Christening" Street) still marks the place that the people descended from the hills into the Dnipro River to be baptized into the one, holy, catholic, and apostolic Church by Greek priests from Constantinople. Although many pagan leaders resisted, Christianity gradually spread from this heartland of Volodymyr's Kyiv-Rus domain to the various outlying principalities and dominions.

These dominions extended hundreds of miles to the north and encompassed, among others, the principality of Vladimir-Suzdal with its village of Moscow. The various "principalities" were then headed by members of the royal Kyivan "Rurik" family, though their subjects were often very dissimilar to the dominant population of Kyiv-Rus. But Volodymyr's acceptance of Christianity for all his dominions obligated even this remote territory, where the Russian nation was born and began to take shape. Hence, Russians, just as Ukrainians, trace the beginnings of their Christianity to 988. In subsequent years, Russians deferred to church authorities in Kyiv and derived most of their early church liturgy and literature from Ukrainian monasteries and ecclesiastical institutions. With the coming of the Mongols and the fragmentation of the Kyiv-Rus state, Russia and Ukraine began to drift further apart and to develop church hierarchy, liturgy, literature, and tradition independent of each other. Today, the presence of a large and dynamic Byzantine Catholic Church in Ukraine and the virtual absence of Catholics in Russia is partly a reflection of the different directions Christianity has taken in these two countries.

For the rest of his life, Volodymyr lived as a sincere Christian. One chronicle writes: "When he had in a moment of passion fallen into sin, he at once sought to make up for it by penitence and almsgiving." Shortly before he died in 1015, he gave away all his personal belongings to his friends and to the poor. Volodymyr is honored by both Russians and Ukrainians as their patron saint. In 1036, his son, King Yaroslav, built the Saint Sophia (Holy Wisdom) Cathedral in Kyiv as a sister of the famous Hagia Sophia in Constantinople. The city of Kyiv then became known as "golden-domed" because of the gold-plated domes of its 600 churches.

When Volodymyr converted his Kyivan-Rus domain, he converted it to the one, holy, catholic, and apostolic Church of that time. Because both Ukrainians and Russians were always greatly influenced by Constantinople, they developed the same rituals as did the Church in the Byzantine Empire, which is also sometimes called the Eastern Church (or Eastern Rite).

Customs in the Byzantine and Latin Rites

In 1054, the Church in Constantinople broke away from the Pope and went into *schism,* refusing to be obedient to the Pope, and became the Greek Orthodox Church. The Russian church hierarchy, as well as some Ukrainian church leaders, followed the example of Constantinople and went into schism, forming

Cathedral of St. Sophia, Kyiv

the Russian Orthodox Church and the Ukrainian Orthodox Church, respectively.

Many Catholics, however, remained loyal to the Pope, but they kept the Eastern rituals and customs. These Catholics are members of the Byzantine Catholic Church (also called the Eastern Rite). They have the same beliefs, the same sacraments, and are loyal to the Pope, but they have different customs. The Byzantine Rite is an important part of the Catholic Church, as emphasized in Pope John Paul II's 1995 document, "Orientale Lumen."

The customs in the Byzantine Rite are somewhat different from the Latin Rite, but the doctrine is the same. The Liturgy involves much more singing, by priest and congregation, than in the Western or Latin Rite Mass. There is also much use made of processions and incense in the Eastern Rites. Baptism is by triple immersion instead of by pouring of water. There is a great devotion to the Blessed Mother in the Eastern Rites, but the rosary is not commonly used. Children receive Holy Communion when they are baptized. They are also Confirmed at the time of Baptism. Holy Communion is received under both species at all liturgies. Some priests are allowed to be married if they are already married at the time they become priests. Some parts of the Liturgy take place behind an icon screen in front of the altar. All of these customs date back to the very early days of the Church. While these customs were changed in the Western Church, they have been kept in the Eastern Church.

Icons and Paintings

Byzantine religious art is also different from what we are used to in the Western Church, and it is quite interesting. In churches in Europe, the main art form we see is sculpture. In the Eastern Church, we see a kind of painting called an *icon*.

The word *icon* means "image" in Greek. Legend has it that the first icon was a miraculous portrait of Christ—which may have actually been the image of Christ on the Holy Shroud—which cured King Abgar of Edessa. Some traditions say that St. Luke painted icons of the Blessed Mother.

There are some important ways in which icons differ from paintings that we normally see. First, icons are not meant to be realistic. The icon painter does not try to reproduce what he sees as a photographer does, nor does he try to make his painting look like real life. Instead, he is trying to show the spiritual side of life, to help us appreciate the holiness of Christ, Mary, and the saints. Second, and as a result of the first point, the icon painting does not have spatial depth. The background is not meant to suggest three dimensions: the icon seems "flat". The reason is that in eternity, in God, there is no "here" nor "there"; everything is present to God. Third, the artist does not try to suggest everyday life. He wants to take us out of our day-to-day existence so that we can concentrate on God. Fourth, the icon painter does not usually portray the sufferings of Christ or the saints, but rather their glorification. Fifth, all icon painters use similar techniques, called *conventions*.

The Trinity of the Old Testament by Andrei Rublev

Conventions, Symbolism and Creation of Icons

In their paintings, we notice many similarities (conventions), even though these paintings were done many years, or even centuries, apart. For example, the Christ Child often has a man's face instead of a baby's face. Mary's veil has a similar style in different icons, and she holds Christ in the same position: in her arms with her head bent toward Him.

An interesting example of the symbolism of icons can be found with the icon of St. Nicholas. He is portrayed as he is transformed by the glory of God. His eyelids are permanently fixed, never to shut in sleep. His mouth is so small that it can sing only the Glory of God. His ears are turned toward the center of his face where they can hear only the voice of the soul.

In an Eastern Church, the icons are placed on a screen called an *iconostasis,* which stands before the altar. Most of the ancient icons that survive today were once part of an iconostasis. When the Communists took over Russia and Ukraine, many people carried the smaller icons away to their houses for safekeeping. Unfortunately, many icons were chopped up by the Communists; others were used as firewood. In one case, three icons were sacrilegiously used to construct a watering trough for cows.

Icons were always painted on wood. The icon artist would hollow out panels of birch or pine so that the wood provided its own frame for the image. Then the artist would season the wood with layers of glue and plaster mixed with powdered alabaster to make a smooth surface for the paint. He would blend each color individually, using rye beer and egg yolks to make the colors adhere. When finished, he covered the painted surface with a layer of oil to protect the painting. Sometimes people would donate jewels and gold or silver to make a crown or a mantle for the figures in the icon.

Once the icon was hung in a church, it would slowly turn dark from the soot from the candles that always burned before it. If the wood was still in good condition when this happened, an artist could paint a new icon over the old one. If the panel was rotten or warped, the icon would have to be destroyed. Since an icon was a holy object, it was considered a sin to burn it or throw it away. So they would wrap the icon in linen and float it away down a river.

Even though the Communists turned the churches into museums and attempted to destroy the icons, many of the icons were still secretly venerated in Christian homes as a reminder of God's loving providence.

Saving "Our Lady of Kazan"

Our Lady of Kazan is probably the most famous of the Russian icons. In 1475, a terrible fire almost destroyed the city of Kazan, which is located about 500 miles from Moscow. After the fire, an eight-year-old girl named Matrona told her mother that Our Lady had appeared to her and told her that an icon was buried under the ruins of her parents' home. Her mother thought the girl was imagining things and paid no attention to her message.

Matrona was telling the truth. Our Lady appeared to her two more times. Then, on a third occasion, a flame shot forth from the apparition, and Our Lady said, "If you do not proclaim the message which I gave you, I will appear in another city, and a grave misfortune will overtake this place."

At last her mother thought there might be something to Matrona's insistent story. She went to the Metropolitan-Archbishop of Kazan, but he wouldn't believe her. So Matrona and her mother went to sift through the ashes of her home. Matrona almost immediately found the icon wrapped in an old cloth. Though it was very old, the paint seemed to shine like new and a light glowed from the image. Many people came to venerate the image, and miracles occurred at the spot, the first being the restoration of sight to two blind men.

Our Lady of Kazan

The Rise and Fall of a Cathedral

Then in 1611, Russia was suffering from what was later called "Times of Troubles". The country was in chaos; Poland and Sweden occupied part of the country; robbers freely roamed and pillaged the countryside. Finally, Prince Pojarski raised an army to try to restore order.

Knowing that divine assistance was needed, the prince and his army spent three days in prayer and fasting before the icon of *Our Lady of Kazan* before their attempt to retake Moscow. On the third day, they successfully stormed the Kremlin and drove out the enemy. The prince then ordered a cathedral built in Moscow to enshrine *Our Lady of Kazan*. The church was completed in 1630.

In 1812, Napoleon's army was on Russian soil and driving toward Moscow. The people prayed to Our Lady of Kazan, and Napoleon fled back to France, leaving most of his army dead in the Russian snows. The Russian people erected a new and larger cathedral for *Our Lady of Kazan*, completing it in 1842. She was venerated there until the Communist takeover in 1917.

The Communists were determined to destroy the faith of the Russian people, since they regard Christianity as their greatest enemy. In 1918, they gathered a large crowd on Red Square to witness their burning of the cathedral of *Our Lady of Kazan*.

They intended this destruction as proof that there is no God. They made plans to erect a new building on the site, so that even the very memory of *Our Lady of Kazan* would be lost.

Events did not turn out as the Communists had planned. The icon was not destroyed, but somehow made its way to England. The image was purchased by the Blue Army of Our Lady of Fatima, which was founded to carry out the conditions of Our Lady for the conversion of Russia. Furthermore, the Communists were unable to build anything on the site of the former cathedral.

As the Blue Army explained, in the days before the Soviet Communist government fell, "a copy of *Our Lady of Kazan*, in blatant response to the atheist challenge, is honored at the center of all icons in the Moscow Cathedral. It must be obvious to all that the militant atheists who still control Russia do not dare remove this copy of the icon from the cathedral because of the Russian people. It is a constant, public reminder of the great miracle on Red Square. It recalls that favorite Russian mystery of Christ, which ultimately defeated those who taunted Him to 'Come down from the Cross!': the Resurrection." In 2004, the Vatican donated the original icon of *Our Lady of Kazan* to the Moscow Patriarch, who returned it to the people of Kazan in 2005.

Chapter 22
Review Questions

1. Whom did Princess Olha marry? When was she baptized? Where was she baptized?
   _____

2. What did Princess Olha try to do to bring Catholicism to Kyiv-Rus?
   _____

3. Who was Volodymyr (Vladimir)? _____
   _____

4. When and how did Volodymyr become a Catholic? _____
   _____

5. List three things that Volodymyr did to prove that he became a good Catholic.
   _____
   _____

6. Russian Catholicism derived their liturgy and literature from where?
   _____

7. What does *schism* mean?_____

8. Some of the Ukrainian and Russian Catholics followed Constantinople and formed which two churches? _____

9. Most of the Ukrainian and Russian Catholics followed the Pope and are members of the _____ Rite of the Catholic Church.

10. While the customs are different between the Roman Rite and the Eastern or Byzantine Rite, the _____ are the same.

11. How is the singing different in the Mass or Liturgy?
    _____

12. How are the processions and incense different?
    _____

13. There is a great devotion for the _____ in the Eastern Rite.

14. When do children receive Holy Communion in the Eastern Rite? _____

15. When are children confirmed in the Eastern Rite? _____

16. Some parts of the Eastern Liturgy take place behind an _____.

17. All of these customs were in the early Roman Rite, but were _____ in the Western Church and kept in the Eastern Church.

18. Byzantine art is different from Roman Rite religious art. In the Roman Rite, we see paintings and sculpture in the churches; in the Eastern Rite, we see a kind of painting called an _____.

19. Traditions say that _____ painted icons of the Blessed Mother.

20. The icon painter tries to show _____

21. The icon does not have special depth; the icon seems _____ because in eternity, everything is _____ to God at once.

22. The icon painter does not try to represent _____ life.

23. The icon painter does not try to represent the sufferings of Christ and the saints, but rather their _____.

24. The icon painters use similar techniques called _____.

25. In an Eastern Catholic church, the icons are placed before the altar on a screen called an _____.

26. Icons were always painted on _____.

27. Sometimes people donate _____ for a crown in the painting.

28. An icon is considered to be a _____ so it could not be burned nor thrown away.

29. The most famous Russian icon is _____

30. In 1475, after a fire, an icon was rescued from the ashes, and _____ began to occur at the spot.

31. What did Russian Prince Pojarski and his army do in 1611 before attempting to recover Moscow from the enemy? _____

Chapter 23

Jadwiga's Wedding Ring

In 1370, King Casimir the Great of Poland was killed in a hunting accident, leaving no son to succeed him. Poland might have been plunged into civil wars if it had not been for Casimir's foresight in naming his nephew, King Louis of Hungary, as his heir. Louis ruled the two countries well, but even more important for Poland's future was the daughter born to Louis and his wife Elizabeth in 1371, whom they named after the great Polish saint, Jadwiga.

Louis and Elizabeth had no sons, so Louis wanted to prevent problems by marrying his daughters to powerful princes and willing his kingdoms to these couples. The older daughter, Mary, married Sigismund of Bohemia. Little Jadwiga was betrothed in 1378, at the age of seven, to William Hapsburg of Austria, who was eight. The Hapsburg family was just beginning to come to power. The betrothal took place in a solemn ceremony with great pomp and feasting. As was customary with middle European royalty, each child would live for a time with the family of the other. Jadwiga went off to Vienna, the Hapsburg capital. She was enchanted with the beautiful new cathedrals being built and was caught up in the lively intellectual life of Vienna. Then William came to live in Budapest, where he learned Hungarian laws and customs on the banks of the Danube.

Louis died in 1381. His daughter Mary was immediately crowned Queen of Hungary with the three-hundred-year-old crown of King St. Stephen, the patron saint of Hungary. The Poles did not want Mary to rule them because they feared that Poland would be united with Hungary and lose its independence. Queen Elizabeth told the Polish noblemen that

Vienna (*Wien* in German) Town Hall

Wawel Castle

Jadwiga could be their queen, but they did not think much of that idea either. For one thing, she was so young that they were afraid she would constantly be returning to Hungary and leaving them without a ruler. Furthermore, they distrusted the Hapsburgs because of their German nationality. They finally presented their terms to Elizabeth: they would accept Jadwiga as their sovereign, but she must promise never to leave Poland and she must not marry William.

Elizabeth was not happy with this arrangement. Could she let Jadwiga go off to Poland without the protection of her husband-to-be? She tried delaying tactics, sending messages, and counter-proposals. The Poles were impatient. They had seen too many troubles caused by instability. They wanted their monarch. Finally, they threatened to choose a king of their own. Elizabeth could not permit this to happen. Her husband had planned carefully for the future of Poland and Hungary. She could not let his efforts be wasted. She agreed to bring Jadwiga to the capital city, Krakow (Cracow), for coronation at Pentecost, 1383.

The Poles were delighted, but one nobleman, named Ziemowit, had plans of his own. He would take his 500 knights, intercept the royal procession, seize Jadwiga and marry her, so that he could be king of Poland. He was already for the ambush, but Providence intervened with a spring flood which blocked the passage of Elizabeth and Jadwiga. Ziemowit waited in vain. Then Elizabeth learned of the plot. She communicated with the Polish noblemen: for the safety of her daughter, may she wait until November to come to Poland? The noblemen agreed.

Once again, Elizabeth had misgivings about taking her daughter to Poland. Again, she delayed. November came and went, but Elizabeth and Jadwiga remained in Budapest. Furious, the noblemen appeared in Budapest, demanding their queen. Elizabeth could think of no more delaying tactics. She gave in. In the autumn of 1384, Jadwiga left Budapest in a gorgeous procession, mounted on a white horse, her saddle inset with ivory. However, the splendor of the procession could not distract her from the loneliness in her heart, as she left her family and friends behind.

Coronation of Thirteen year old Queen

When the young queen arrived in Krakow, she was greeted with great rejoicing. Her coronation day was October 15. First the archbishop and the leading nobles and clergymen came to her room where they all prayed for the blessing of God on her reign. Then she went to the cathedral to be crowned, where she took an oath to "respect all the rights, the liberties, and privileges of the people." The coronation was followed by a lavish banquet.

The next day Jadwiga went into the city square to be crowned a second time and to receive the allegiance of the businessmen and merchants of the town.

Though only thirteen years old, Queen Jadwiga took an active part in the government of her new country. She knew that she needed God's help, so she spent long hours on her knees in prayer. She had a special passageway from her apartments to the cathedral so that she could frequently pray before the Blessed Sacrament. She received state visitors from all over Europe, continued her education, sat in the council meetings, encouraged an improvement of manners in the court, and for recreation engaged in needlework.

Though the Polish noblemen had expressed their displeasure with her betrothal to William before she had come to Poland, Jadwiga was convinced that now they would recognize the solemn character of that betrothal and allow her to marry the man she loved. To her shock and surprise, she learned that the noblemen were negotiating with the king of Lithuania, Jagiello, for a marriage contract.

Jadwiga was frantic. She loved William. How could she give him up? What was also frightening was the thought of Jagiello as her husband. He was a pagan barbarian, twenty-five years older than she. All the stories she had heard of the brutality of the Lithuanians convinced her that she could not bear to have this man as her husband.

Unification of Lithuania with Poland

The Polish noblemen told her that Jagiello had made many promises in exchange for the marriage contract. He would unite Lithuania with Poland, restore Poland's lost lands, release Polish prisoners, and most importantly, become a Christian and bring his whole country into the Church. All of these promises would bring immense good to Poland and Lithuania. Jadwiga could see the good, but she was still a frightened girl who had lately been made to leave her family and was now asked to surrender the true love of her life.

Jagiello's brother arrived from Vilno (the capital of Lithuania) to carry on the negotiations. Imagine Jadwiga's feelings when he walked into the room, long-haired, bearded and clad in animal skins. Jadwiga told him firmly that she was pledged to William, and that in any case, she would need her mother's permission to marry another.

The Poles sent off a delegation to Budapest. If Jadwiga had hoped for assistance from her mother, her hopes were dashed. Elizabeth had long hoped to be out of the union with Austria, especially because the marriage would unite Poland and Austria and make Austria much stronger than Hungary. Nevertheless, she loved her daughter and was concerned with her welfare. She told the delegation that she consented to the marriage, but that the final decision must be made by Jadwiga and the Poles.

Now the Austrians took a hand in the matter. William's father sent him off to Krakow to see that the original marriage contract was kept. The Poles allowed William to enter the city, but barred the gate to the Wawel Castle Citadel, which was the royal residence. William took refuge in the Franciscan monastery. The Franciscans had offered their hospitality, but he had another reason for going there. The back of the monastery gardens opened onto the Wawel grounds. So Jadwiga and her ladies would take a stroll to the monastery gardens, while William and his men would enter from the other side. Jadwiga and William had several meetings in the monastery, finding themselves more in love than ever.

Then word came to Krakow that Jagiello was on his way to claim his bride. Jadwiga knew that she must act at once. She decided to follow her heart and sneak out of the castle by a way usually unguarded. She would meet William and flee with him.

The chosen evening came. Quietly, Jadwiga left her apartments. She stole down the halls to the little-used door. To her dismay, she found it guarded by Dimitri of Goray, the aged treasurer of her father and uncle. Jadwiga began to beat on the door, sobbing, begging to be let out. Dimitri tried to calm the weeping queen. He argued that her duty to Church and her country must outweigh her personal feelings.

Though her love for William was powerful, she could not deny his arguments. She was not an ordinary girl who could follow her heart. She was a queen. Upon her decisions depended the future of thousands of people. If she refused to marry Jagiello, Lithuania would not be converted; souls would be lost to Christ.

She could not take that on her conscience. She must put aside her personal feelings and make a sacrifice for the greater glory of God and the good of her people. Still in tears, she allowed Dimitri to lead her back to her room. She wrote a letter to William, asking him to leave Krakow forever.

She spent all the next day at the cathedral, praying before the crucifix, asking Christ for the strength to bear her cross. Our Lord was to answer her prayers in ways that she could not at the time have suspected.

Having accepted what she perceived to be God's will for her, Jadwiga was now curious about her husband-to-be. Somewhat frightened by the stories she had heard about the Franciscan missionaries martyred trying to convert Lithuania, about the paganism and slavery and polygamy in that land, she sent a trusted knight to meet Jagiello, ordering him to return quickly with a report. To her relief, the knight reported that Jagiello was good-looking and courteous.

A Handsome Barbarian Converts

Finally, the King of Lithuania and the Queen of Poland met. Jagiello was deeply moved by the beauty of Jadwiga and was in awe of her civilized manners and education. Jadwiga saw nothing to fear in the handsome barbarian, who seemed to want to do nothing so much as to please her.

On February 18, 1386, three days after the meeting, Jadwiga and Jagiello were married. Poland and Lithuania were united as their monarchs wed, and the people called the union of Poland and Lithuania the "wedding ring of Jadwiga." On March 4, Jagiello was crowned King of Poland, the beginning of the Jagiellian Dynasty and of 200 years of Polish glory. Almost immediately the king and queen made a four-month tour of Poland to gain the support of the people. They were cheered and feasted wherever they went. The people were impressed with Jagiello's willingness to learn the customs and manners of civilized Poland. As for Jagiello

Wawel Cathedral

and Jadwiga, they were finding that their marriage was not merely one of political and religious advantage, but was built on a deep and growing love.

In the midst of her happiness, Jadwiga received sad news. Her mother Elizabeth had been killed by rebellious nobles in Hungary. Jadwiga was deeply hurt, but she could not let her personal sorrow distract her from her duties.

In January of 1387, Jadwiga and Jagiello journeyed to Lithuania. On Sunday, February 17, Jagiello led a procession up the icy path of a hill on which rose the image of the red-eyed fire god Perkinas. On the altar burned a perpetual fire; before this altar the pagan priests sacrificed a white horse each spring. Jagiello smashed the image to bits and extinguished the fire. The people expected a bolt of lightning to strike him dead. Instead, Jagiello planted a cross, before which he knelt to sing the *Te Deum*. Next to the fire altar was a sacred wood,

Sigismond Chapel of Wawel Cathedral

infested with sacred serpents. Jagiello cut down the sacred oaks and killed the snakes.

The old false god was dead; the people surged forward to receive the baptism of the new and true God. They were taken to the riverbank in groups, because the numbers were so large, for the ceremonies of baptism. They were given Christian names and received white linen mantles as symbols of their new life of grace; the mantles were personally bestowed by the king, who had brought them from Krakow. Some 30,000 were baptized in the first months of Lithuania's conversion.

The pagan temple near the royal castle was destroyed, and Jagiello laid the cornerstone of a new cathedral. Wayside shrines were set up all over the country. The new religious beliefs of the Lithuanians also came to be reflected in their laws. Jagiello signed a document securing to all men their property rights and equality before the law, protecting workers and their families, outlawing forced labor, and providing for just judges. All these gains for the people of Lithuania came from Jadwiga's sacrifice.

Upon her return to Krakow, Jadwiga learned that her brother-in-law had seized Red Ruthenia (Galicia) from Poland and was attempting to hold its rich fertile land. Jadwiga rode to Red Ruthenia at the head of an army of enthusiastic soldiers. A few skirmishes were fought, but it was soon obvious that the people of Red Ruthenia wanted Jadwiga, not Sigismund. The usurper was forced to withdraw.

Jadwiga and Jagiello also had to cope with the Teutonic Knights, who in 1390 invaded Lithuania. The Teutonic Knights marched into the capital city, Vilno, burning part of it, including a newly built church. Polish knights arrived just in time to save the castle and drive out the Germanic knights.

Then a quarrel broke out between two of Jagiello's brothers, Witowt and Skirgiello. Jadwiga personally attended a peace conference to resolve the disagreements. She first reconciled with Witowt, who pledged his loyalty to Jagiello, but Skirgiello continued to rebel. Finally, Jadwiga arranged a meeting with him and brought about his reconciliation. The brothers agreed that all future disputes would be referred to her. On her journey to and from these conferences, the people cheered their peace-making queen.

In January of 1395, Jadwiga saw her sister for the first time in years when the Hungarian queen came to Krakow for a visit. Jadwiga prepared great banquets for Mary's visit. We have the menu of one such banquet: one large and eight small pigs, sixty-two chickens, sixteen geese, sixteen partridges, turnips and beets for the men; two cows, two hams, sixty chickens, seven hares, eight partridges, seven small pigs, turnips, carrots and beets for the women. The men had twelve cheeses, seven pounds of butter, and a cheesecake made from 200 eggs. At these feasts, food was always provided for the poor, so that they could share in the celebration.

The visit would be the last time the sisters would see each other. In May, after her return to Hungary, Mary died after a fall from a horse. Jadwiga turned to the Blessed Mother for consolation in her grief.

Poland's Golden Age

In 1396, Jagiello and Jadwiga celebrated their tenth wedding anniversary. The accomplishments of those ten years had been great. The first and immediate accomplishment had been the union of the two countries, followed by the conversion of Lithuania. They had rebuilt Vilno, making it a Christian city with many churches. Throughout both countries they built or remodeled hospitals, schools, monasteries, and churches. They visited the sick and unfortunate and listened to the appeals of the people. The Scriptures had been translated into Polish, and the Church had been reformed. Poland was recognized as the most advanced kingdom in Europe as it experienced a Golden Age of art and culture. In all things Jadwiga and Jagiello ruled as equals, sharing all decisions.

Working Miracles

Jadwiga's holiness was an example to all, and stories of miracles circulated. One such story was of a sick beggar covered with sores, neglected by all others. Jadwiga washed him with her own hands until a light shone in the dark corner where he lay. The beggar rose, completely healed.

On another occasion, Jadwiga was taking part in a Corpus Christi procession. During the procession, the son of a coppersmith fell into the river and drowned. Jadwiga left the procession and kneeling beside the body, threw her mantle over it. Soon the weeping mother felt the boy's hand grow warm in her own. From that time, when any member of the coppersmith guild died, the guild members threw a silken mantle over the coffin in commemoration of Jadwiga's miracle.

The Teutonic Knights remained a problem, and many of Jagiello's advisers urged him to attack them. Jadwiga and Jagiello, however, were strongly opposed to any war except for defense. Finally in June, 1397, Jadwiga was appointed to go to the border to negotiate with the Teutonic Knights regarding the restoration of occupied Polish lands. The Knights met her dressed in their white capes and helmets topped with peacock feathers. They had no intention of yielding an inch, but Jadwiga managed to get some of Poland's land back.

In 1399, Masses and prayers of thanksgiving were offered in every church in Poland and Lithuania because Jadwiga was going to have a child. The Pope ordered a *Te Deum,* and three Masses were offered in the Wawel Cathedral.

The baby, a girl christened Elizabeth, was born on June 22. The rejoicing soon turned to mourning when the baby died. The king did not even arrive before she died, since the baby had not been expected until July. Even more tragically, the queen became ill, and it was soon apparent that she would not recover. She asked that one-half of her possessions be given to the university, the other half distributed among the poor. She requested a simple funeral and to be buried near her baby.

Queen Jadwiga died on July 17, 1399. In the Wawel calendar for that day, the following inscription is written:

> Today at noon died Jadwiga, Queen of Poland — unwearied creator of divine culture, protectress of the Church, administrator of justice, servant of all virtues, humble and beneficent mother of orphans, who in her time has had no equal of royal blood in the eyes of men in the whole world.

Her body rests beneath a beautiful marble effigy in Wawel Cathedral. She is venerated as a saint.

Chapter 23
Review Questions

1. King Casimir of Poland arranged for the King of _____ to rule Poland as well.

2. What was the name of the baby born of King Louis of Hungary and his wife Elizabeth in 1371?
   _____

3. Jadwiga was betrothed to Willam _____ of Austria when she was only seven years old.

4. Why did the Polish people not want King Louis' daughter Mary to rule them?
   _____

5. Why did the Polish people not want King Louis' daughter Jadwiga to rule them?
   _____

6. What were the terms the Polish leaders gave to accept Jadwiga as their ruler?
   _____

7. In 1384, Jadwiga left Budapest, Hungary, and traveled to the city of _____ in Poland.

8. In the cathedral in Krakow, what was the oath that Jadwiga took?
   _____

9. Jadwiga was crowned a second time in the city square of Krakow to obtain the support of which two groups?
   _____

10. As Queen of Poland, what were some of the things that Jadwiga did in addition to praying in front of the Blessed Sacrament?
    _____

11. Why was Jadwiga upset that the leaders of Poland wanted her to marry Jagiello, the King of Lithuania? Give three or four reasons.
    _____

12. What were four promises that Jagiello had made if Jadwiga married him?
    _____
    _____

13. What was the response of Jadwiga's mother, Elizabeth, in regard to the marriage with Jagiello?
    _____

14. What were the reasons Dimitri of Goray gave to Jadwiga why she should marry Jagiello rather than the man she loved?

15. What was referred to as the "wedding ring of Jadwiga"?

16. How did the king and queen gain the support of the Polish people for the new king?

17. List several things that Jagiello did to make Lithuania reject paganism and adopt Christianity.

18. List the four things that Jagiello did for his people of Lithuania as a result of accepting Christianity.

19. What was the capital city of Lithuania? Who attacked it in 1390? Who drove out the invaders?

20. List some of the Christian activities accomplished by Jagiello and Jadwiga by the time of their tenth wedding anniversary.

21. What were two of the stories of miraculous events because of Jadwiga?

22. Why did the king and queen not attack the Teutonic Knights when they occupied Polish lands?

23. What caused the death of Queen Jadwiga?

24. To whom did Jadwiga give her possessions?

25. What were some of the titles that the people of Poland gave to their beloved queen at her death?

Chapter 24

The Black Madonna's Fort

The Poles have a great devotion to a painting of the Blessed Mother with an extraordinary history. The painting is known as the Black Madonna or Our Lady of Czestochowa (pronounced Ches-to-hov-a).

The painting is said by some to have been done by St. Luke, but nobody really knows its origins. During the time of King Louis (Jadwiga's father), the painting hung in a castle in Louis' territory. The castle was besieged by Tatars (not Tartars). One of them shot an arrow which came through the window of the chapel and struck the face of the Virgin, leaving a scar. At that moment what had been broad daylight became dark night. The Tatars panicked and ran away.

Louis then decided that the picture should be moved to a more secure place. He gave orders to have the painting put in a carriage and brought to Silesia. The horses were hitched to the carriage, and it set off. When the carriage stopped off at the Polish town of Czestochowa, the horses would not move. No matter what the drivers tried, the horses remained rooted to the spot.

In Czestochowa was a small chapel on a hill, called Jasna Gora or "Bright Hill." The image was placed in the chapel, and the horses were able to move again. The people concluded that Our Lady wanted to stay in Czestochowa. A large church and monastery were built to house and protect the image.

Then in 1430 on Good Friday night, a band of Czech Hussites (a wildly anti-Catholic group) attacked the monastery. They killed five monks and seized sacred vessels and the image of the Blessed Mother, loading it on a cart. They drove the cart to the bottom of the hill, and once again the horses would not move. One of the Hussites, furious, grabbed the picture and threw it to the ground. Another drew his sword and slashed the picture twice. But when he raised his sword a third time, he was struck by a bolt of lightning, coming out of a cloudless sky. The Hussites fled, leaving the picture lying in the mud.

When the monks saw that the Hussites were gone, they came down and retrieved the image. It was repaired, though the scars remain to this day, and a new church was built, surrounded by strong walls and a moat.

In the 1600s, Poland was beset by enemies on all sides: Cossacks, Turks, Tartars, Russians. Somehow Poland managed to fend off these enemies, but, in 1655, disaster

Our Lady of Czestochowa

struck. The king of Sweden was Charles Gustavus, a fierce and ferocious Lutheran Protestant. He invaded Poland, taking Warsaw in September, 1655, and then Krakow. King John Casimir, abandoned and discouraged, took refuge on the borders of Silesia, leaving Poland to its fate. All that remained unconquered was the fortress/monastery of Czestochowa. Some Catholic noblemen, led by Stephan Zamoyski, came to the monastery and vowed to die in defense of Czestochowa. They consecrated themselves to Our Lady. The abbot, Augustine Kordecki, called the monks together. He asked them if they wanted to surrender. To a man, they said no.

Word came that the Swedish army was on its way, four thousand strong. Abbot Kordecki said Mass before the altar of the Black Madonna. Then he carried the Blessed Sacrament in procession along the walls, blessing the cannon, cannon balls, bullets and barrels of powder, so that they could be used in defense of the monastery and for the glory of God.

Monastery Under Attack

The Swedes arrived under General Muller and besieged the monastery. Hoping to obtain an easy victory, they sent a message to Abbot Kordecki, asking the monks to surrender. Abbot Kordecki later explained his answer: "It was no longer the hour to write, but take up arms. We answered by the mouths of our cannon."

The Swedes were furious and launched a three-day attack with grenades and incendiary projectiles, trying to set fire to the monastery buildings. By night, they dug trenches leading up to the walls. The monks ordered Catholic hymns to be sung during the battle, giving the defenders courage, while infuriating the Swedes. Some of the Swedes' bombs ricocheted. One aimed at the chapel bounced back and landed among the Swedes. A Polish nobleman, Sir Peter Czarniecki, sallied forth at night with a brave detachment of soldiers.

He managed to maneuver to the rear of the Swedes. He killed the commander of artillery, seized two cannon, and returned safely to the monastery, losing only one man.

The attack having failed, the Swedes resorted to psychological pressure. They asked a Polish nobleman who had defected to the Swedes to argue with the monks. He presented two arguments to Abbot Kordecki and his men. First he said, "Why continue to hold out when everyone else has surrendered?" Then he argued, "Moreover, the aim of a religious order is to abstain from temporal affairs. What do you have to do with the turbulence of war, you whose rules call you to solitude and silence?" The response of the monks was to organize an around-the-clock prayer vigil in the chapel. Abbot Kordecki answered the Polish defector, "Thus to the limit of our forces, we shall defend all the rights of God and of men."

The Swedes then kept hostage the two monks who had brought this last message, threatening to kill them if the monastery would not surrender. Kordecki's response was, "Let them die, then, that by their blood, they may obtain an honorable liberty; while as for us, we swear that we shall dedicate ourselves

Czestochowa Shrine, Jasna Gora, Poland

courageously and confiding in the help of God Almighty, to the defense of the sanctuary." General Muller sent one of the monks back, but told him to return or the second monk would suffer a terrible death. The Monk told Abbot Kordecki of the enemy's great strength, but counseled against surrender because God's will was more powerful than any foe. This monk then went back to Muller to say that he was only a slave so he had no power to negotiate anything. The second monk was sent to put pressure on Abbot Kordecki, but he told the Abbot that he was more than willing to die to protect Our Lady's shrine. He returned to Muller with no consolation for the Swedish general. In a fury, Muller said that he would hang the two monks the next day. They replied: "Why may we not die today, if we must be immolated tomorrow for God, for King, and for our Fatherland?" Muller ended up postponing the hanging, and the monks were saved, as he realized that threats were to no avail with men who were willing to die for God.

The Swedes vented their anger with a bombardment of the fortress, followed by a message to Kordecki that if the Poles surrendered, none of the defenders would be harmed. Kordecki replied that he had no reason to believe Muller's word, since he had taken the monks as prisoners though they were only messengers traveling under a flag of truce. Frustrated, General Muller permitted the monks to return to the monastery. He then unleashed a heavy attack, but the Polish knights drove it back.

On December 7, a Polish knight named Peter Sladowski, who had been captured by the Swedes, was sent to the fortress to persuade the monks to capitulate. Instead he urged them not to give up. The Swedes were getting desperate. The local people were turning against the invaders who were murdering priests and profaning churches.

Next Muller sent a Tatar to try to persuade the monks to surrender. The Tatar was not really on either side, but when he saw how courageously the monks were holding out, he encouraged them to hold fast so as not to permit "swine and perjurers to occupy the place consecrated to the Most Pure Virgin."

The Swedes launched another attack in a dense fog. The defenders could not see them to fight back. Kordecki ordered more prayers to be said. The sun came out, the fog drifted away and the Swedes were repulsed. In spite of their continued successes, the constant fighting was wearing down the outnumbered defenders. Some of them were even beginning to think that they might have to surrender. Kordecki encouraged them with these words:

What Faith is ours, what love, what gratitude to God so generous to us — that such a small damage to our earthly comforts is able to turn us away from the guard and protection of the chest

Gnieyno Cathedral

containing the celestial treasures of the eternal King? Let us consider that it is by far more prudent for us to defend the integrity of the House of God, the Holy Faith, and at the same time our own liberties, than for us to lose all and, in addition to that, to go into exile and eternal slavery.

Having tried everything else, General Muller now tried bribery, offering silver and jewels if Kordecki would surrender. Kordecki scornfully rejected the bribe, saying, "The glory of God and the protection of the sacred things is more important for us than all the treasures in the world."

Then Zamoyski and his men sallied forth on December 20, with a surprise attack on the Swedes' trenches. He lost only one man, though the Swedes had to suspend their attack for two days because of their great losses.

The Swedes suffered a further setback during a banquet given by General Muller. A cannonball came through his tent and landed right in the middle of his fine meal.

Kordecki requested a truce for Christmas Day, but the Swedes attacked anyway. They had cannon balls and incendiary shells raining down on the fort and a new kind of shrapnel-like shell which exploded and scattered pieces of lead. Finally they were forced to withdraw when their main cannon exploded.

Our Lady Intervenes

On December 26, after thirty-eight days of siege, the Catholic monks and nobles were almost out of provisions. Despite this, they continued their celebration of Christmas. Muller heard them laughing and singing and concluded that they must have ample provisions. Discouraged, he considered withdrawing. Then he saw in the sky a vision of a Lady which he described as follows: "Something of the celestial and divine, which frightened me from the beginning, shone in her face." Some of the Swedish soldiers also saw a Lady on the walls. "She obliged us to cover our eyes," they said, "and bow our heads." Sometimes she would point with a sword. Muller concluded that he was fighting an enemy much stronger than he was. He withdrew his army and lifted the siege.

The heroism of the defenders at Czestochowa inspired the rest of Poland to rise up in rebellion against the Swedish invaders. John Casimir returned from his hiding place, and the people rallied around him. On June 30, 1656, Warsaw was liberated and the Swedes driven out of Poland. The king solemnly proclaimed Our Lady of Czestochowa as the Queen and Mother of Poland, and she has been so venerated ever since. To this day, the shrine at Czestochowa is the most popular one in Poland.

Main Altar
Shrine of Our Lady of Czestochowa

Chapter 24
Review Questions

1. According to tradition, who painted the famous Polish painting known as the Black Madonna or Our Lady of Czestochowa? _____

2. King Louis of Poland moved the painting to a safer place after it was damaged by an arrow from a _____ soldier.

3. The carriage containing the painting was pulled by horses that would not move past the town of _____.

4. What was the name of the small chapel called "Bright Hill" in English? _____
_____

5. What was built there to house the painting? _____
_____

6. What anti-Catholic group attacked the monastery which housed the famous painting?
_____

7. How did the attacking soldiers damage the painting? _____
_____

8. To protect the painting and the monks, what was built around the church?
_____

9. In the 1600s, who was the King of Sweden who was a Lutheran Protestant?
_____

10. Which two major cities in Poland were conquered by the Swedish king?
_____

11. Only the one fortress/monastery remained to be conquered. Who was in charge of the men protecting the monastery? _____
_____

12. Who was the abbot in charge of defending the monastery? _____

13. How many men in the Swedish army were ready to attack the monastery?
_____

14. What did the abbot do when he knew the Swedish soldiers were coming?
_____

15. Who was in command of the Swedish soldiers attacking the monastery?
_____

16. Describe what the monks were doing during the battle.
_____

17. Who was the Polish nobleman/hero who captured two cannons from the enemy?
_____

18. What did the Swedes do with the two monks they held hostage?
_____

19. Why were the Polish people turning against the Swedes?
_____

20. Who was the hero throughout the battle with the Swedes? Why?
_____

21. Who was the Catholic Polish nobleman who led a surprise attack on the Swedes in their trenches?
_____

22. What did the Catholic monks and nobles do on Christmas which fooled the enemy?
_____

23. What was the vision that the Swedish general Muller saw in the sky?
_____

24. Why did General Muller give up the attack?
_____

25. What was the effect that the thirty-eight day resistance had on the rest of the Polish citizens?
_____

26. What title did the King of Poland give to the Blessed Mother?
_____

Chapter 25
Suffering Poland

The Catholic people of Poland have had to endure many sufferings in their long history. Once Poland even disappeared from the map. All during the nineteenth century, the land of Poland was divided among Russia, Prussia, and Austria. In the Prussian and Russian sections, the Polish people were persecuted, as attempts were made to force them to change their religion, their language, even their culture. All of these attempts failed, as oppression only made the people stronger Catholics and more devoted to their heritage.

Finally, after World War I, the Versailles Treaty brought Poland back into existence, with boundaries considerably eastward of where they are today.

Poland's long-awaited independence lasted only twenty years (1919 to 1939). Soon the Nazi threat loomed over Poland. The leaders of Poland tried to compromise with Hitler and also sought alliances with England and France for protection.

On September 1, 1939, the Nazi *Blitzkrieg* ("Lightning War") rolled across Poland's borders. Conventional warfare required an entire army to move forward until it met an opposing army. The Blitzkrieg sent motorized columns of tanks and other vehicles, supported by aircraft, speeding ahead of the rest of the troops and devastating everything in their path. Then the infantry would follow to wipe up what remained of the opposition. No one had ever tried such a strategy before, and some German military leaders feared that the motorized columns would be cut off and eliminated. However, the Blitzkrieg into Poland worked to perfection.

Katyn Forest Memorial, Poland

The Poles had only a few outmoded tanks and planes. The British and French declared war on Germany but were able to give no aid to Poland beyond sending over a few planes to drop leaflets exhorting the Poles to fight harder. On September 17, Poland's sufferings increased when the Soviet Union declared war and invaded from the East, forcing the Poles to fight a two-front war when they were scarcely able to fight one. The Poles behaved with great heroism, especially in Warsaw, which was subjected to savage aerial bombardment and reduced to ruins.

On September 27, Warsaw capitulated, and on September 28, Russia and Germany signed an agreement partitioning Poland. Germany annexed part of Poland outright and named the rest of its section "Wartegau," which it controlled. One and a half million Poles were deported, many forced to labor in Germany, the rest sent to "Wartegau." Jews were forced into ghettoes where they faced starvation. All Polish high schools and colleges were closed, all art treasures confiscated. The Russians deported one and a half million Poles to Siberia, launched a religious persecution and massacred 10,000 Polish army officers at the Katyn Forest.

In spite of these tremendous disasters, Poland would not bow to its new masters. Alone among all the countries the Nazis conquered, no natives joined the new government set up by the Nazis. A Polish exile government was formed in Paris in October 1939, with Paderewski elected president of the national council. Many Polish soldiers escaped after the surrender and formed an army which fought in France. When France fell to Germany, these men went to England. Many flew with the Royal Air Force.

Poland's Home Army

In Poland itself a resistance movement was formed to wage guerrilla warfare against the Nazis. Calling itself the Home Army, these men and women fought heroically on many fronts. They set up radio transmitters and receivers to communicate with London. They had to move their radio sets constantly so that the German devices could not locate them, but they managed to keep in touch with the Allies. Since the Germans had closed all schools except primary schools, the women provided education. The Home Army disrupted food shipments to the Germans and smuggled food to Poles in cities to supplement

Home Army in 1944

Monument to the Warsaw Uprising

their starvation rations. (Once, a pig was transported in a railway car disguised as a peasant woman!) They sent information to London about the concentration camps and helped those Jews who had managed to remain outside the ghettoes. They sabotaged German vehicles and harassed the German occupation forces. They used their radios to broadcast directly to the Polish people to keep alive their hope and to encourage them to resist the Germans.

Gradually, the German attitude toward the Jews in Poland and in all German-controlled lands hardened. In October of 1940, they built a wall around the Warsaw Ghetto. The wall, ten feet high and eleven miles long, enclosed 840 acres in the northern slums of Warsaw, into which the Nazis crowded half a million Jews. The daily food ration was only 300 calories. To live, the Jews had to smuggle in food.

Then on July 22, 1942, the Nazis began what they called a "resettlement" policy, but which was actually the Nazi "Final Solution," or extermination of the Jews. The Jews in the Warsaw Ghetto were told that some of them would be taken east to "family camps," where they would have more room, proper food and productive work. Each day a train would pull out of the station, pulling boxcars crammed with Jews. This procedure kept up until only 60,000 Jews were left in the Ghetto.

The Jews who had left on the trains had not gone east to "family camps." They had gone west, to Auschwitz, probably the most notorious death camp of all. Thousands of Jews, Poles and other innocent people, including many Catholics, were murdered in Auschwitz.

Knights of the Immaculata

Out of the darkness and degradation that was Auschwitz shone a bright light that still shines in Heaven — St. Maximilian Kolbe.

Maximilian was born on January 8, 1894, not far from Lodz, in Poland. He entered the Franciscan seminary and was sent to Rome to complete his training. In 1917, the year that the militant atheism of Communism came to power in Russia, Maximilian founded a militant order of a far different kind, the *Militia Immaculatae*, Knights of the Immaculata. Maximilian envisioned these knights as a spiritual army to bring the entire world under the Immaculata's rule of love.

Ordained in 1918, Father Maximilian returned to Poland in 1919. In 1922, he began the publication of a monthly magazine, *The Knight of the Immaculata*, the official publication of the knights. Though Father Kolbe faced many difficulties — lack of funds, lack of proper equipment — the magazine appeared regularly and its circulation grew.

In 1927, Maximilian founded *Niepokalanow*, the city of the Immaculata, about twenty-five miles from Warsaw. Twenty Franciscans lived there, imitating as closely as possible the life and spirit of St. Francis, the founder of the Franciscan order. Within a short time this new Marian center became known throughout the country. In his work Father Maximilian always relied on divine Providence and the spirit of sacrifice of the Polish people. He was not disappointed; as early as 1929, he was able to found a minor seminary to prepare boys for their future labors as missionaries.

In 1930, Father Maximilian himself became a missionary, leaving Poland with four Brothers to undertake a mission in the Far East. He founded a house called Garden of the Immaculata and published a Japanese version of the magazine. The mission grew rapidly. He returned to Poland in 1936, his Japanese mission firmly established.

War clouds now hung over Europe, but Father Maximilian's work prospered. Before the outbreak of World War II, Niepokalanow had become the largest Franciscan community in the world. It numbered 772 members in 1939. The presses kept turning out more and more copies of the various publications; 800,000 copies of the *Knight* were being printed each month. On December 8, 1939, after Poland had fallen, Niepokalanow inaugurated its radio station. To speed up the distribution of his publications, Father Maximilian thought of establishing his own airstrip and sent two Brothers to take a pilot training course. But his successes aroused the fury of the Nazis. Father Maximilian was arrested and sent to Auschwitz.

In Auschwitz, though he was brutally treated, Father Maximilian remained peaceful and joyful, trusting in God's loving Providence. Then in 1941, during the summer, a prisoner escaped from Auschwitz. The Nazi practice in such cases was to bring all the prisoners in the cell block from which the escapee had gone and force them to stand outside, whatever the weather, until the prisoner was found. If he were not found, ten men would be chosen at random to die in the starvation bunkers of the punishment cells.

The prisoner was not found. The Nazi guards went down the row of half-starved haggard prisoners to choose those who were to die. They pointed to one man. He cried out, "No, please, I have a family."

Another man stepped forward and asked to die in his place. "Who are you?" the guards asked.

"I am a Catholic priest." The guards did not particularly care who died, so long as their quota was met. They added Father Kolbe to the line and marched the ten men off to the starvation bunker.

The Nazis were accustomed to hearing pitiful cries for mercy from the dying prisoners in the punishment cells. This time, though, they heard prayers and hymns. Somehow the prisoners seemed to be living longer than usual. Finally, the survivors, including Father Kolbe, were injected with carbolic acid. Father Kolbe entered Heaven on August 14, 1941.

To this day, the Polish people mark the cell where he died with flowers and candles. Father Kolbe's memory still shines brightly in Poland, having survived two of the most brutal tyrannies known to man.

While Fr. Kolbe represents the spiritual opposition to Nazi tyranny, others tried physical opposition. Twice during the Nazi occupation Poland rose up against her oppressors. The first was the Warsaw Ghetto Uprising 1943, and the second was the Warsaw Uprising of 1944.

Fighting Back the Nazis

On January 18, 1943, the Nazis had scheduled a roundup of Jews in the Warsaw Ghetto for the death camps. The Jews, for the first time, fought back, and the Nazis were forced to back off. This hardened the determination of the Jews to fight again, and it hardened the determination of the Nazis to wipe out the Jews and the Ghetto.

At 6:00 A.M. on April 19, sixteen officers, 850 German soldiers, a tank and two armored cars entered the Central Ghetto. The Jewish Fighting Organization, under the command of twenty-four-year-old Mordecai Anielewics, had prepared as best they could. They had 1500 fighters, both men and women, a few automatic rifles, some mines, several thousand grenades and molotov cocktails, and a pistol apiece. Some of the weapons had been smuggled in by the Home Army; others, they had made themselves. People who could not fight were hiding in underground bunkers. The odds were uneven and the Germans thought that they would have an easy time rounding up the Jews. As they marched to Nalewki Street, a small group of Jews with pistols and home-made bombs routed the German force without a casualty of their own. The Jews set the tank on fire with a molotov cocktail and forced the armored cars to retreat; by the end of the day, the Nazis realized that this would be no easy victory.

The next day, the Germans had little more success. At one gate, the Jews detonated a huge mine, leaving eighty Germans dead or wounded. The Nazis now decided that they could not take the Ghetto by battle, so they would burn it and the people in it.

On April 21, they began the slow and systematic burning of the Ghetto, to drive the people out of the bunkers to their deaths. The Jewish Fighting Organization would not surrender. They forced the Germans to fight for every inch of territory, but they could not stop the deadly fires.

Some of the Jews were able to escape the Ghetto through a tunnel to a Franciscan church on the other side of the wall. Others took the perilous route, through the sewers, to be met by Polish resistance fighters on the other side. Several hundred escaped.

The rest of the Ghetto was doomed, but the fighting did not cease until May 16. For twenty-eight days, the poorly armed Jews held off the Nazi War Machine. It was one of the greatest humiliations the Nazis had faced. In frustration they reduced the Ghetto to rubble, but they could not erase from people's minds the heroism of the Warsaw Ghetto Uprising.

The second Warsaw Uprising was led by the Home Army, who hoped to drive the Nazis out of Warsaw and free Poland. The uprising began on August 1, 1944, with the Soviet Army just outside the city. The Home Army believed that the Soviets would come to their aid as they fought against their common enemy.

The Poles fought heroically, but the Germans cut off the city so that no supplies could get in. The Poles expected the Soviets to send airdrops of supplies. The few supplies that the Soviets dropped were dropped without parachutes. The Soviets refused to allow the Allies to use their bases to land planes, so that the Allies were unable to do much to help the Home Army. The Warsaw Uprising was crushed.

Soviet Takeover

On October 2, a capitulation agreement was signed. All surviving members of the Home Army were taken into captivity; civilians had to leave the city only with what they could carry. Then Warsaw was destroyed. The Poles had lost 200,000 of their best people and seventy percent of their capital city, the brain center of the most widespread and determined resistance movement in Europe. That was exactly what the Soviets had wanted.

With the Home Army annihilated, the Soviets were able to take over Poland easily and establish a Communist government in power.

For over forty years, Poland remained under tyrannical rule.

The Nowa Huta Church

Just as the Poles refused to give in to the Nazis, so they refused to give in to the Communists. The story of the Nowa Huta Church is a good example.

Nowa Huta was a new city built near Krakow, built to house the 200,000 workers who would labor in the New Lenin Steelworks. The Communists decided to make the city into an ideal socialist city, that is, a city without God. When the plans were drawn up for the city, no space was allotted for a church, even though almost all of the Poles were strong Catholics.

The people would not accept the Soviet plans. For a time they attended Mass at a small wooden chapel on the edge of the city, rain or shine, winter or summer. Then they began pestering the authorities to build a church.

They so annoyed the government that in 1956 permission was given to build a church, and the people set up a large wood cross on the building site. The church itself would not come so easily into existence.

Building materials, machinery and electric power all had to come from the Communist authorities. There was never electricity before five in the afternoon. The men had to mix cement by hand because they were not permitted the use of a cement mixer. The men had to do almost all the work on the church in the afternoons and evenings after they finished their long, exhausting day of work at the steel mill.

Stone by stone, the church slowly rose, designed in the form of a ship, an ark, crowned with a steel mast in the shape of a cross. The church would be named in honor of Mary, Queen of Poland. The pastor of the parish, Father Jozef Gorzelany, described the building of the church this way:

> Churches are often built for people who never come to them. People often build churches for themselves in order to satisfy their own ambition. We have another end in view. Our church is a house of God in which His people too can live. We are building the church for our children and grandchildren and for all who come from afar. Every stone shall be a grace, a sign of grace received and shared with others.

At last the church was completed. In the city where no church at all was supposed to stand, this huge church is crowded every Sunday. Each of the five Sunday Masses is attended by 10,000 people. *Corpus Christi* processions draw 40,000 participants. In May, nearly 2,000 children receive First Communion.

God prevailed in the supposedly godless city, and He still reigns in the hearts and minds of the Polish people, who never gave way to their Communist oppressors.

Typical roadside memorial

Chapter 25
Review Questions

1. The Polish people were independent for only _____ years, from 1919 to _____.

2. The German Nazis, attacking Poland in September, 1939, did not use conventional warfare in Poland. The used a tactic called Blitzkrieg. Describe this kind of warfare.
   _____
   _____

3. Who declared war on Poland and invaded them from the east?
   _____

4. By the end of September, what did Russia and Germany do to the land of Poland?
   _____

5. How many Poles were deported from Poland and sent to work in forced-labor camps in Germany?
   _____

6. Where were the Jews forced to live?
   _____

7. Where were thousands of Polish army officers massacred by the Russians?
   _____

8. Did any Poles join the new government set up by the Russians? Where was the exile Polish government located?_____

9. What was the name of the Polish resistance movement formed to resist the Nazis?
   _____

10. List at least four things that the Polish resistance movement did to fight against their enemies.
    _____

11. What did the Germans do to the Jews in Warsaw?
    _____

12. In 1942, what was the "resettlement" policy of the Nazis toward the Jews?
    _____

13. What kind of education did Maximilian Kolbe have?

14. What was the order founded by Kolbe? What was the goal of the order?

15. What were some of the successes of Father Kolbe in Niepokalanow?

16. Where did the Nazis send Father Kolbe? _____

17. What happened with Father Kolbe in the German prison camp?

18. Tell the highlights of the first Warsaw Ghetto Uprising in 1943.

19. How did some of the Jews escape?

20. In October, 1944, what happened to the surviving members of the Polish Home Army? What happened to the city of Warsaw?

21. Why were the Russians so easily able to take over Poland and establish a Communist government? How many years did Poland remain under their rule?

22. Tell the story of the Nowa Huta Church. What kind of a city did the Communists build? Where did the people attend Mass? How did the people manage to build a church? What is the name of this church?

23. Tell something about this church today.

Chapter 26
Survival of the Faith

The Mystery of the Passion, Death, and Resurrection of Our Lord is continually re-enacted in the life of the Church, Christ's Mystical Body. One such story is that of Christianity in Japan.

As the Protestant Revolt slashed gaping wounds in Christ's Mystical Body in Europe, the Catholic Church, reformed and revivified through the efforts of the Council of Trent, Popes Paul III and Pius V, and the great Catholic monarchs Charles V and Philip II, reached out to previously unknown lands to bring the Gospel of Christ to people who had never known Him. Leading the missionary explosion were the Jesuits, St. Ignatius Loyola's great army of dedicated priests. The greatest missionary of them all was Ignatius' close friend, St. Francis Xavier.

St. Francis Xavier

In 1540, Ignatius said farewell to Francis, the two men realizing that they would probably never see each other again. The king of Portugal had asked for missionaries to take the Gospel to the Portuguese colonies in India, and Francis had eagerly accepted the assignment. After achieving great success in India, Francis went to Malaysia, where he met a Japanese, one of the few who traveled outside Japan. Francis converted him, baptizing him with the name of Paul. Paul asked Francis to return with him to Japan to bring Christ to his people. In 1549 Francis arrived in Kagoshima, Japan.

Francis received permission from the local officials to preach and to baptize, but his main goal was the capital city, Kyoto, where he hoped to convert the emperor. While waiting for a ship to take him to Kyoto, Francis baptized over 100 Japanese; so successful was he that the Buddhist *bonzes* (Buddhist monks) became worried and persuaded the officials to deny Francis permission to make any more converts. Francis then went to Hirado, where he baptized another 100, and then began the overland journey to the ancient capital of Kyoto.

He arrived in the middle of January, 1551, but stayed only eleven days because he quickly learned the nature of the Japanese political system. Though the Japanese had an emperor, the emperor was powerless. The real power resided in a chief minister, or *shogun*. The emperor, though living in luxury and surrounded with ceremony, was only a figurehead. Francis realized that his plan to convert the country by converting the emperor was not possible.

Upon learning that the *daimyo* (local chieftain) of Yamuguchi was a powerful leader, Francis visited him as the official ambassador of the viceroy of India, taking him the gifts originally intended for the emperor. Though Francis did not convert the daimyo, he so impressed the official that his permission to

Pope Paul III

168

preach and make converts was renewed. Within two months, he had baptized 500 Japanese, including *samurais* (members of the noble-military class), and bonzes. Francis traveled throughout the country, making converts and establishing churches, until he was called back to India. The foundation he had established was to serve the Church in Japan well in the future.

The first Christian daimyo in Japan was Omura Sumitada, baptized in 1563. Though he may originally have been partially motivated by the hope of gaining commercial advantages from the Portuguese, his conversion proved sincere and his whole city joined the Church. In fact, Omura may have been guilty of excessive zeal, as he ordered the destruction of pagan temples and the burning of images. Finally, anti-Catholic forces launched a rebellion aimed at Omura's death and the substitution of his adopted son as daimyo, as well as the death of Father Torres, leader of the Jesuit mission. The rebels burned Omura's castle, but he and his family escaped to a nearby castle where they held out against great odds until help was sent by Omura's father. The rebels burned the Catholic church, but the priests fled to a Portuguese ship in the harbor where they were safe until Omura put down the rebellion.

In 1568, Father Vilela started a mission in Nagasaki, where he soon converted some 1,500 Japanese, thus founding what was to be the strongest Catholic community in Japan. The missionary remodeled a pagan temple into a church, which he named All Saints Church.

The Jesuits also made plans to build a splendid church in the capital city. Though Kyoto had few Christians, the Catholics wanted a beautiful church there to rival the many lovely pagan temples. The only plot of land the missionaries owned was quite small and the neighbors refused to sell the adjoining land because of their hostility to Christianity. So the missionaries designed a three-story church. This building angered the bonzes because the church was higher than their Buddhist temples. Nevertheless, in spite of the opposition, the church was dedicated on August 15, 1577, in honor of the Assumption of Our Lady.

From 1570-1578, after the conversions of a number of ruling princes, large numbers of persons joined the Church. After 1590, the government began to harass the Church, but Christianity continued to spread. Then new enemies appeared: the Protestant Dutch and English traders who began entering Japan in 1600. William Adams, an Englishman rescued from a shipwreck, became close to the shogun Ieyasu Tokugawa. The Portuguese feared the man's influence, so they offered to help Adams return to England. He refused. Then the Jesuits tried to convert Adams to Catholicism. They failed. Adams, meanwhile, told Ieyasu that Portugal intended to conquer Japan by means

St. Francis Xavier

of the Christian missions. Dutch ships began attacking Portuguese ships.

Ieyasu eagerly believed all that the Englishmen told him, the more so because he himself was hostile to Christianity. He began looking for an excuse to begin overt persecution of the Church. The pretext he sought came at the end of 1613. Hasegawa Sahyoe, governor of Nagasaki and a fierce enemy of Christianity, reported to Ieyasu that the Christians of Nagasaki had adored a criminal at the time of his execution. The truth was that when the Nagasaki Christian was about to be executed for a minor crime, his Christian brethren knelt down to offer prayers for his soul. This act of Christian charity was interpreted as "adoration of a criminal." Ieyasu exclaimed, "A law which teaches such things is from the devil."

Persecution and the Great Martyrdom of Nagasaki

On January 27, 1614, Ieyasu issued a decree marking the beginning of the persecution. Representing Christianity as a danger to the Japanese nation, Ieyasu ordered all missionaries to leave Japan and all Japanese Christians to return to the religion of their ancestors. Missionaries in Kyoto were ordered to leave in five days and proceed to Nagasaki for deportation. Most left, though a few went into hiding. Many Christians also chose exile, rather than abandon their newfound faith. Ieyasu told the wives of these voluntary exiles that if they remained in Japan, they would not be harmed; but the wives, nevertheless, joined their husbands in exile.

Ieyasu ordered Itakura, the governor of Kyoto, to draw up a list of Christians in the capital city. When he did so, he found 4,000 names. Fearful that Ieyasu would punish him for allowing Christianity to spread so widely in the capital, Itakura drew up another list, omitting children and servants, leaving a total of 1,600. Ieyasu was still furious at even that abbreviated number. In reality, Kyoto had about 7,000 Christians.

Ieyasu called upon Okubu Tadachika, daimyo of Odawara, to launch the persecution in Kyoto. Tadachika arrived in Kyoto toward the end of February with 300 armed men. They tore down churches, burnt the materials and threatened to deliver all Christians to death at the stake if they would not apostatize (give up their faith). His threats were ignored. Tadachika then urged relatives, friends and neighbors of the Christians to use whatever tactics of persuasion they could devise to "reform" the recalcitrant Christians, but this method too was unsuccessful. Finally, Tadachika ordered the arrest of the Christian women who lived near the Jesuit church in a sort of convent under the direction of Julia Naito. If they refused to give up their faith, all of them would be bound and led through the streets of the city. Julia hid the nine youngest of her companions in the houses of friends, but she with the other nine prepared for the ordeal. The women were tied hand and foot, put into rice bags and carried two by two, dangling on sticks, through the streets of

St. Francis Baptizes an Oriental Queen

Kyoto. Outside the city they were thrown down on the snowy ground and exposed to the cold. Throughout the ordeal they were exhorted to give up their faith, but they held fast. Ieyasu was still reluctant to shed blood, so he finally ordered the Christians into exile when his tortures proved of no avail.

As the missionaries waited in Nagasaki for a ship to carry them into exile, they clung to hopes that the order would be canceled. For three weeks, they held processions through the city, praying that they might remain in Japan. When word of these processions reached Ieyasu, he thought that the missionaries were organizing a rebellion. He immediately dispatched an expeditionary force to Nagasaki to put down the supposed rebellion, only to have them discover that the people were holding the processions for prayer, not fighting.

All the churches remaining in Japan were torn down and the debris burnt. The last of the missionaries went into exile in November, 1614.

Ieyasu died in 1616. He had wanted to eliminate Christianity from Japan but had not been prepared to kill Christians as a means of doing so. His son and successor, Hidetada Tokugawa, had no such scruples. He began ordering the execution of scattered Christians until finally, in 1622, in what was called the "great Martyrdom of Nagasaki," twenty-three Christians were burnt at the stake and twenty-two other Christians (most of whom had served as hosts for priests), with their wives and children, were beheaded.

On January 31, 1623, Hidetada retired from the office of shogun. The new shogun, his son Iemitsu Tokugawa, was the most vicious of the persecutors. Persecution spread throughout the entire country. In December of 1623, for example, seventy-four Christians were burnt. In 1624, mass martyrdoms took place. In 1627, Catholics were burnt at the stake, tortured and killed in hot sulphurous springs. Iemitsu's goal was not so much to kill Catholics as to make

The Death of St. Francis Xavier

them apostasize. He therefore ordered more fiendish tortures which prolonged the suffering so that the victim would be more likely to give up his Faith than to remain steadfast until death brought release. One such torture was to roast the victim over a slow fire. The majority of the Christians would not give in.

In 1637-1638, the Shamabara rebellion occurred. The rebellion began as a protest against fiscal exploitations of the poor peasants in Arima. When the government offered forgiveness to the pagans who would lay down their arms, most of them did so. The government then told Christians that their only choices were death or apostasy, so the Christians kept up the rebellion which was thereby transformed into a religious war. The overwhelmingly superior government forces finally captured the rebel army and their wives and children. All of them preferred death to apostasy and were beheaded. The number of victims of the Shimabara holocaust is estimated at between 35,000 and 37,000. Not a single Christian was left in Arima, which until 1612 had been almost entirely Christian.

The Closed Door Policy

In order to discover who were Christians, the Japanese government introduced the practice of *efumi* or picture treading in 1627. Those suspected of being Christians were ordered to trample on a picture of Christ or His Mother. The government also offered rewards to anyone who informed against a priest, brother, catechist or Christian layman. In 1634, Japanese were forbidden to go abroad, lest they become Christians. Only an occasional Dutch ship and some Chinese junks were permitted to land in Japan, and the coast was heavily guarded. For more than 200 years, from 1638 to 1854, Japan was virtually cut off from the rest of the world. (This is known as the Closed Door Policy.)

Some missionaries did try to sneak into Japan, but they were invariably captured and killed. Martyrdoms continued. In 1649, 23 were martyred; in 1650, 74; in 1658, 411; and in 1697, the last great known martyrdom claimed 35 victims.

In 1708, Father John Baptist Sidotti succeeded in landing in Japan. He was at once arrested and brought to trial. Sidotti's courage and intelligence created a feeling of respect so that he was merely sentenced to life

Japanese Martyrs

imprisonment rather than to torture and death. He was imprisoned and treated humanely for about seven years. However, he could not cease being a missionary. He converted and baptized his guard, whereupon he was thrown into a dark cell, dying shortly afterward from starvation and exhaustion on November 16, 1715.

When the Portuguese colonists in Macao attempted to send a ship for trading purposes only, the entire crew was thrown into jail. Refusing to apostasize, they were beheaded. A message was sent from Japan to Macao: "So long as the sun warms the earth, let no Christian be so bold as to come to Japan, and let all know that if King Philip himself, or even the very God of the Christians, or the great Buddha contravene this prohibition, they shall pay for it with their heads."

Underground Missionaries - Keeping the Faith Alive

Nevertheless, in spite of being deprived of priests, in spite of the continued practice of *efumi*, in spite of being totally cut off from the rest of the Mystical Body—except in the all-important matter of prayer— Christianity in Japan survived. The missionaries had trained many lay catechists because of the shortage of priests, so the laity was used to taking responsibility. Every Christian community had its own secret catechist who taught prayers and Christian doctrine as well as several Christians designated as baptizers. In order to ensure that the Latin formula for Baptism was transmitted exactly, every baptizer had a disciple whom he trained to take his place when he died. The Christian village elders were charged with keeping the Church calendar and a number of leaders announced the weekly feasts and days of fast and abstinence.

In the time of the missionaries, the Catholics had memorized their basic prayers, and these they passed down intact to their children. During the 200 years of isolation, parents taught their children the Our Father, Hail Mary, Sign of the Cross, Apostles' Creed, Ten Commandments, Hail Holy Queen, Confiteor, and Mysteries of the Rosary. Even doctrinal treatises were sometimes memorized and transmitted to later generations. For example, the ten-chapter *Doctrine* prepared by the Jesuits was preserved almost verbatim from 1591-1892.

Since the Christians were deprived of all sacraments except Baptism and Matrimony, they relied on perfect contrition for a happy death. Therefore *A Treatise on Contrition* was copied many times and passed down over the centuries. Holy objects had to be guarded and hidden as priceless treasures. Christians used statues of the Buddhist goddess of mercy, Kwannon, as substitutes for statues of Mary, to avoid detection by the police in their periodic raids of suspected Christian homes.

Finally in 1854, Commodore Perry of the United States persuaded the Japanese to negotiate a commercial treaty with the U.S. The Closed Door was at last reopened. In 1859, a treaty negotiated with the French included a clause abolishing *efumi* and giving French citizens permission to build churches and practice the Catholic religion. On January 5, 1860, the French priest Father Mermet opened a chapel, the first Christian house of worship in Japan since 1614. However, he was not permitted to make converts.

On March 17, 1863, Father Petitjean in his church at Nagasaki saw about fifteen people outside. He opened the door. They came in and looked around. Father Petitjean knelt down before the altar and began to pray. Three women knelt down beside him. One of them whispered, "All of us have the same heart as you." Another asked, "Where is the statue of the Santa Maria?" Petitjean led the group to the Blessed Mother altar; all knelt down and wept for joy. One exclaimed, "Yes, this is indeed Santa Maria. Behold her divine Infant in her arms." One of the women remarked,

"We celebrate the Feast of Our Lord on the twentieth day of the cold month. We were told that at midnight of that day He was born in a stable. Then He grew up to manhood in poverty and suffering to die for us on the Cross in His thirty-third year. At present we are in the season of sorrow. Have you also these feasts?" "Yes, we have today the seventeenth day of Lent." Then they spoke of St. Joseph, whom they knew to be the foster father of Our Lord Jesus.

More visitors came to the church so that the priests became alarmed that the police might interfere. They therefore warned the people to come only on days of very bad weather or in the very early or late hours, so that the police did not know what was going on. Soon a priest began visiting the Christians at Urakami to instruct them. They met mostly during the night and in hidden places, such as in a garden, among the bushes or in the mountains. During the following months many more Christians were discovered. At Urakami about 1,300 Christians contacted the priests, and about an equal number were discovered in the neighboring mountains. As the Christians came out of hiding, joyous at having priests among them once again, the authorities became aware of their existence and began to harass them. In Nagasaki sixty-three were imprisoned; chapels were plundered and Catholics were tortured and imprisoned. In 1870, 3,290 Catholics were deported.

However, Japan was no longer isolated from the world. The European governments, with whom Japan was now trading, put pressure on the government to end its persecution of Christians. Finally in 1889, a new constitution granted complete freedom of worship. The approximate number of Christians who were in touch with priests when the persecution ended was 14,000, a monument to the courage of the Japanese in holding to their faith in spite of 200 years of persecution and isolation. The largest Catholic community was in Nagasaki.

Franciscan house in Nagasaki founded by Fr. Kolbe

From 1873 to 1945, prejudices against Christianity were many, and conversions few. In 1945, 8,500 Catholics were killed by the atomic bomb dropped on Nagasaki, thus wiping out the largest Catholic community which had survived the persecution. The house built by Father Maximilian Kolbe was one of the few buildings that survived the atomic blast.

After the war the number of baptisms rose rapidly. Japan's Catholic population in 1997 was about 450,000.

Thus did the Christians of Japan relive in their own history Christ's Passion, Death, and glorious Resurrection.

Chapter 26
Review Questions

1. St. Francis Xavier converted a single Japanese, one of a few who traveled outside of Japan in the 1540s. The Japanese asked Francis to return with him to Japan to bring Christ to the Japanese people. In what year did Francis Xavier arrive in Japan?
   _____

2. The king of Portugal wanted Christianity brought to the people in the _____ in India.

3. The religious leaders in Japan were Buddhist bonzes or Buddhist _____.

4. Francis converted and _____ the Japanese quickly and easily, but the government officials started denying him permission to do so.

5. The daimo was a local chief and a very _____ leader.

6. With permission from the daimo in the city of Kyoto, Francis converted how many Japanese in only two months? _____

7. Those who were converted included some former monks, as well as nobles and members of the _____ class.

8. Francis traveled throughout the country, making converts and establishing _____.

9. The first Christian local chief was baptized in 1563, and his whole _____ converted with him.

10. Which country provided a ship for protection for the priests when anti-Catholic rebels burned the Catholic church headed by Father Torres? _____

11. In 1568, Father Vilela started a mission in the major city of _____, where 1500 Japanese were converted in All Saints Church.

12. Which order of priests was instrumental in the conversions in Japan?
    _____

13. In which major city of Japan was a three-story church built in 1577, in honor of the Assumption of the Blessed Mother? _____

14. There were many conversions to the Catholic Church until 1600 when an Englishman named William Adams began to influence the most important government official. What was the terrible lie that he told the Japanese official?
    _____

15. The Japanese official, Ieyasu, began persecution of Christians in 1614. What was his "reason"?
    _____

16. What was the decree of Ieyasu, the most powerful government official?
    _____

17. Describe some of the persecutions that the Christians of Kyoto had to suffer.
    _____

18. What did the missionaries and people in Nagasaki do while they were hoping for a change in the order?
    _____

19. What happened to all the Catholic churches in Japan?
    _____

20. In what year was the last of the missionaries sent into exile from Japan?
    _____

21. What was the great martyrdom of Nagasaki in 1622?
    _____

22. What happened to the Christians between 1623 and 1627?
    _____

23. What was the Shamabara rebellion of 1637 and 1638?
    _____

24. What was *efumi*?
    _____

25. What was the Closed Door Policy, from 1638 to 1854? Why did Japan have this policy?
    _____

26. In 1708, Father John Baptist Sidotti landed in Japan. What happened to him?
    _____

27. What happened to Portuguese traders and crew when they attempted to land in Japan in the 1700s?
    _____

28. List some of the things that Japanese Catholics did to keep the faith for themselves and for their children, for over 200 years.

    _____

    _____

    _____

29. What historic event happened in 1854?

    _____

30. Which group was allowed to practice the Catholic religion? _____

31. In 1860, which French priest was allowed to open a chapel? What was he not allowed to do?

    _____

32. What happened with Father Petitjean, a French priest, in 1863 in his church at Nagasaki?

    _____

33. How did the Christians try to protect themselves in the years in the 1860s?

    _____

34. Once the Catholics were discovered, what did the government do to them? How many were deported in 1870 from one city alone?

    _____

    _____

35. Once European governments started trading with Japan, what did they pressure the Japanese government to do?

    _____

36. When did a new Japanese constitution grant freedom of worship? How many Christians were identified in Japan at that time?

    _____

37. Where was the largest community of Catholics living?

    _____

38. What happened to the Catholics in 1945 in Nagasaki?

    _____

    _____

Chapter 27
Forbidden Country

China, the largest country in Asia, has always been a difficult land for Catholic missionaries to penetrate. The Chinese were more or less agnostic. They did not worship God, but neither did they deny His existence; they simply did not seem to care very much.

The Catholic missionary who had the most success in China was the Italian Jesuit, Matteo Ricci. In 1578 Matteo left Italy, which he would never see again, for India. After an unpleasant six months' voyage, Matteo arrived on September 14. He studied in the Jesuit college in India, was ordained, and then in 1582 was sent to Macao, a small Portuguese-controlled territory on the Chinese mainland, near Hong Kong.

Father Ricci Gains Entry

The following year a Chinese soldier arrived in Macao with a letter from Wang Pan, the governor of Shiuhing Province. Wang Pan was interested in Westerners, who had only recently come to the Far East. Ricci's companion, Ruggieri, boasted to the soldier of Ricci's mathematical ability, which was considerable, and told the Chinese that Ricci possessed clocks, maps, and spheres. All of these inventions and accomplishments impressed the Chinese and so he invited Ricci and Ruggieri to come to China.

The Jesuits could not believe their good fortune. China was most inhospitable to foreigners, believing them far inferior to the Chinese, lumping together all non-Chinese under the title "barbarians." Now these two Italians had received an invitation to China, largely on the strength of Ricci's ability to solve complicated mathematical problems. The two men agreed that they would receive a better welcome if they imitated Chinese dress and customs. So they chose the dress and appearance of Buddhist *bonzes*, shaving their heads and wearing gray cloaks.

Matteo Ricci, painted just before his death.

When they arrived in Shiuhing, they were made to stay in a ramshackle building outside the city reserved for "barbarians." When the governor finally granted them an audience, Ricci did not dare mention Christianity because it would have been far beyond the comprehension of his listeners. So he addressed the governor as follows:

> We are religious who serve the King of Heaven, and come from the farthest parts of the West — that is, from India — all we ask is a piece of land away from the commercial distractions of Macao, where we can build a house and pagoda. There we will remain serving Heaven until we die. We beg your Excellency to help us. We shall give no trouble. We intend to seek alms for our food and clothing and shall remain indebted to your Excellency for the rest of our lives.

The governor was impressed and gave Ricci and Ruggieri a small plot of land, but he made a number of conditions. The Jesuits had to speak Chinese, dress Chinese, eat Chinese, observe Chinese customs, marry only Chinese women, and bring no more new barbarians in.

Despite the favor of the governor, the Jesuits were not well received. Their first convert was a dying, poor man who had been thrown out of his home. He could not understand the difficult doctrines of Christianity, but he repented of his sins and expressed his belief in the Lord of Heaven. The priests baptized him just before he died. The behavior of the foreigners puzzled the Chinese. Why did these men take care of this poor old man who could do nothing for them? They finally devised an explanation that satisfied them: they convinced themselves that the old man had jewels in his head and that Ricci and Ruggieri took him into their home to cut them out.

Governor Wang was transferred, and the new magistrate ordered the Jesuits to leave China. The Jesuits could not bear to leave when so little had been accomplished, so they convinced him to withdraw the order. However, they could not stay where they were, and he ordered them to move to a Buddhist monastery called the Pagoda of the Southern Flower. Ruggieri was recalled to India and replaced by another Jesuit, Almeida. The two men went to the monastery to find it totally irreligious and corrupt, with the monks living there with their wives and children, in complete violation of Buddhist custom. The head of the monastery was afraid that Ricci and Almeida had been sent to reform the Pagoda of the Southern Flower, and was much relieved when they told him they only wanted some land of their own on which to build a church. He gave them some, but it was in a swampy and unhealthy place. Almeida fell ill with a fever and died soon after.

Alone now in the vast and inhospitable country, Ricci set about making himself known and respected. Since he had been allowed to come to China in the first place because of his mathematical ability, he now began to use it to impress people so that they would listen to his teachings on Christianity. He even learned Chinese chess, which is played with 278 pieces on a board with 361 positions.

By 1592, Ricci had made just fifteen converts in his new location. His mission had been attacked by a gang of drunken rowdies and he had been wounded on the hand by a hatchet blow. It seemed to him that he must make a drastic change in his methods if he were ever to make a significant number of converts.

Ricci had gradually come to realize that Buddhist *bonzes* were not respected in China,

Great Wall of China

and that his adoption of Buddhist garb had meant that the Graduates (the educated class) would have no respect for him or for his teachings. So he decided to adopt the dress and customs of a Mandarin, who was a type of Graduate. At the same time he moved to Nanking, in the north of China.

Mandarin dress consisted of an ankle-length silk robe with loose, flowing sleeves. The mandarin wore a high square black hat, which resembled a bishop's miter, and slippers. Ricci had to let his hair and beard grow long. He refused, however, to follow the custom that required that he spend half an hour combing his hair and letting his nails grow to be six inches long!

The Mandarin class also required complicated etiquette. For example, when Ricci went to visit a mandarin friend, each had to take a chair, test it to be sure it was solid, dust it thoroughly (though it was already perfectly clean) and then offer it to the other as worthy of him. They drank tea from porcelain bowls and ate crystallized fruits with silver chopsticks. After Ricci returned home, a servant from his host would arrive at Ricci's house to bid him good-bye in the host's name, a compliment Ricci was obliged to return through his own servant.

Strengthened by God's Promise

Shortly after Ricci arrived in Nanking, his request for permission to remain there was refused, and he was ordered to leave. Disappointed, he decided to sail down the river to the smaller town of Nanchung. Standing on the deck of the boat, Ricci bemoaned his misfortune. Suddenly, he noticed a shadowy figure where there had been no one before. The figure spoke to him, "So you are traveling to destroy the ancient religion of this country and establish a new one?"

Ricci replied, "Are you God or the devil, that you know my secret?"

"I am not the devil," the figure answered. "I am God."

"O Lord," begged Ricci with tears streaming down his cheeks, "since You know my plans, why do You not help?"

God promised that Ricci would be allowed to enter both capital cities of China (Nanking and Peking) and then disappeared. Ricci felt a deep inner peace and knew that no matter how discouraging circumstances might appear to be, God was with him and would care for him.

In Nanchung, Ricci called on a doctor whom he had known in earlier days in China and was invited to a banquet with many important people present. During the five-hour banquet, Ricci impressed all the guests with his knowledge of the fine points of Mandarin etiquette and his learning on many subjects.

During the course of the banquet, the doctor began to boast of Ricci's amazing memory. The other guests demanded a demonstration, so the doctor handed a book to Ricci and opened to a page with 400-500 Chinese characters on it. Ricci looked over the page and then handed the book back to the doctor. Disappointed, the doctor asked, "You decline?"

Replied Ricci, "I think I have it memorized already."

Temple in the Forbidden City

A gate in the Forbidden City

The doctor and the guests all agreed that he could not possibly have memorized it; he had barely had enough time to read the page through. So Ricci stood up and recited the entire page perfectly. The guests were silent for a moment and then the doctor said, "You must have seen the book before." Ricci merely smiled and suggested that they write down 500 characters at random and let him try again. They did. He again recited them perfectly, and then proceeded to recite them backwards. This amazing feat so impressed the Chinese that Ricci began to receive many invitations and offers of support.

With this kind of assistance, Ricci was able to obtain a sponsor for a trip to Peking, the residence of the emperor. Ricci was delighted to be in the chief city of China at long last, but soon found that his ultimate goal of meeting the emperor was far from being realized. The palace guard hated Mandarins and would only listen to Ricci's request if he offered sufficient bribes, for which Ricci did not have the resources.

Ricci spent two months offering gifts to the guard, but their only response was that he might consider letting him into the Forbidden City (where the emperor actually lived) if he could show him how to change mercury into silver. Since such an attainment was beyond Ricci, as it is beyond everyone else, he decided to return to the south of China.

The trip was a nightmare. It was winter and the roads were in such terrible condition that sometimes Ricci could barely tell where the roadway was. He came down with a fever and was sometimes so ill that he had to dismount and sit on the snow-covered ground. So weak he could scarcely sit on his horse, his whole body shaking with pain, Ricci decided that he must find a place to rest. He knew that a friend lived nearby and managed somehow to reach his house. When he arrived, he was told that his friend had moved fifty miles away. Barely conscious, he covered the fifty miles and then collapsed on his friend's threshold. He lay at the point of death for several days, but finally his inner reserves of physical and spiritual strength brought him back to health and he went on to Nanking.

In March of 1600, Ricci was joined by James Pantoja, the first Spanish missionary to come to China.

A friend, Li Pen-ku, invited Ricci to dinner to debate his beliefs with a famous scholar named Huang San-hui, before an audience of about twenty-five other guests. Huang began by challenging Ricci's belief in an omnipotent Creator, saying, "Each one of us is, in every respect, as great as that Lord."

"Well, then," said Ricci, "I do not want to give you the trouble of creating another Heaven and another earth, but I should like to see you make — let us say a brazier, like that one over there."

When the guests applauded Ricci's clever answer, Huang tried to get out of the dilemma by saying that the images in our mind of any object were a new creation, and in that sense we were creators, just like the Lord of Heaven.

Ricci's answer: "Take a shining surface, for instance. When it is placed opposite the sun or the moon, it reflects those planets. But no one would claim that the surface creates the sun and the moon or the other objects it reflects."

The guests approved Ricci's argument, but Huang grew angry and began to insist that there was no difference between the real world and the world of the mind. Li was forced to intervene and lead his guests in to dinner, where they interspersed their eating with so much talk that the banquet went on until three in the morning.

Once again, Ricci obtained permission to visit Peking, and he and Pantoja obtained passage on a canal boat. In Peking, Ricci and Pantoja were confined to a house outside the walls and required to submit their gifts to the emperor. Ricci had no idea if the emperor would ever see the gifts, but he paid a high fee to have delivered a flowery, flattering letter written to the emperor requesting an audience.

For the next few days, Ricci heard nothing and assumed that all his efforts had been wasted. Then, more than a week later, he received an urgent letter, summoning him to the Forbidden City immediately. It seemed that one of the gifts sent to the emperor, a chiming clock, had run down and no longer struck the hours. The emperor was displeased and wanted the clock running again.

Ricci could hardly contain his joy as he and Pantoja hastened to the Forbidden City where no Westerner had ever gone before. Everywhere he looked he saw the imperial dragon — an image made of a camel's head, deer's horns, hare's eyes, bull's ears, snake's neck, carp's scales (of the lucky number of eighty-one), eagle's claws, and tiger's paws.

When they arrived in the palace, the chief of protocol met them and begged them to show him how to regulate the clock. Surprised at the chief's ignorance, Ricci said he would be happy but that it would "require two or three days." The Jesuits were escorted to the college of mathematicians where they spent the next three days teaching them everything about clocks, and watching them feverishly take down every word, fearful for their very lives if they failed to learn how to keep the clock striking.

During the three days, Ricci received many questions from the emperor about

European life. In the answers he sent back, he indicated his desire to remain in the Forbidden City. When the work on the clock was finished, the emperor was so pleased that he promoted his mathematicians and raised their pay. Still, Ricci could not see the emperor. In fact, he learned, no one saw the emperor except his palace guard and his wives. He did not even go out in public for fear of assassination and shame at his unsightly body.

Yet the people regarded the emperor as the Son of Heaven, the only one in the whole nation worthy of offering the sacrifices to heaven that would bring prosperity to the people. Twice a year, dressed in a robe embroidered with dragons, the emperor would climb to a white marble altar and offer food, silk, a bull, and precious stones to the mysterious life-giving heaven. The Chinese had no real belief in God, but they did feel themselves under the influence of forces outside their control, which must be honored if their lives were to proceed in peace and prosperity.

By this time the emperor had run out of questions for the Westerners, and they were escorted from the palace, still having had no direct contact with the "Son of Heaven." Ricci and Pantoja were then moved into the Castle of Barbarians where most foreigners were required to stay. Their room was bare and unfurnished, but they did at least have a place to say Mass.

Ricci still received visits from high ranking officials who had become his friends during his stay in Peking. And then, much to his amazement, he received word that he, Pantoja, and some of the other "barbarian" ambassadors had been granted an audience with the emperor. First, they had to be rehearsed in the proper techniques of bowing to the emperor. They were dressed in red silk and given ivory tablets to cover their mouths, so that when they spoke, their breath would not touch the emperor.

Precisely at dawn the ambassadors were ushered through the Gates of Supreme Harmony and Heavenly Purity into the courtyard of the Throne Hall of Assured Peace. At the north end, approached by three flights of white marble stairs, stood the emperor's throne, still empty. Behind the throne was a balcony with a slatted blind. An official called out, "Kneel down," and all knelt. Then they were ordered to rise, move forward, and bow to the empty throne, beating the floor with their heads and calling out, "Ten thousand years." Each group of ambassadors performed this ceremony. All the while the throne remained empty. Then they were escorted out of the Forbidden City, having had a ceremonious audience with an empty throne. They later learned that the emperor was behind the blind, watching them, but they never saw him at all.

Ricci obtained permission to move out of the Castle of Barbarians to live in the city of Peking itself. He made his first Peking converts, including a nobleman married to the emperor's sister-in-law, two sons of the imperial doctor, and a nephew of the Minister of Justice.

In 1603 Ricci published *A True Disputation about God*, a dialogue between a Chinese and a Western Graduate, to explain those Christian beliefs which could be proved through natural reason, such as the existence and nature of God. Ricci showed the error of *metempsychosis*, the belief that souls traveled from body to body. He told how the Son of Heaven had become man and summarized the life of Christ. The book was very popular and went through many editions.

By 1610, Ricci had been in China for twenty-seven years; there were 2,500 Christians in the country and a novitiate with eight Brothers. Ricci had an endless succession of visitors and an exhausting correspondence as he had to answer every letter that came to him disputing points in his books. All of these activities were in addition to his spiritual activities to which he devoted most of his time and strength.

On the evening of April 30, 1610, Ricci returned home after a series of visits. Exhausted and in pain, he lay down on his bed but sleep would not come. Two days later, he was still worse, so Pantoja called in doctors. They could do nothing for him, so on May 8, he made a general confession. Next morning, when Holy Communion was brought to his room, despite his weakness he knelt on the floor before the Sacred Host. The next day he became delirious but by the afternoon of the tenth, he regained consciousness and received the Last Rites. At seven o'clock that evening, as the sun was setting in Peking, Matteo Ricci peacefully died.

Ricci's efforts bore fruit. In 1692, the government issued an Edict of Toleration, giving full legal rights to Christians. There were soon 300,000 Christians in China.

The Chinese Rites Controversy

Then a major tragedy occurred. Ricci and the other Jesuits had always done everything they could to accommodate Chinese customs so that the Chinese would be more willing to accept Christianity; at the same time, they were careful not to compromise Christian doctrine or moral teaching. An example were the rites honoring the dead, because the Chinese had great respect for their ancestors. The Jesuits permitted the ceremonies, so long as their converts clearly believed that they were only honoring the dead, not worshipping them. In the eighteenth century other missionaries came into China. They believed that the Jesuits had actually compromised with Catholic doctrine and strongly condemned the Jesuit practices.

The dispute, known as the Chinese Rites Controversy, was taken to the Vatican, where a commission of cardinals ruled against the Jesuits. Christianity lost its respect in the court and hence among the people. Christianity slowly began dying out in China.

In the early twentieth century, new missionaries began to make headway again in China, and in 1939 the Chinese Rites decision was reversed. The number of Christians in China grew to three million.

When the Communists took over China after World War II, they launched a vicious persecution of Christianity in China. One of their first targets was the Legion of Mary. The Legion of Mary is an organization of laymen and laywomen who have a special devotion to the Blessed Mother. They promise to spend at least two hours a week in apostolic work, such as visiting the sick, distributing Catholic literature and persuading fallen-away Catholics to return to the Church. The Legion of Mary was strong in China. The Chinese Communists kept lists of members of the Legion. When they came into control of the government, they began to arrest, torture and kill every single Legionary they could find. They knew that if they could stamp out devotion to Our Lady, they would be close to destroying the Church.

They also arrested or expelled foreign missionaries and set up a mock church with a few priests who cooperated with them. At the present time, the only Christian religion permitted by the Communist government is the state-controlled church, which has few members. We have no way of knowing how many Catholics in the underground Church continue to hold fast to their faith in secret, refusing to let the Communist government take from them what is more precious than life itself, their Catholic religion.

Chapter 27
Review Questions

1. The Catholic missionary who had the most success in China was Father Matteo Ricci. Of what nationality was Father Ricci? Of which religious order?

2. What was the ability that Father Ricci had which attracted the Chinese?

3. What did Father Ricci own which was of interest to the Chinese?

4. What did the Chinese believe about all non-Chinese? What did they call all non-Chinese?

5. Why did Father Ricci and Father Ruggieri dress in Chinese clothes and appear like Buddhists?

6. When Father Ricci asked for a small piece of land, the governor gave it to him under certain conditions. What were those conditions?

7. What did the priests do for the dying Chinese man?

8. What kind of land did the head of the Buddhist monastery give the priest? What was the result?

9. What did Father Ricci do to get people to listen to his teachings?

10. To which major city did Father Ricci move?

11. What were some of the things Father did to look like a member of the mandarin class?

12. Describe the vision that Father Ricci had as he was entering Nanchung.
    _____

13. What impressed the Chinese guests in Nanchung?
    _____

14. Father Ricci was able to find a sponsor for what? Did he ever meet the emperor?
    _____

15. Who was the first Spanish missionary in China who joined Father Ricci in 1600?
    _____

16. Both priests went again to Peking to visit the emperor. Did they ever see him? _____

17. What did the two priests do for three days in the college of mathematicians?
    _____

18. Did the Chinese [in general] believe in God? _____

19. Father Ricci finally received permission to live in the city itself, in Peking. What finally happened while he was there? _____

20. What was the name of the book published by Father Ricci? _____

21. What did Father Ricci explain in his book? _____

22. In which year did Father Ricci die? _____

23. What happened in 1692? How many Christians were there soon after?
    _____

24. What was the Chinese Rites Controversy? What happened when the Vatican cardinals ruled against the Jesuits? What happened when the Vatican reversed its decision in 1939?
    _____
    _____
    _____

25. What did the Communists do to persecute the Christians in China?
    _____
    _____
    _____
    _____

Chapter 28
Teacher of Reality

India's people are primarily of the Hindu religion (82%). The beliefs of Hinduism deny the goodness of creation. Hindus also believe in reincarnation: that the soul comes back to earth many times in different bodies, sometimes even in the form of an animal. At one time, another popular religion in India was Buddhism. The Buddhist religion began as a way to escape from reincarnation. Buddha taught that a person could avoid being reincarnated if he purified himself of any attachment to anything material, including his own body, often by torturing himself. He could then be "dissolved" into *Nirvana*, a sort of "big blob of nothingness." Christianity came to India with the Apostle Thomas, and the first Christians' descendants, known as "Thomas Christians," still live in India.

Father Roberto de Nobili

The first concentrated missionary effort in India began with the Jesuits in the 1500s. St. Francis Xavier was the first Jesuit missionary, and he was quite successful. After he went on to Japan, he was followed by Roberto de Nobili, who gave fifty-two years of his life to India.

De Nobili was born in Rome in 1577 to one of Italy's most noble families. He entered the Jesuit novitiate in Naples in 1596 at the age of nineteen and studied hard because he knew that only those with good academic records could go to foreign missions. Roberto longed to be sent to India. He did so well that he was ordained early, in 1603, and received his longed-for assignment to the land of cobras and reincarnation.

On the voyage, they survived storms and becalming in the doldrums, where it was so hot that the sun melted their candles. They lived on dry biscuit and water so foul that they had to drink it through a piece of cloth to filter out the worms. Many of the

The ruins of St. Paul's Church in Macau, destroyed by fire during a typhoon in 1853. It was built in 1602 by Christian refugees who fled persecution in Japan. For many years Macau was Christianity's main outpost in the Far East.

passengers came down with scurvy from lack of vitamin C because they had no fresh fruit or vegetables. Finally, the ship crossed the equator and rounded the Cape of Good Hope at the tip of Africa.

De Nobili finished his studies at the Jesuit College of St. Paul's in Goa, the capital of Portuguese-controlled India, 250 miles south of Bombay. He was then sent to Cochin at the end of 1605.

Father De Nobili soon became acquainted with the complicated social structure of India known as the "caste system." The Indians believed that all men were divided into groups called castes. A man is born into his caste, must marry in it, must observe the customs of it, and will die in it. If a man does not conform to the customs of his caste, he can be expelled from it and become an "outcaste," which is worse than being in the lowest caste (the untouchables) because he has no caste at all and is deprived of the funeral rites which ensure his continued existence and reincarnation. The higher the caste, the stricter its customs. The three highest castes were the Brahmins (the priestly and learned caste), the Rajas (warriors), and the Vaisyas (farmers or traders). The ordinary people were in the fourth caste or Sudras, which was divided into more than a thousand subcastes.

The Portuguese, when they came to India, did not seem to the Indians to belong to any caste and, therefore, did not fit into Indian society. Furthermore, the Portuguese had told the Indians that if they became Christians, they must abandon all caste customs. Thus, there had been almost no converts to Christianity and the Indians had little respect for the Portuguese.

Joining the Brahmins

De Nobili, observant and perceptive, decided that the only way he could bring Christ to India was to join a caste and to adopt as many of their customs as he reasonably could. He began by eliminating beef from his diet (Hindus would never eat beef), speaking only Indian dialects, frequently bathing (as did members of the higher castes), and sitting cross-legged. He decided to join a class of Brahmins called *sannyasi*, who took vows of poverty and were devoted to the contemplation of God and the problems of philosophy.

When de Nobili suggested his plan to his superiors, they were shocked. What priest had ever worn only a red ochre cloth, shaved his head, and lived on rice and herbs? Father de Nobili's superior decided to refer the matter to the bishop. The bishop was a little worried because some of the *sannyasi* were extreme in their attempts to free themselves from dependence on the body. Some would stare at the sun until blind; others would stand on one leg or keep an arm stretched high until it dried up. But, finally, the bishop decided that de Nobili could adopt some of the *sannyasi* customs, but not the clothing.

Delighted, de Nobili organized his house along strictly Indian lines and began getting

St. Francis Church, Cochin India
Built in 1503. It is the oldest European church in India.

used to their customs. Every day, he had to wash himself thoroughly. He could not eat meat or eggs. His rice and vegetables could not be touched by a man of lower caste. Seated on the ground, he must take his rice with the top of the fingers of his right hand. He must drink water only once, when he had finished eating, pouring it into his mouth from a distance. After his meal, he poured water out of the drinking vessel to wash his right hand clean.

Gradually, men of the three highest castes came to see him, men who had formerly spat contemptuously as he passed or uttered pious prayers to avert bad fortune. For the first time in 2,000 years, since the time of Alexander the Great, a European had won the respect of high caste Indians.

In February 1609, de Nobili opened doctrine classes for a group of young men and held a series of debates with a local teacher. They debated the unity of God (since the Hindus believed that all men were in a sense God), unity of body and soul (since the Hindus believed that the same soul could inhabit many bodies through reincarnation), and the true meaning of suffering (since the Hindus believed that suffering had no purpose, except in self-torture to free one from dependence on the body). The arguments achieved their purpose, and de Nobili baptized several of the men, including the teacher, giving him the name Albert. De Nobili became their *guru*, or spiritual teacher and spiritual master.

Finally, he was given permission to adopt the full life-style of a Brahmin, including the red silk robe. Now he had to live an even stricter life: give up all amusements, eat only one meal a day, and wear a rectangular mark on his forehead to indicate a man of learning. De Nobili did not mind the extra restrictions, because he could offer them up to God as penance. The Portuguese, however, were shocked.

Having become a Brahmin, de Nobili was now to wear a special insignia made of strands of thread. He chose five strands: three of gold which he used to symbolize the Trinity, and two of white which he used to symbolize the soul and body of Christ. He also attached a cross to his thread, to symbolize the Redemption.

As a Brahmin, de Nobili was required to learn the language of Sanskrit and to learn the great epic poems of India, the *Vedas*. Father de Nobili was the first European to know of the *Vedas* in the 2,500 years of their composition. The first was the *Rig-Veda*, a collection of over a thousand hymns addressed to the gods. The second was the *Yapur Veda*, a collection of sacrificial formulas. The third, *Sama Veda*, described the worship of the goddess Indra for whom India was named. There were other *Vedas* as well. De Nobili hoped to take what was good out of them to show the relationship to Christianity.

Tattuva Bodhakar

This task was not easy. Indian philosophical beliefs were almost totally contradictory on every point to Christianity. The Indians denied individuality, believing in one universal soul. They did not believe in reality. They believed that there is no true or false, good or evil, right or wrong. All is nothing and nothing is all.

The meager diet and difficult life exhausted de Nobili. He was also tormented by flies and white ants, which gorged on everything in sight, and by the blazing heat which alternated with the torrential rains of the monsoon season. Father de Nobili spent his spare time translating the Gospel but had many difficulties. India did not have the same kind of animals or seasons as were in the Gospels. The Indians did not like wine and considered fishermen a polluting caste.

Despite the hardships, de Nobili persevered and by Easter 1609 had made a total of fifty converts. His Indian friends decided that he needed an Indian name, one that would identify what he stood for. They chose the name *Tattuva Bodhakar,* which means Teacher of

Reality. Thus did they contrast de Nobili with Indian religious teachers who refused to admit that the world or anything else was real.

The work was too much for one man to handle, and de Nobili requested an assistant. His Jesuit superiors sent him Emmanuel Leitao, who arrived in Brahmin dress with his feet worn out by walking in wooden sandals. The work was so exhausting that Leitao soon had to return home, and de Nobili was left to continue his work alone. On the feast of the Annunciation, in 1610, he had a great triumph: the opening of his first church, built in Indian style.

In 1610, he had the idea of establishing a seminary to educate Indians for the priesthood, while still preserving as many of the Indian customs as possible. He, therefore, had to familiarize himself with the difficult and complicated system of Brahmin education.

First, the student would study the Vedas with a guru but without any books. The lessons were given out of doors and if any notes needed to be taken they were written on loose sand. Next, the student would study what were called the "limbs of the Veda," subjects necessary for the proper understanding of the Veda, such as phonetics, grammar, and astronomy. All lessons had to be memorized. Next, the student would go to the university where he specialized in one of the six classic systems: liturgy, metaphysics, psychology, cosmology, logic, and yoga (control of breathing or concentration of thought to overcome the five hindrances: the world, the sensation of one's own existence, sympathy, antipathy, and the will to live). Much of the teaching in these areas would contradict the other areas, but since the Indians did not believe in truth or falsity it did not really matter to them.

De Nobili also learned of an amusing legend associated with the university. Supposedly, Siva (the Indian god of death) had appeared as a professor and given the

The Taj Mahal in Agra, northeast India, is considered one of the Seven Wonders of the World.

university a bench of solid diamond on which only a faultless scholar could be allowed to sit. One day a poet came by and wanted to sit on the bench but was refused permission because he was of a lower caste. He was, however, given permission to lay his poems on one end. Immediately the bench disappeared, leaving the professors who had been on it afloat in a lotus pool. And that was the end of the diamond bench.

De Nobili decided to base his lectures on the system of logic, since as far as he could tell that was the system most compatible with Christianity. He was able to deliver some lectures, but the seminary never came into being because of a lack of funds and opposition from the Portuguese authorities in Goa. He then petitioned Rome for permission to use Sanskrit as a language for Mass in place of Latin, but was refused. He was able, however, to write many books in Sanskrit. In one of his books, he made the following argument to refute the notion that the world was God: "If the world were God, it should be eternal and infinite; having an infinite number of men with an infinite number of hairs on an infinite number of heads."

Some Portuguese objected so strongly to de Nobili's methods that they complained to Rome, accusing him of being close to apostasy. Even some of his friends in Rome believed the rumors and wrote to him reprimanding him for his behavior. These misunderstandings were most painful for de Nobili.

The General, or head, of the Jesuits, Father Acquaviva, wrote to de Nobili's provincial superior in India, Pero Francisco, warning against the adoption of Indian customs to the detriment of Christianity. Pero Francisco, who did not like de Nobili's methods, used the letter as an excuse to forbid de Nobili to use Indian customs at all. Shocked, de Nobili traveled to Cochin for a conference with Pero Francisco. When he arrived, exhausted by his long journey across the mountains, Pero Francisco refused

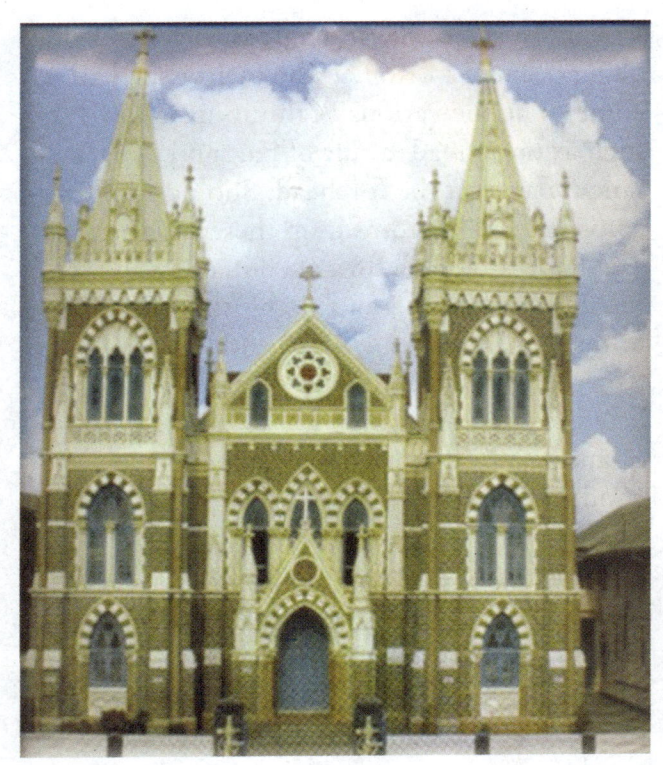

Mount Mary Basilica, dedicated to Our Lady of Fatima

even to speak to de Nobili because he was still in his red silk robes. Though he could hardly set one foot in front of the other, de Nobili continued another day's journey to the residence of Archbishop Rose. The archbishop welcomed him and returned with him to Cochin. But Pero Francisco still refused to talk to de Nobili. Instead he put a number of restrictions on de Nobili's actions and, finally, in August 1613, told him that he was forbidden to baptize anybody. De Nobili was heartbroken, lonely and frustrated, but he continued to teach Catholic doctrine, praying for the day when he could once again bring converts into Christ's Church.

Thus he labored on for two years, until the death of Pero Francisco in August of 1615. The new Provincial, Gaspar Fernandez, invited de Nobili to come for a conference. Father Fernandez was shocked by what he saw. Though only thirty-eight, de Nobili's emaciated body and lined face made him seem much older. His obvious holiness and learning so impressed Father Fernandez that he gave de Nobili permission to baptize once more.

The issue of the Indian customs was still being debated in Rome. The main issue had come to be the various Brahmin insignias such as the thread, a tuft of hair and a mark of sandal paste on the forehead. Should the Indian converts be allowed to keep these insignia? The Pope ordered a formal conference in Goa, including de Nobili and Archbishop Da Sa, to be held February 4, 1619. Archbishop Da Sa was hostile to de Nobili and would not listen to any arguments. He accused de Nobili of apostasy and sent off to Rome a decree condemning him.

The Pope did not act hastily but appointed another commission, under the chairmanship of Peter Lombard, an Irish bishop exiled from his country by the English. The commission ruled in 1622 that the insignia were social symbols, not religious, and would be permitted.

De Nobili was much relieved but physically and mentally exhausted. Nevertheless, he decided to go on a missionary journey around south India. In one town he was told by the inhabitants that they already had enough gods of their own (the number of Hindu gods was estimated at 330,000,000). He made the acquaintance of a *nayak* or local king, and so impressed him that on Christmas Day, 1625, the nayak, his mother, wife and daughters were all baptized.

De Nobili now felt that he had concentrated on the higher castes long enough; now it was time to preach Christ to the poor. He converted and baptized many untouchables. This angered some of his former friends among the higher castes, who attacked him and beat him with a bamboo rod.

By 1630, the Indian mission consisted of three self-contained mission centers. For the protection of the missions, de Nobili needed the help of Tirumala, who was Nayak of Madurai, and known as Lord of the Holy Mountain, the most powerful king in south India. Tirumala was devoted to his elephants. When he went to war, the elephants were clad in steel plates, with large scythes attached to their trunks, each carrying a dozen soldiers in a reinforced *howdah*. He fed chicken, eggs, and butter to his more than 300 elephants. Almost every day he held an elephant parade. On special occasions he would dress in his gold-embroidered robe and turban, don his earrings of eight large pearls, his necklace and bracelet of diamonds, and mount his biggest elephant, whose tusks were sheathed with gold, to sit on a velvet blanket spangled with pearls. No one was admitted to his presence without money, and his favor would be retained only until someone came with a bigger present.

Tirumala was impressed with de Nobili's learning and granted him a license to preach and to build churches wherever he pleased. Father de Nobili never had a chance to talk to Tirumala himself about Christianity because he was always watching his elephants, or spending time at plays, concerts and dances, which *sannyasi* were forbidden to attend.

De Nobili Imprisoned

1640 was an ominous year in the Indian calendar; it marked the end of a sixty-year cycle when any catastrophe might occur and, therefore, any preventive action was considered justified. While Tirumala was away, one of his assistants decided that de Nobili was a threat to the peace of the ominous year and ordered the priest imprisoned. Actually, he was not so concerned about the ominous year as he was about his own greed. Since priests used gold chalices, he thought they were rich. A recent convert rushed to de Nobili to warn him that his arrest had been ordered. De Nobili started hiding his vestments and sacred vessels, but the soldiers arrived and found everything. Father de Nobili was put into a miserable dungeon and restricted to a handful of rice a day. The sixty-three-year-old priest suffered greatly, and his suffering was increased when he learned that some of his converts were being tortured to reveal the location of the supposed treasure.

Finally Tirumala returned, and de Nobili was released, but he was not allowed to return to his church or his house. He was forced to live in the palm-thatched hut he had lived in twenty-five years before.

A major problem, still unsolved, was how to minister to both the high and low castes. De Nobili learned of a group of middle-class holy men, called *pandaraswamis*, who were permitted to speak to both Brahmins and lower castes. De Nobili began to train some of the Jesuits to be *pandaraswamis*. The first was Baltazar da Costa who in three years baptized 2,500 Indians.

De Nobili decided to ask Tirumala to extend his special protection of him to the other missionaries. However, he could not go to the nayak without a gift. He decided that an organ would be a properly impressive gift. Impressing Tirumala wasn't easy because he had become quite greedy. Almost at the beginning of de Nobili's visit, he began hinting about the gift, so de Nobili had the organ brought in. The nayak had never seen one before. De Nobili had also brought along an organist who played for the Indian king. Tirumala was delighted. He granted the special protections and even said that he would see that de Nobili's stolen property was returned.

De Nobili wanted to die in his mission, but the Provincial, in 1644, ordered the now almost blind Jesuit priest to the Jesuit college in Ceylon where he could rest and be attended to. When he had arrived years earlier, there was not a single Christian in the area. Now there were 4,183. His motto had been "To open the door of India to Christ." The door was now indeed open.

De Nobili so longed for India that after two years he was allowed to return to Mylapore. While there, he wrote to his sister Ludovica, a mistress of novices in a Roman convent:

Be careful that you teach nothing which is not, by God's grace, found doubly in you, for it would be a hateful thing if she who teaches the young brides of Christ did not prove her words by her deeds.

De Nobili was only explaining what he himself had done all his life: he had lived the Christian message that he taught so well.

He spent eight years in Mylapore and then fell into his last illness. His mind was still clear; and ten days before his death, he finished a volume of poetry. He then dictated this declaration:

It is my wish that all I have written be in conformity with the mind of our Holy Mother the Roman Catholic Church. I beg that she deign to correct anything erroneous or objectionable or likely to give offense, which may have escaped me.

Then he signed his name as he wished it to be remembered: *Tattuva Bodhakar*, Teacher of Reality.

Roberto de Nobili, Teacher of Reality, died January 16, 1656, and was buried in Mylapore, the site of the martyrdom of St. Thomas the Apostle.

St. Thomas Cathedral, Madras, India

Chapter 28
Review Questions

1. What is the name of the main religion in India? Name another popular religion of India.

2. Who was the apostle who first came to India?

3. Who was the first Jesuit missionary to go to India?

4. Of what nationality and of what religious order was Roberto de Nobili?

5. Who controlled India? What was the capital city of India?

6. The Indians believed that all men were divided into what kind of groups?

7. What did the Catholic Portuguese tell the Indians that they must do if they became Christian?

8. What did de Nobili decide was the only way to get converts?

9. What were the effects of Father de Nobili's new lifestyle?

10. In 1609, Father opened a catechism or doctrine class. What were some of the issues they debated? Who was the first person baptized?

11. What upper class did Father enter? What was his special insignia?

12. What are the Vedas of India? What did Father hope to do with them once he learned them?
    _____

13. What were the Indian beliefs that were contrary to the truth of Christianity?
    _____

14. What did Father's Indian name mean in English? Why was this name important?
    _____

15. What did Father de Nobili open in 1610? _____

16. Father discovered that the Indians did not mind that the subjects they studied contradicted each other. Why did they not mind?
    _____

17. Father's superiors did not always understand his methods. Which sacrament was he at one time forbidden to give for two years? _____

18. A Vatican commission in 1622 ruled that the insignia that Father wore was not a religious symbol but a _____ symbol.

19. Who was the influential person Father baptized on Christmas Day in 1625?
    _____

20. Father finally began to baptize the lowest classes, called the _____.

21. By 1630, Father de Nobili had established three mission centers, but he needed the protection of the most powerful _____ in South India.

22. Father was finally granted a license to preach and to build
    _____

23. Father de Nobili began to train Jesuit priests to be _____ class holy men so they could speak to both the high classes and the lower classes.

24. In three years, one Jesuit priest baptized _____ Indians.

25. Father Robert de Nobili, who died in 1656, signed his name "Tattuva Bodhakar," which means _____ in English.

Chapter 29

Roses in Winter

Our Lady of Guadalupe is the patron saint of all the Americas, north and south. Within ten years after she appeared to a poor Indian named Juan Diego near Mexico City, eight million Indians were baptized. To this day Mexicans are deeply devoted to the Virgin of Guadalupe. Here is a play about the apparitions at Tepeyac Hill.

Narrator: It is December 9, 1531. Juan Diego is on his way to Mass.

Mary: Juanito, where are you going?

Juan: My Lady, I am on my way to Mass.

Mary: Understand, my dear son, that I am the ever Virgin Mother of the true God, in whom we live, the Creator and Maker of Heaven and earth. It is my desire that a church be built here to my honor where I shall spread my love and protection. I am your merciful Mother and a loving Mother to your fellow men who love me and trust me and seek my aid. Go now to the house of the Bishop and tell him that I send you to make known my great desire to have a church built in my name here.

Juan: Dearest Lady, joyfully I am on my way to do as you ask. With your permission, I take leave of you. (Juan goes to the Bishop's house.)

Narrator: Juan is at the Bishop's house. It is the same day.

Bishop: What do you want, my son?

Juan: I have heard beautiful music and seen a strange light. A Lady, the Mother of God, has told me to ask you to build a church to her honor on the hill where she stood. Please, your excellency, heed her request.

Bishop: Where did you see this lady?

Juan: On Tepeyac Hill, outside the city.

Bishop: Are you sure you were not dreaming, or imagining that you saw her?

Juan: No, Your Excellency. She was truly there, as real as you are to me.

Basilica of Guadalupe

Our Lady of Guadalupe

Bishop: I'll think over what you have said. Come back in a few days.

Narrator: Juan returns to the hill. It is the same day.

Juan: My sweetest Lady, I obeyed your command and went to the house of the Bishop. After great difficulty, I saw him and gave him your message exactly as you had instructed. The bishop received me kindly and listened closely, but when he answered me, I knew that he did not believe me. Dearest Lady, I know that he thinks I am making up the story. Please send someone else better known and more respected to carry out your wish. I am only a poor Indian, and no one believes me.

Mary: My dearest son, I have chosen you. It is through your help that my purpose will be accomplished. Go again to the Bishop tomorrow. Tell him that it is I, in person, Holy Mary, ever Virgin, Mother of God, who sends you.

Juan: Sweetest Lady, I will joyfully carry out your desire. I will return tomorrow afternoon to tell you what the Bishop answers. With your permission, I take leave of you, my sweet Lady.

Narrator: It is the next day, Sunday, December 10. Juan arrives at the bishop's house.

Juan: Your Excellency, I saw the wonderful Lady again. She said that you must build a church on the hill. She said that she is truly the Mother of God.

Bishop: My son, I am interested in what you have to say. Perhaps you can bring me some sign from the Lady as a proof that she is the Mother of God and that she definitely wants a temple built at Tepeyac Hill.

Juan: Your Excellency, I promise that I will bring you this proof. Please excuse me now. (Juan leaves.)

Bishop: Servants, come here.

(Two servants enter.)

Servants: Yes, Your Excellency?

Bishop: Follow that Indian, see where he goes, watch everything he does and report to me. (Servants follow Juan a short distance.)

1st Servant: Where has he gone? He has disappeared.

2nd Servant: He was by that stream and now I can not see him any more. We must go back and tell the Bishop.

Narrator: As the surprised servants return to the Bishop, Juan is at the hill.

Juan: My Lady, the Bishop has asked me for a sign. He wants proof that you are truly from Heaven.

Mary: So be it, my son. Come back tomorrow morning so that you may obtain the proof for the Bishop. With my sign, he will believe you and no longer will he doubt you or suspect you. Know that I will reward you for your trouble. At dawn tomorrow, I shall await you here.

Narrator: Juan returns home. His uncle is very ill. He spends the next day taking care of him. Now it is Tuesday, December 12 at Juan Diego's home.

Cathedral of Guadalajara, Mexico

Uncle: Juan, I fear that I am going to die. Please go to the monastery and bring a priest that I may receive the sacraments.

Juan: I go immediately. (Juan goes out.) I was supposed to see the Lady yesterday, but my uncle was ill. She is probably waiting for me now. I will go around the other side of the hill so that she won't see me.

Narrator: Juan goes around the other side, but the Lady is there.

Mary: What troubles you, Juanito? Where are you going?

Juan: I am ashamed, my Lady, that I did not come to see you. My uncle is dying and I must get a priest. Then I will return to you and deliver your message. Forgive me, my Lady, and be patient with me. I am not deceiving you. Tomorrow I will accomplish your desire.

Mary: There is nothing to fear. Do not fear this illness or any other sorrow or affliction. Am I not here beside you? I am your merciful Mother. Have I not taken you unto myself? What more do you need? Let nothing distress or disturb you. As for your uncle's illness, it is not unto death. At this moment I ask you to believe that he is already cured.

Juan: Thank you, my Lady. Now I will take the sign to the Bishop.

Mary: Go, my son, to the summit of the hill where you first saw me. There you will find a great variety of roses. Gather them and bring them to me.

Juan: I go at once. (Juan gathers the roses and wraps them in his tilma.)

Mary: (arranging the flowers in his tilma) My dear son, these roses are the sign which you must give to the bishop. Tell him in my name you are my ambassador and worthy of confidence. When you reach the bishop, unfold your tilma and show him what you carry, but only in the presence of the Bishop. Tell him that I sent you to the top of the hill and that you gathered the flowers there. Repeat the story completely so that the Bishop will believe you and will build the church.

Juan: I go at once.

Narrator: It is the same day. Juan comes to the Bishop's palace. The servants make fun of him.

1st Servant: It's that foolish Indian again.

2nd Servant: Look, he's carrying something in his tilma. Let's see what it is.

Juan: No, I'm not allowed to show it to anyone except the Bishop.

1st Servant: Who says so? Come on. Show it to us. (Juan clutches his tilma to himself.)

2nd Servant: We're the Bishop's servants. You're just an ignorant Indian. You have to do what we say. (He pulls the tilma away from Juan.)

Narrator: When they pulled the tilma open, the roses appeared only as if they were painted on the tilma.

1st Servant: Is that all you're showing the bishop? Painted flowers?

2nd Servant: He certainly won't pay any attention to you now.

(The bishop's secretary comes out.)

Secretary: The Bishop will see Juan Diego now. You servants, get on about your business. (The servants hurry away and Juan goes to meet the Bishop.)

Juan: I saw the Lady again. She asked once more that a church be built on the hill. She gave me a sign of her presence which I have in my tilma.

Narrator: Juan unfolds the tilma and the roses fall to the floor, but everyone looks at the tilma, which has a miraculous picture of Our Lady.

Bishop: Juan Diego, my son, you have truly been visited by the Mother of God. We will build the church she requests and in it we will place this miraculous image of Our Lady. Let us march in procession, carrying the image and praising the Mother of God for her great favors. (All march out, carrying the image and singing a hymn in honor of Mary.)

Narrator: The miraculous image remains to this day, clear and bright, though normally the picture should have faded and the cactus fiber tilma crumbled to dust centuries ago. Scientists have found no natural explanation for the image. The only explanation is a supernatural one: that Our Lady has given us her portrait to show her special love and care for all of the people of the Americas, north and south.

* * *

After Our Lady's visit to Guadalupe, dedicated missionaries continued to spread the Catholic Faith throughout the New World. Among the saints that have blossomed forth from the soil of the western hemisphere is Mariana, the Lily of Quito.

Mariana de Quito

On October 31, 1618, in Quito, Ecuador, Doña Mariana Parades gave birth to her eighth and last child, a beautiful little daughter. Little Mariana loved to be told stories about Christ and His Blessed Mother. Almost the first words she learned to say were her prayers.

When she grew up, she took private vows of poverty, chastity, and obedience and said that she wanted to be known as Mariana de (of) Jesus. She transformed her room into a place of prayer, and set aside another room to receive the poor and the sick. She spent one hour a day weaving and sewing to earn money for the needy.

Mariana's home became a free clinic for the sick, a school for uneducated Indian and

Negro children, and a kitchen for the hungry. No one was ever turned away. Mariana had a huge basket from which she handed out loaves of bread to all who lined up in front of her door. No matter how many came, the basket was never empty. Was it a miracle? Probably, but Mariana herself never talked about where the bread came from.

People came to her with all sorts of problems. A woman named Juana de Sanguesa ran into Mariana's room and knelt down close to her. Within seconds, her husband Juan rushed in with a dagger in his hand. Mariana rose and said quietly, "Calm yourself. What manner of crime are you contemplating? Repent the great sin which you are about to commit!" He stepped back, then left the room. Afterward, the marriage between Juan and Juana became blissfully happy, with never a moment's trouble.

In 1645, Quito suffered one disaster after another. First, came earthquakes which split the ground. Then, epidemics of measles and diphtheria brought death. Finally, the volcano Pichincha erupted with fiery lava all over the countryside. The people felt that God was punishing them for their sins.

So, on the fourth Sunday of Lent, March 26, Father Alonso de Rojas, Mariana's confessor, preached a shocking sermon. He offered himself as a victim, asking that he might die to save others from the punishment they had brought on themselves. Immediately Mariana rose. She said that she would ask God to take her life in place of the priest's. She offered her life "in defense of her country, her compatriots, and her kindred." After Mass she returned home where she became very ill. She never left home again. From that moment, earthquakes ceased, plagues abated, and the deadly volcano was again quiet.

Mariana had offered her life for her people and the offering was accepted. She died on May 26, her face beautiful and peaceful in spite of the sufferings she had undergone. The people were so impressed by her sacrifice that they repented of their sins and came to confession and Holy Communion in great numbers. Her sacrifice was not in vain.

Cathedral, Quito, Ecuador

Chapter 29
Review Questions

1. Who is the patron saint of both North and South America?

2. What is the Indian's name to whom the Blessed Mother appeared in 1531?

3. Near which city did the Blessed Mother appear? What was the name of the hill?

4. Who did the Lady say she was?

5. What did the Lady want to have built there?

6. Why did she want to have a church built?

7. The Lady said she was a merciful and loving Mother. What three things did she say that men do?

8. What did the Lady ask Juan Diego to do?

9. What did the bishop want to see?

10. Why did Juan not want to return to the hill the next morning?

11. What did Juan gather in his tilma?

12. What did the Lady say was the "sign" Juan was to give to the bishop?

13. What appeared on the tilma when Juan opened it to show the roses?

14. How does the picture on the tilma look today?

15. When was Mariana, the Lily of Quito, born?

16. What private vows did Mariana take?

17. What were some of the charitable works that Mariana did?

18. What was the miracle of the loaves?

19. What happened in Quito in 1645?

20. What did the priest offer to do?

21. What did Mariana offer to do?

22. What happened to Mariana after her offer?

23. What were the changes in Quito after Mariana became ill?

24. What happened to the people in Quito after Mariana died?

Chapter 30

Our Lord's Grandmother

Canada, our neighbor to the north, has one province (their equivalent to our states) that is very different from the others. Quebec province was originally settled by Frenchmen and has a Catholic heritage. After France was defeated by Great Britain in the French and Indian War, ending in 1763, all of Canada became British territory. Canada is now an independent member of the British Commonwealth. Although the majority of Canadians are Protestant, Quebec still retains its French Catholic heritage. Visiting the capital, Quebec City, is like visiting a French city. Not far from the capital is the most famous shrine in Canada, the Shrine of St. Anne de Beaupré (St. Anne of the Beautiful Prairie). The history of this shrine, dedicated to Our Lord's grandmother, will tell us much about the Catholic Faith in Canada.

Good Saint Anne

The French sailors who came to Canada from the Old World brought with them a devotion to the saint they called Good Saint Anne. At that time it was a long and dangerous journey across the Atlantic. The ships were not made for the high seas, and shipwrecks were frequent. The voyage up the St. Lawrence River was scarcely safer. Just before the Island of Orleans, the river is wide and rough with many sandbars. The sailors built a small church on the island in St. Anne's honor, in thanksgiving for her intercession in their dangerous voyages. Whenever a ship's crew would arrive safely at the site of the church, they would fire off a salute as a sign of joy because they knew that the dangers of navigation were past.

The first miraculous cure in the history of St. Anne de Beaupré was that of Louis Guimont, a crippled farmer of the locality. In March of 1658, he placed three small stones in the foundations of the first chapel, then being built, and he was suddenly and permanently cured. Miracles have occurred at the shrine ever since. In one of the chapels of the modern shrine, the visitor can see stacks of crutches left there as offerings by pilgrims who have been cured through the intercession of St. Anne.

The Shrine of Beaupré possesses relics brought from France. The first, a fragment of the finger of St. Anne, was brought to Beaupré by Bishop François de Montmorency Laval, the first Bishop of Quebec, who has since been beatified. On March 12, 1670, the relic was first offered for public veneration. The largest relic possessed by the shrine is part of the arm of St. Anne. This relic is kept in the St. Anne Chapel of the shrine. Together with the

Shrine of St. Anne de Beaupré

miraculous statue standing in front of it, in a glory of golden rays, this relic is the object of all the pilgrims who come to Beaupré. The sight of this relic is moving because here is the arm which carried the Immaculate Mother of God.

The Indians who roamed through eastern Canada were among the first pilgrims to come to the new little shrine. The Jesuits who had evangelized the Indians had shared with them the devotion to Mary's mother which has characterized Frenchmen since the earliest days of Christianity in France. The Hurons were the first tribe to go to Beaupré on an organized pilgrimage. In June 1671, accompanied by their missionary, Father Chaumonot, the Hurons traveled in their bark canoes down the river to Beaupré, singing hymns in honor of Mary and her holy mother.

When they reached the shrine, the chiefs presented gifts. The mothers placed their children under the protection of St. Anne. Later, other tribes came from more distant spots. For nearly two centuries, Algonquins, Montagnais, Iroquois, and other tribes came each year to make the novena preceding St. Anne's feast day and to celebrate the feast itself, July 26, at the shrine. Often they brought with them the bodies of relatives whose dying wish had been to be laid to rest near the shrine. Seventy-one Indians are buried in the old cemetery.

In 1690, England attacked Quebec. On October 1, the English Admiral Phipps anchored before Quebec with a fleet of 35 vessels manned by 2,000 men. A force of fighting men came from Beaupré to resist the invaders. They were led by Pierre Carré, whose house stood near the shrine. He brought his men to the shrine to kneel before St. Anne. They were to fight an enemy who outnumbered them three to one, but they put themselves under the protection of their patron saint.

On October 2, the English landed several hundred soldiers. Pierre Carré made his way

Miraculous Statue of St. Anne de Beaupré

at the head of his brave soldiers from Beaupré and opened fire. The enemy was amazed at this resistance from a small band of men. They had to retreat in disorder toward the ships, abandoning cannon, weapons, and a flag. Later Carré brought the flag to Beaupré and laid it at the feet of St. Anne in thanksgiving for the victory won through her intercession. The Quebec colony was saved.

For almost 200 years, birchbark canoes, dinghies and sailing boats were the main means of transportation for pilgrims to the shrine. Beginning in 1844, steamships came regularly to the shrine. An adequate pier was not available at first. Travelers had to climb up a ladder fifteen or twenty feet high to reach the first stage of the wharf. From there, they had to walk in Indian file along a narrow, unsteady gangway. "When you have done this once," concluded a not too enthusiastic pilgrim, "you won't do it again for the pleasure of the thing, and you'll need a hearty devotion to start all over again." In 1875, a real pier was built. By 1877, carriages could go right down the pier to help transport invalid pilgrims. By 1890, a bridge was built over the St. Charles River, and soon trains took the place of boats. Now, most pilgrims come by highway.

In 1759, war broke out again between France and England. General Montgomery pillaged and burned most of the houses on either side of the river. Despite the order of the English commander to spare the churches, several were destroyed. At St. Anne, only the church and four houses escaped the flames. Fire was set to the church three times, but it died out by itself. The residents of the town hid in the woods, carrying with them the furniture, church vestments, and sacred vessels from the shrine. The priest remained with his people and gave them courage. Several days later, it was learned that Quebec had been captured and that Canada was now in the hands of the British. The people left the forest. Scarcely able to hold back their tears, they returned to their village to find heaps of ruins. The church still stood, giving the people hope for the future.

Eventually, this church was destroyed. On the morning of March 29, 1922, a terrible fire broke out in the church. Flames leaped to the sky and the people watched, horrified. Their eyes turned toward the statue of St. Anne at the top of the church. They could barely make it out through the smoke and flames. It was made of wood coated with a thin layer of copper, so that it was sure to burn. However, when the roof sagged, the statue remained erect on the crumbling wall. Sadly, though, within three hours the church was a heap of ashes. The people did not despair. Instead, they resolved to build a new church, bigger and more beautiful than ever. The church they built is the one now standing on the site, the beautiful basilica of St. Anne de Beaupré.

First Station of the Cross at the Shrine of St. Anne de Beaupré

Chapter 30
Review Questions

1. Quebec, in Canada, was settled by people who were of which nationality and religion?
   _____

2. When did all of Canada become British territory?
   _____

3. Though most of Canada is Protestant, which part is Catholic?
   _____

4. Who came to Canada and brought the devotion to Good Saint Anne?
   _____

5. Why did the sailors build a small chapel dedicated to St. Anne?
   _____

6. Who was Louis Guimont?
   _____

7. Who was the first bishop of Quebec? What relic of St. Anne did he bring to the chapel?
   _____

8. When was the first relic offered for veneration?
   _____

9. Of which religious order were the priests who evangelized the Indians of Canada?
   _____

10. Who were the first tribe of Indians to make a pilgrimage to the Shrine of St. Anne? What year did they make it?
    _____

11. What other tribes visited the Shrine of St. Anne?
    _____

12. In 1690, England attacked Quebec. What was the name of the English Admiral? How many vessels and men did he have with him?
    _____

13. Who was the leader who defended Quebec? What did the men do before the battle?
    _____

14. What happened at the battle? Why were the English defeated?
    _____

15. In 1759, the English again attacked Quebec. Who was the English General? What damage did he do?
    _____

16. What happened to the church in 1922?
    _____

17. What is the church or basilica that is now standing?
    _____

St. Anne de Beaupre ceiling

Tomb of Julius II, by Michelangelo

Bibliography

Chapter 1
Guarducci, Margherita. *The Tomb of St. Peter*. New York: 1960.
Milne, James Lee. *St. Peter's*. Boston: 1967.

Chapter 2
Canady, John. *Masterpieces by Michelangelo*. New York: 1979.
Coughlan, Robert. *The World of Michelangelo*. Time-Life Library of Art, New York: 1966.

Chapter 3
Dupre, Maria Grazia Ciardi. *Raphael*. New York: 1954.
Wallace, Robert. *The World of Leonardo*. Time-Life Library of Art, New York: 1966.

Chapter 4
Jorgensen, Johannes. *Saint Catherine of Siena*. London: 1938.
Undset, Sigrid. *Catherine of Siena*. New York: 1954.

Chapter 5
Carroll, Warren H. *Isabel of Spain, The Catholic Queen*. Front Royal, Virginia: 1991.
Walsh, William Thomas. *Isabella of Spain*. New York: 1930.

Chapter 6
Auclair, Marcelle. *Teresa of Avila*. Garden City, New York: 1953.
Peers, E. Allison, ed. *The Autobiography of St. Teresa of Avila*. Garden City, New York: 1960.

Chapter 7
Robinson, R. A. H. *Contemporary Portugal, A History*. London: 1979.
Walsh, William Thomas. *Our Lady of Fatima*. New York: 1958.

Chapter 8
Kurth, Godefroid. *Saint Clotilda*. London: 1898.
Wallace-Hadrill, J. M. *The Long-Haired Kings and Other Studies in Frankish History*. New York: 1962.

Chapter 9
Macaulay, David. *Cathedral: The Story of its Construction*. Boston: Houghton Mifflin, 1973.
von Simson, Otto. *The Gothic Cathedral*. New York: 1958.
Swaan, Wim. *The Gothic Cathedral*. London: 1969.

Chapter 10
Gies, Frances. *Joan of Arc; The Legend and the Reality*. New York: 1981.
Pernoud, Regine. *Joan of Arc*. New York: 1988.
Sackville-West, Victoria. *Saint Joan of Arc*. New York: 1938.

Chapter 11
Daniel-Rops, Henri. *The Protestant Reformation*. Garden City, New York: 1963.
Parker, Geoffrey. *The Dutch Revolt*. Penguin Books: 1985.

Chapter 12
Copplestone, Trewin. *Rembrandt*. Seacaucus, New Jersey: 1974.
Foote, Timothy. *The World of Brueghel*. Time-Life Library of Art, New York: 1968.
Philip, Lotte B. *The Ghent Altarpiece and the Art of Jan Van Eyck*. Princeton: 1971.

Chapter 13
Ashe, Geoffrey. *The Discovery of King Arthur*. London: 1985.
Barber, Richard. *The Arthurian Legends*. Totowa, New Jersey: 1979.

Chapter 14
Bury, J. B. *Life of St. Patrick*. London: 1905.
Hanson, R. P. C. *Saint Patrick, His Origins and Career*. New York: 1960.

Chapter 15
Jorgensen, Johannes. *Saint Bridget of Sweden*. London: 1954.
Mollat, Guy. *The Popes at Avignon*. New York: 1963.

Chapter 16
Scott, Franklin D. *Sweden: The Nation's History*. Minneapolis: 1977.
Weibull, Curt. *Christina of Sweden*. Stockholm: 1966.

Chapter 17
Birch, J. H. S. *Denmark in History*. London: 1938.
Daniel-Rops, Henri. *The Church in the Dark Ages*. Garden City, New York: 1962.

Chapter 18
Lamb, George. *Brother Nicholas*. New York: 1954.
McSwigan, Maria, *Athlete of Christ*.

Chapter 19
Marek, George. *Beethoven: Biography of a Genius*. New York: 1969.
Schmidt-Georg, Joseph. *Ludwig Von Beethoven*. New York: 1970.

Chapter 20
Anceiet-Hustache, Jeanne. *Gold Tried By Fire: St. Elizabeth of Hungary*. Chicago: 1963.
Sinor, Doris. *History of Hungary*. New York: 1959.

Chapter 21
Barber, Noel. *Seven Days of Freedom: The Hungarian Uprising 1936*. New York: 1974.
Kovrgi, Bennett. *Communism in Hungary from Kun to Kadar*. Stanford: 1979.

Chapter 22
Dvornik, Francis. *Byzantine Missions Among the Slavs: Saints Constantine-Cyril and Methodius*. New Brunswick, New Jersey: 1970.
Iswolsky, Helene. *Christ in Russia*. Milwaukee: 1960.

Chapter 23
Halecki, Oscar. *Jadwiga of Anjou and the Rise of East Central Europe*. Boulder, Colorado: 1991.
Jasienica, Pawel. *Jagellonian Poland*. Miami: 1978.

Chapter 24
Macinkowski, K. *The Crisis of the Polish-Swedish War, 1655-60*. Wilberforce, Ohio: 1952.
de Oliveira, Plinio Correia. *The Siege of Czestochowa*.

Chapter 25
Davies, Norman. *God's Playground: A History of Poland*. New York: 1904.
Micewski, Andrzej. *Cardinal Wyszynski*. New York: 1984.

Chapter 26
Boxer, Charles R. *The Christian Century in Japan*. London: 1951.
Lauren, John. *The Catholic Church in Japan*. Rutland, Vermont: 1954.

Chapter 27
Cronin, Vincent. *The Wise Man from the West*. Garden City, New York: 1957.
Dunne, George H. *Generation of Giants*. Notre Dame, Indiana: 1962.

Chapter 28
Cronin, Vincent. *Pearl to India*. New York: 1959.
Muggeridge, Malcolm. *Something Beautiful for God*.

Chapter 29
de Madariaga, Salvador. *Hernan Cortes, Conquerer of Mexico*. Chicago: 1955.
Carroll, Warren H. *Our Lady of Guadalupe and the Conquest of Darkness*. Front Royal, Virginia: 1983.

Chapter 30
Keyes, Frances Parkinson. *St. Anne, Grandmother of Our Saviour*. New York: 1955.
Talbot, Francis X. *Saint Among Savages*
Talbot, Francis X. *Saint Among the Hurons*.

Index

A

Adams, William 169
Adoration of the Magi 15
Alfonso, Prince 28, 32
Alfonso the Fat 29, 30
allegro 121
Almeida 179
Alvastra 94
Alvastra, Peter of 95
Amsterdam 70, 74, 77, 80
Anatomy Lesson of Dr. Tulp 75
Andrew, King of Hungary 126
Andrew the Apostle 4
Annals of Wales 80
Anne, Saint 203
Annunciation 14, 190
Anskar, Saint 106
apprentice 7, 14
apse 3
Aragon 29, 31, 33, 44
arcade 57
arch 57, 58
Auschwitz 162, 179, 180
Avalon 82

B

Badon 80, 81
baldachino 4
baroque 4, 77
basilica 2, 4, 50, 89, 103, 113, 120, 136, 205
Beaupré 203, 204
Bedivere 82
Beethoven, Karl 122
Beethoven, Ludwig van 120, 121, 123
Bella Brigata 23
Bernini 4, 103
Black Madonna 114, 154
Boabdil 33
Bobadilla, Beatriz de 29
Brahmins 188, 193
Bramante 2, 4, 9
Bruges 9
Budapest 133, 135, 136, 146, 147, 148
buttress 57, 58
buttress, flying 57, 58

C

Caesar, Julius 50
Camelot 82, 83
Camlann 80
Canute the Great 108
Carré, Pierre 204
Carrillo, Archbishop 29
Casimir the Great 146
caste system 188
cathedrals, Gothic 56, 57, 59
Catherine of Siena, Saint 21, 97
Catherine, Saint 62, 65, 66
Cattedra 4
Cauchon 65, 66
Chalons 51
Charles I of Spain; also Charles V, Holy Roman Emperor 34, 168
Charles II, King of England 87
Charles VII of France 64
Charles X Gustavus 102
Chartres Cathedral 58
Childebert 53
Childeric 51
Chinese Rites Controversy 184
Chinon 63, 64
Christiana 100, 101, 102
Church in the Attic 71
classical 2, 120, 121
clerestory 57
Clodomir 52, 53
Closed Door 172, 173
Clothair 53
Clotilde 51, 52, 62
Clovis 51, 52
Cochin 188, 191
Columbus 32, 33
Compiegne 64
concerto 121, 122
Constantine 2, 50, 52
Convention 160
Cracow 147, 148, 150, 155, 165
Cromwell, Oliver 87
Czestochowa 154, 157

D

dauphin 62
David 8, 10, 18, 22, 58, 77
Della Porta 3
Den Bosch 71
Denis, Saint 44, 50, 56, 64
deNobili, Roberto, see Nobili
Descartes 101
Diego, Juan 196, 197, 198, 199
discalced 39
Doctor of the Church 21, 25, 39, 41

dome 3, 31
Domremy 62
drum 3

E

efumi 172, 173
Einsiedeln 113
Elaine 44, 83
Elizabeth 146, 147, 148, 149, 151
Elizabeth I of England 87
Elizabeth of Hungary, Saint 126, 127, 128
Elizabeth of Portugal, Saint 45, 46, 47
Emperor Concerto 122
Enrique IV 28
Eroica 121, 161, 164
Esztergom 133, 136

F

Fatima, Our Lady of 47
Ferdinand 29, 31, 32, 33, 34, 44, 45, 100
Fidelio 121
Fifth Symphony 121
First Symphony 121
Flue, Nicholas von 114
Forbidden City 181, 182, 183
Francis I 18
Francisco, Pero 191
Freedom Fighters 136
fresco 10
Friedrich 109

G

Genevieve, Saint 51
Geoffrey of Monmouth 81
Giron, Pedro 29
Goa 188, 191, 192
Gorkum 69
Gothic 56, 57
Granada 30, 31, 32, 33
Great Schism 97
Greek cross 2, 3
Gregory XI, Pope 24
Grummore 83
Guadalupe, Our Lady of 196
Guimont, Louis 203
Guinevere 82
Gustavus Adolphus 100
Gustavus II Adolphus, King of Sweden 100

H

Hamburg 102, 107
Hapsburg, William 146
Harold Bluetooth 108
Haydn 120
Heiligenstadt 121

Heiligenstadt Testament 121
Helena 2, 4
History of the Britons, The 81
History of the Kings of Britain 81
Home Army 161, 164
Huygens, Constantin 75
Hymn to Joy 123

I

icon 3
Idylls of the King 82
Incarnation Convent 40
Interior Castle 41
Irenaeus, Saint 50
Isabel 29, 31, 32, 34, 37
Isabel of Portugal 28
Isleif 109

J

Jadwiga 146, 147, 148, 151, 154
Jagiello 148, 150, 151
Jasna Gora 154
Jewish Fighting Organization 164
John of the Cross, Saint 40
Jon Aresson 109
Juan 31, 32, 34
Juan II 28
Juana 31, 34, 37
Julien le Pauvre, Saint 51
Julius II 2, 9

K

Katherine 93, 96, 97
Katyn Forest 161
Knights of the Immaculata 162
Kolbe, Maximilian 162, 174
Kordecki, Abbot Augustine 155, 156
Kyoto 168, 169, 170

L

lancet 57, 58, 59
lantern 3, 51
Last Judgment, The 10
Last Supper 16, 17, 18
Latin cross 3
Laval, Bishop 203
Lily Maid of Astolat 83
Longinus 4
Lough Derg 88
Louis, King of Hungary 146, 154
Louis the Pious 106
Luna, Alvaro de 28
Lyon 50, 51

M

Maderno 3
Madonna 9, 114, 154, 155
Madrigal de las Altas Torres 28
Magnus II 94
Malory, Thomas 82
Mandarin 180, 181
Marburg 128
Mariana of Quito 199
Martyrs of Nagasaki 170, 171, 172
Mary and Sigismund 146, 150
Medici 15
Medici, Lorenzo di 7, 8
Medraut 80, 82
Meeting at Emmaus 77
Meinrad 113, 114
Mendoza 30, 33
Merovee 51
Michelangelo 3, 7, 8, 9, 10, 11, 17, 18
microcosm 56, 57
Mindszenty, Cardinal 133, 134, 135
Missa Solemnis 123
Mona Lisa 18
Money-Changer 74
Mordred 82
Morte, D'Arthur Le 82
Moses 10
Muller, General 155, 156, 157
Mylapore 193
mystical marriage 22, 40, 41, 96

N

Nagasaki 169, 170, 171, 173, 174
Nanking 180, 182
Napoleon 51, 114, 121, 122
nave 3, 57
nayak 192, 193
Nero 1
Nicholas V 2
Niepokalanow 163
Nightwatch 76, 77
Nineteen Holy Martyrs of Gorkum 69
Ninth Symphony 123
Nirvana 187
Nobili, Roberto de 187, 188, 189, 190, 191, 192, 193
Nowa Huta 165

O

Olaf 107, 108, 109
Once and Future King 82, 83
Orleans 63, 64, 203
outcaste 188
Oxenstierna, Axel 100

P

Pagoda of the Southern Flower 179
pandaraswamis 193
Pantoja 182, 183, 184
Paris 50, 51, 53, 56, 58, 64, 66, 161
Pastoral 121
Patrick, Saint 87
Paul III 3, 168
Peking 180, 181, 182, 183, 184
Pellinore 83, 84
Peter, Saint 1, 2, 4, 70
Pieck, Nicholas 69
piers 3, 4, 57
Pieta 8, 11
plinth 4
Plunkett, Oliver 87, 88
Pothinus, Saint 50

Q

Quebec 203, 204, 205

R

Ranft 117
Raymond of Capua 24
recant 65, 66
Reims 52, 63, 64
reincarnation 187, 188, 189
Remi, Saint 52
romantic 121
Rome 1, 2, 8, 24, 66, 81, 94, 95, 96, 97, 102, 134, 136, 187, 191, 192
rose window 59
Rouen 65, 66
Ruggieri 178, 179

S

Saint Joseph's Convent 39
Saint-Denis, Church of 50
Saint-Étienne, church of 50, 51
Sangallo 3
Santa Hermandad 31, 33
Santa Maria, Monastery of 16
Santiago de Compostela 94
Saskia 75, 76
schism 24, 65, 97
Segovia 30, 31, 40
Sforza, Lodovico 15
shogun 168, 169, 171
Sidotti, Father John Baptist 173
Siena 21, 23, 97
silent walk 71
Sistine Chapel 9, 10
Sistine Chapel ceiling 9

St. Peter's 9
St. Peter's Basilica 2, 3, 4, 10, 96, 103
stained-glass 57, 87
stigmata 24
Stoning of St. Stephen 74
Sutcliffe, Rosemary 84
Sweet Mother 71
Sweyn Forkbeard 108
Sword at Sunset 84
Syndics of the Drapers' Guild 77

T

Tattuva Bodhakar 189, 193
Tennyson, Alfred Lord 82, 83
Tepeyac 196
Teutonic Knights 150, 151
Thuringia 126
Tirumala 192, 193
Tokugawa, Hidetada 171
Tokugawa, Iemitsu 171
Tokugawa, Ieyasu 169
transepts 2
triforium 57
Trondheim 109
tympanum 58

U

Ulf 93, 94, 96
United Provinces 74
Urban V 96, 97

V

Vadstena 95, 97
Vaucouleurs 62
vault 57
Vedas 189, 190
Veronica 4
Verrocchio 14
Villena 29, 30
Villena, Marquis de 29
Vilno 148, 150, 151
Virgin and Child with St. Anne 17

W

Waergeuzen (Watergeuzen) 69
Warsaw 155, 157, 161, 162, 163, 164
Warsaw Ghetto 162, 163, 164
Wartburg 126, 127, 128
Wartegau 161
Wawel 148, 151
White, T.H. 82
William III of England 88

X

Xavier, Saint Francis 168, 187
Ximenes 33

Z

Zakar, Andrew 134
Zamoyski, Stephan 155

HISTORY 7
CATHOLIC WORLD CULTURE ANSWER KEY

These answers are very brief. It would be best if the students wrote complete sentences.

Chapter 1: The Mother Church of Christendom

1. A basilica is a rectangular-shaped church with columns dividing it into three lengthwise sections.
2. Transepts are aisles.
3. A Greek Cross is a cross with four arms of equal length.
4. The apse is the back section of a church.
5. The dome is the huge rounded roof.
6. The lantern is the decoration on the top of a dome.
7. The nave is the center aisle in a church.
8. A Latin Cross is a cross with three short arms and a longer bottom arm.
9. The term "baroque" refers to an ornate, highly decorative style.
10. The baldachino is a canopy (over the altar).
11. The plinth is the base of a column.
12. "Cattedra" is the Latin word for "chair/throne" and the basis for our word "cathedral."
13. St. Peter was the man chosen by Our Lord to be the head of the Church. St. Peter chose Rome as the center of his missionary work, and was martyred there by Nero in 67 A.D.
14. Constantine was the first Christian Roman Emperor. He legalized Christianity in 313 with the Edict of Toleration.
15. Nicholas V was the pope who decided to rebuild St. Peter's.
16. Julius II was the pope who was responsible for the major portion of the rebuilding.
17. Bramante was the architect hired by Pope Julius II to rebuild St. Peter's. He tore down the old church, but did little new construction.
18. Sangallo was the next architect hired. He built a huge, expensive model of his design, but his plans were never put into effect.
19. Paul III was the pope who hired Michelangelo to work on St. Peter's.
20. Michelangelo worked on St. Peter's after his conversion, and built the base of its dome.
21. Della Porta was the architect who finished the dome of St. Peter's.
22. Maderno was the architect who changed the design of St. Peter's from a Greek cross to a Latin cross.
23. Bernini was the dedicated Catholic artist who designed the interior of St. Peter's in the Baroque style.
24. Longinus was the Roman soldier who pierced Christ's side with a lance and later converted to Christianity.
25. Helena was the mother of Constantine; she found the true cross.
26. Andrew was the apostle who was martyred on an X-shaped cross.
27. St. Peter was executed by Nero. He was crucified upside-down outside of Rome, in an area called the Vatican.
28. Constantine chose to build a church over the burial site of St. Peter.
29. It had fallen into disrepair, especially during the Babylonian Captivity, when the popes were living in France, rather than Rome.
30. The thirteen statues are of the eleven apostles, the Risen Christ, and St. John the Baptist.

Chapter 2: Genius in Marble

1. Fresco is a method of painting on wet plaster.
2. An apprentice is a person in the process of learning a craft.
3. The *Pieta* is a marble statue of Our Lady holding the crucified Christ.
4. The *David* is a 17-foot statue of the Old Testament David, and it symbolizes the ideal young man.
5. The *Bruges Madonna* is a statue of Our Lady holding the Infant Christ.
6. The Sistine Chapel ceiling is one of Michelangelo's most famous works. It shows the creation and fall of man.
7. The *Moses* is a statue of Moses seated with the Ten Commandments. He symbolizes the ideal mature man.
8. The *Last Judgment* is a painting of the Last Judgment, which is on the back wall of the Sistine Chapel.
9. Michelangelo was born in 1475 in Florence. Over his lifetime, he lived in Florence, Bologna, and Rome. He began stonecutting after his mother died, while living with a stonecutter's family between ages 6 and 10.
10. He persuaded his father to apprentice him to a painter.
11. Thirteen
12. Michelangelo's earliest paintings show that he had a great talent and was far superior to his fellow students and even to his master.
13. Michelangelo secretly studied anatomy through dissection at the local hospital.
14. Michelangelo's earliest existing statues are on St. Dominic's tomb.
15. twenty-three
16. Michelangelo believed that contemplation of physical beauty could bring man closer to God, and that true art is made noble and religious by the mind that creates it.
17. "divine"
18. He is saying that art, for all its beauty, and for all the time and effort he spent on it, is vain when compared with the salvation of his soul.
19. His mother died when he was six. He studied anatomy illegally. He did not pay his taxes. He was put in jail. He took more work on himself than could be handled, and wore himself out.
20. Answers will vary.

Chapter 3: The Artist of Mysteries

1. Leonardo da Vinci lived from 1452-1519. His native country was Tuscany. He did most of his work in Florence and Milan.
2. Verocchio was the artist to whom da Vinci was apprenticed. He taught the latest methods in painting to da Vinci, which led da Vinci to invent depth-effect techniques still in use today. He painted the *Baptism of Christ*, a part of which was actually painted by da Vinci.
3. Lodovico Sforza was important because it was while da Vinci was working for him as an engineer that he devised many of his well-known inventions.
4. Francis I was the King of France who paid da Vinci to be his companion until da Vinci died in 1519. If he had not done this, da Vinci would have died in poverty without recognition.
5. The *Annunciation* was da Vinci's first complete painting.

It is noteworthy for its realistic plant detail and the sense that real communication is occurring between the angel and Mary.
6. The *Adoration of the Magi* is da Vinci's first major work, an altarpiece. It is very detailed and shows the affect of the Incarnation on all of humanity.
7. The *Last Supper* is da Vinci's masterpiece. It captures the moment when Christ reveals to the Apostles that one among them will betray Him. It is notable for the fact that emotion is expressed throughout the bodies of the figures, not just in their facial expressions.
8. The *Virgin and Child with St. Anne* is an unfinished work, originally designed as an altarpiece. The Blessed Mother as an adult sits on St. Anne's lap, while Christ plays with a little lamb. Although an unusual construction, the painting conveys unity and warmth among the generations of Christ's family.
9. The *Mona Lisa* is da Vinci's famous portrait of a woman with a mysterious smile.
10. Da Vinci was interested in everything around him; he was a dreamer, and full of foresight; drawn to mystery.
11. human flying machine, tank, bombshell, parachute, cloth-shearing machine, cannon, eyeglasses, chariot with horizontal blades
12. *The Last Supper* has been heavily damaged by dampness, floods, and unsuccessful attempts at restoration. The badly designed wall upon which it was painted also caused the painting to crumble and crack.
13. Accumulated dust and paint from inept restoration attempts was removed until the original painting was exposed. Then a shellac coat was applied to protect it. Currently, the most modern technology is being used to discover da Vinci's original intentions and restore the painting accordingly.
14. fifteen
15. He learned how to achieve the effect of depth by using lines that converge on a central vanishing point.
16. the use of light and dark to create three dimensions (chiaroscuro); very precise detail; unusual and puzzling or mysterious expressions on faces.
17. He used live human models.
18. A carefully detailed landscape serves as the background for the figure of the mysterious woman.
19. Leo X
20. Answers will vary.

Chapter 4: Bride of Christ
1. Siena was the birthplace of St. Catherine, mystic and Doctor of the Church.
2. The "Bella Brigata" was the "Happy Brigade," the company of St. Catherine's followers. She taught them how to be Christ-centered in the midst of a busy life. She taught them to start reform with reforming themselves. She also taught them how to make every action a prayer and how to find God in everything.
3. Raymond of Capua was St. Catherine's confessor. She told him that she had received the stigmata.
4. He was a weak man, but one who did really love the Church. Catherine's traveling to Avignon and eloquent arguments persuaded him to return to Rome.
5. St. Catherine had a vision in which Christ betrothed her to Himself. The Blessed Virgin gave her away. St. John the Evangelist, St. Paul, and King David attended. Christ gave her a pearl and diamond ring, which only she could see afterwards.
6. The five wounds of Christ borne on the body of one who loves Him.
7. Refusal to accept the pope's authority.
8. One who has contributed greatly to the wisdom of the Church.
9. St. Catherine was born and lived most of her life in Siena. She lived from 1347-1380. As a young girl, she spent much time in prayer, never felt called to marriage, and never went out to parties. At 16, she took the Dominican habit as a laywoman in the 3rd order. For three years she lived in a room at the top of the house, and communicated with no one but her confessor.
10. After the Mystical marriage, Christ asked St. Catherine to return to her family and take up an active life.
11. St. Catherine nursed the sick, counseled the troubled, and helped the poor.
12. The repentance of two robbers on their way to execution, and the healing of her sick friend, Matteo. She also experienced visions, and eventually received the stigmata.
13. Catherine received the stigmata in a vision just after receiving Holy Communion on Laetare Sunday in 1375. The stigmata caused her great suffering.
14. Catherine was the one who persuaded Pope Gregory XI to return to Rome, ending the Babylonian Captivity.
15. *The Dialogue of St. Catherine*
16. It is a conversation between God and the soul.
17. Catherine died a beautiful, prayerful, and peaceful death after great physical suffering in 1380. She was surrounded by her spiritual children.
18. He meant that it was only because of His help that she was able to overcome the temptations. Also, God allows those He loves the most to be most closely united with Him in intense suffering.
19. All she did for her neighbor was for the love of God and in obedience to His will.
20. Both were gently outspoken and unafraid of telling the truth. They devoted themselves to the weak and the poor.

Chapter 5: The Catholic Queen
1. Because her Catholic Faith influenced every aspect of her life, both personal and public, and because she achieved so much for the Catholic Church.
2. Isabel was born in 1451, in Castile. She spent her early childhood in poverty, while her mother went insane, her brother died, her father died, and the new king (her brother) tried to arrange marriages for her with evil men.
3. Juan II was Isabel's father and the king of Castile. Juan II was a weak man and not a good husband, father, or king. He allowed his court to fall into disorder and immorality, and was incapable of protecting his family from the evil people with whom it was surrounded.
4. Isabel fasted for three days, and prayed that God would deliver her from having to marry Giron. On his way to Castile for the wedding, Giron choked to death.
5. Don Alvaro de Luna looted the crown, gave Church property and money to unworthy people, and had a huge influence on the moral decay of the court. He might have tried to poison the queen. The king finally executed Alvaro after he had pushed one of the queen's friends from a window.
6. Enrique IV was Juan II's son by his first marriage. He became King of Castile in 1455, and his court was very corrupt. He did not support his family with generosity, or even fairness. He and his friends invented blasphemies

for fun. He would act with excessive leniency or excessive severity. He gave bandits permission to collect taxes.
7. The Marquis de Villena led a rebellion against Enrique in 1465. After his brother died, de Villena wanted Isabel to marry Alfonso of Portugal so that she would leave the country.
8. because Enrique was still the rightful king, even if he was evil
9. Archbishop Carillo helped Isabel by arranging her marriage with Ferdinand of Aragon, while encouraging her to delay her marriage with Alfonso of Portugal.
10. Ferdinand disguised himself as a muleteer, and traveled with two friends dressed as merchants.
11. Aragon was important because it was the most powerful and prestigious kingdom in Spain after Castile.
12. She was crowned with great ceremony and much rejoicing from the people on December 13, 1474. After her coronation, she went straight to the cathedral to pray.
13. No money or troops, a corrupt government and Church, economic chaos, trouble with the Moslems, and Portugal attacking them
14. They traveled to cities of Spain, gathering troops, and melting down precious metals from the churches for money. At first their army was defeated, but later they launched a surprise attack and defeated Alfonso's troops.
15. They re-established the Santa Hermandad (the Holy Brotherhood) to keep law and order.
16. She rode from town to town, listening to the people's complaints and judging their cases.
17. At Christmastime of 1481, the Moslems raided across the Granada borders, killing and enslaving numerous Christians.
18. Ferdinand's army did not have enough big guns. Isabel rode from town to town, restoring morale and gathering artillery.
19. Isabel carried out a systematic plan to defeat the Moslems. She organized an army and organized the purchase of new equipment. She organized a "hospital" which traveled with the army, with field nurses to care for the sick and wounded, a new idea of warfare. When one of her army forces was ambushed and captured, she decided to besiege two neighboring castles occupied by the Moslems. She organized 6000 men to build a nine-mile road, by which they moved cannon to attack and beat the Moslems.
20. It was important because it showed the determination of the Spanish armies, and demoralized the Moslems.
21. Granada, the capital city of the three million Moslems who lived in Spain, was so low on food that, in desperation, they asked to begin negotiations for peace. Isabel allowed the Moslems to keep their language, customs, and property.
22. Isabel worked closely with Cardinal Ximenes in ridding the Spanish church of such evils as the selling of indulgences. Together they anticipated many of the complaints that Luther would have, rooting out the problems before the Protestant Revolution even occurred, and allowing Spain to remain free of the Protestant influence.
23. Because of the work of Queen Isabel and Cardinal Ximenes, the Spanish church's evils were already remedied by the time of the Protestant Revolt in the other European countries.
24. Due to the work of Queen Isabel, Spain remained a devoutly Catholic country until the current age.
25. Answers will vary. They were strong and active Catholics who restored the Faith to Spain's people, and strengthened the Church against the evils, both the Moslems and abuses within that had grown up in it.

Chapter 6: God Alone Sufficeth

1. St. Teresa was born in 1515 in Avila, Spain. She spent her whole life in Spain, though her later years were occupied with travel throughout the kingdoms as she started new convents.
2. She ran away to be a martyr, and after she was caught, she tried to make herself into a nun, attempting to build a convent in her backyard.
3. She struggled with determining her vocation and with submitting her very strong will to God's will.
4. She was convinced that her spiritual life was taken care of simply by the fact that she was in the convent. She soon realized that she was still very sinful, and she began to do extreme penances. She made herself very sick, and close to death. Her family finally had to remove her from the convent.
5. Don Pedro was Teresa's uncle. He taught her how to pray, how to meditate, and to rely on God.
6. Teresa underwent great suffering with sickness for three years, but this cured her of self-love, and caused her to become very serious about doing God's will.
7. Teresa realized this was the only way to start the reform so badly needed in the Carmelite order—the reform she knew God desired. It was called St. Joseph's convent. Her nuns vowed to live in poverty.
8. The nuns went barefoot (hence the name "discalced"), and lived in enclosure (never leaving the cloister). Their emphasis was upon mutual charity, detachment from material things, and humility. The community's living expenses were paid by spinning.
9. after a visiting priest from the New World made her aware of the need for conversion and reform throughout the world
10. St. John of the Cross was the reformer of the male Carmelites. He helped Teresa reform the worldly Carmelite convent. He became the nuns' confessor, as well as St. Teresa's personal spiritual director.
11. The Carmelite friars arrested St. John because they did not want reform.
12. First Mansion: the soul overcomes temptation to mortal sin.
13. Second: the soul overcomes venial sin.
14. Third: the soul overcomes most sins but is still imperfect.
15. Fourth: the soul overcomes selfishness.
16. Fifth: the soul concentrates on prayer.
17. Sixth: the soul prays without effort.
18. Seventh: the soul is in total union with God.
19. Mary appeared to him and showed him the way to escape. He then tied strips of cloth together, by which he climbed out the window. When pursued, he escaped by entering a cloister and hearing confessions.
20. Her body remained incorrupt and regained the beauty it had possessed in youth.
21. St. Teresa was canonized in 1622.
22. Doctor of the Church
23. First, we learn that sanctity is not easily acquired—that it must be worked at; we must overcome many trials.
24. Second, we learn that we must always do God's will, no

matter what, and that all difficulties will be overcome if we but trust in Him.
25. Third, we learn that if any activity is to succeed, we must first be very close to God in prayer.
26. Finally, we learn that prayer first, last, and always is the most important thing.

Chapter 7: Roses and Bread
1. St. Elizabeth of Portugal was born in Zaragoza, the capital of Aragon. She lived at the court in Zaragoza until her marriage to the King of Portugal. The royal court of Aragon was very immoral.
2. When she was twelve, she was married off to Denis of Portugal in a political match meant to forge an alliance between Aragon & Portugal.
3. One could assume that Elizabeth did not love Denis because it was a political match, and because she was only twelve at the time.
4. She shamed her husband and her brother into making peace by making the personal sacrifice of giving away her possessions.
5. She caused quarreling parties to reconcile with each other; sponsored the building of churches; set up a college for orphan girls, training them in farming & giving them farms from her own estates.
6. because of her purity and goodness
7. The page was saved from being killed by going to Mass.
8. The workmen asked Elizabeth for help, and when she gave them roses because she had nothing else, the roses turned into gold coins.
9. Her husband became unfaithful to her and banished her from the court.
10. Her son ignored her, and schemed to seize the throne of his father.
11. She refused to do anything that would cause suffering and bloodshed.
12. She trusted in God alone to take care of the problems of the court.
13. She rode into the midst of the battle, risking death in order to stop her husband and son from fighting each other. This impressed them so much that they did stop fighting.
14. St. Elizabeth became a Poor Clare and devoted herself to the poor.
15. She washed the feet of twelve poor people every Holy Week.
16. A seriously wounded leper was healed, both of his wound and his disease.
17. The day before she died, even though she was suffering from a tumor and blood poisoning, she arranged and oversaw the reconciliation of her son and the King of Castile, who had been warring with each other.
18. On her deathbed, Queen Elizabeth of Portugal saw the Blessed Mother.
19. We should ask St. Elizabeth's intercession for our country, for peace, for the carrying out of just wars only, and for awareness of the sufferings of the innocent.
20. Answers will vary. Because of her great charity, because of her love for all her people, and because of her great emphasis on both justice and peace.

Chapter 8: Eldest Daughter of the Church
1. the Pyrenees and the Alps, and by the Rhine River
2. Paris
3. Lyon; St. Pothinus
4. bishops
5. Paris
6. He was beheaded. The statues depict St. Denis carrying his own head under his arm. This is based on the legend that after being beheaded, St. Denis's head was being kicked around by the jeering crowds; he rose up alive and carried his head four miles away before setting it down with himself lying beside it.
7. Jupiter, and named St. Etienne, or St. Stephen's Church
8. the "Scourge of God"
9. St. Germain
10. She cared for the sick, crippled, and poor.
11. a hospital, the Hotel Dieu
12. by the intercession of St. Genevieve, by the efforts of four armies united against them, who were able to force them into retreat
13. because of her beauty; because of his desire to have Burgundy as an ally; because he believed a Christian wife would bind his Roman subjects more closely to him
14. While losing a crucial battle, Clovis became so desperate that he prayed to Clotilde's God, Jesus Christ, asking Him to deliver them, and promising to believe in Him if his army should be granted victory.
15. Christian Europe
16. St. Remi
17. He met St. Genevieve, the protectress of Paris, and seeing her courage, he grew ashamed and withdrew his forces from Paris.
18. Once Clovis had withdrawn, Genevieve opened the gates of Paris to him, and the city was peacefully drawn into the Frankish kingdom.
19. The Parisians called St. Genevieve "Daughter of Heaven," "mother of France," and the "patron of Paris."
20. moderation
21. convents and monasteries
22. sons
23. charity
24. prayers
25. "Eldest Daughter of the Church"

Chapter 9: Spires in the Sky
1. because God was glorified in every aspect of life: art, music, literature, and customs
2. Gothic
3. to give glory to God and bring souls to Him
4. the Church of St. Denis
5. eternal
6. a copy of something but on a smaller scale
7. universe
8. height
9. pointed
10. lancet
11. flying buttresses
12. Solomon's Temple
13. nave
14. three
15. stained-glass windows
16. salvation history
17. Old Testament times
18. St. John the Baptist
19. Easter
20. detail

21. religion
22. Judge
23. twelve apostles
24. salvation
25. know, love, and serve God

Chapter 10: Saint in Armor
1. Joan of Arc was born in 1412 in Domremy, in the Lorraine province of France.
2. As a child, Joan helped take care of the communal herd of the village.
3. Joan began to hear the voices.
4. St. Michael the Archangel, St. Catherine, and St. Margaret
5. the Hundred Years' War
6. Prince (Dauphin) Charles
7. because he was too cowardly to try to assert himself before the British
8. sixteen
9. Robert de Baudricourt
10. adventurous young soldiers
11. Joan's goodness
12. to lead Charles to Reims to be crowned
13. as a common man
14. That he (Charles) was to be anointed and crowned in the city of Reims, and that he was to be the light of the Kingdom of Heaven
15. by telling him of three things that he had prayed for on the last All Saints Day, none of which he had ever mentioned to anyone
16. The white flag was fringed with silk, and depicted the world, supported by two angels, with a portrait of Our Lady, the words "Jesus," and "Maria," as well as the fleur de lis (the lily symbol of France).
17. that every soldier must go to confession
18. She asked the English to surrender and thus save lives.
19. Orleans
20. Reims
21. Compiegne
22. the Burgundians
23. Pierre Cauchon, Bishop of Beauvais
24. Rouen
25. five

Chapter 11: Martyrs and Miracles
1. Spain
2. 1568
3. Nineteen Holy Martyrs of Gorkum
4. 1572
5. St. Antony van Willehad, who was ninety
6. Calvinist pirates
7. Lumey
8. Pieck was the leader of the nineteen martyrs. He was also the youngest of these martyrs (38).
9. William, Prince of Orange
10. Eucharist, Mass
11. the Pope
12. They refused to flee when the town of Gorkum was captured by the Calvinist pirates, and were imprisoned, tortured, and hanged.
13. Two of the four who apostatized later repented, and one of them was hanged by the same Lumey who had martyred the Nineteen.
14. Amsterdam
15. The Catholics would use code names for the private houses and secret places where Mass was said.
16. Catholics were not permitted to have processions.
17. The Host was not burned when thrown into a fire, but an image of the Holy Spirit appeared in the flames. This happened in the 14th century, and the miracle was commemorated by a procession.
18. They had "silent walks." These were silent processions in which the people simply traversed the streets in silence, without praying out loud.
19. One of the secret Mass places was the attic of a businessman. When he died, his heirs sold the building to a non-Catholic because they needed money. Instead of reporting the Catholics, however, this Protestant rented out the attic to the Catholics and allowed them to continue having Mass in his attic. This attic still goes by the name of "Our Dear Lord in the Attic," and Mass is still said there once a month.
20. Den Bosch
21. Brother Wouter
22. Mass is still said in the Attic Church once a month.
23. 1853
24. plague
25. Answers will vary.

Chapter 12: Portraits that Breathe
1. Rembrandt lived from 1609-1669.
2. Calvinist
3. Protestants
4. paintings
5. Amsterdam
6. lighting, detail, and multi-figured excitement
7. an interest in costuming and hidden light sources
8. etching
9. He arranged them in a triangular composition, rather than the typical row or crescent shape.
10. He used a triangular composition, with figures attentively observing the dissection, while portraying the individual reactions: some were interested in what was going on, some were bored, some disgusted.
11. The horror of the Crucifixion is emphasized most.
12. movement
13. Christ bathed in sunlight, breaking bread with his surprised disciples. The light comes from a window.
14. think
15. rising
16. David
17. *The Prodigal Son*
18. moving, emotional scenes
19. rich, warm
20. beauty

Chapter 13: Kings and Crowns
1. England
2. the sixth century (or the 500's)
3. *Annals of Wales*
4. the cross of our Lord, Jesus Christ
5. Saxon
6. Blessed Mary, ever Virgin
7. the Roman civilization in Britain

8. his devotion to Christ and to the Blessed Mother
9. monasteries
10. Guinevere
11. Excalibur
12. Sir Lancelot
13. Sir Thomas Malory
14. Alfred Lord Tennyson
15. Elaine
16. T. H. White
17. Merlin
18. Camelot
19. King Arthur and his knights admirably live the Christian virtues through chivalry. He is the brave hero fighting greed, pride, and violence of human nature, including his own human weaknesses. The dream of Camelot became a symbol for justice and peace in this fallen world.
20. The message assures us that with every victory we win against the Saxons (the culture of death), the more the culture of life will survive, and the less completely the good shall be hidden (engulfed) by the evil. The light we expect to return is Christ.

Chapter 14: Prayers and Penance
1. the fifth century; in Ireland after his childhood
2. They arrived in the 900s. They burned churches, killed innocent people.
3. Brian Boru, by leading his men into battle with a crucifix in his hand
4. King Henry VIII and Queen Elizabeth I
5. They massacred whole towns of Irish Catholics, broke into churches, smashed stained-glass windows and statues.
6. secret
7. Mass
8. hanged
9. King William III
10. Catholics could not own land, could not attend schools, and could not practice their religion.
11. on Mass rocks
12. Penal rosaries were small, one-decade rosaries that could easily be hidden.
13. Penal crosses were crucifixes carved out of peat—the fuel burned to heat their homes—so that they could easily be hidden amongst the peat baskets on the hearth.
14. The Irish were simple, did not require huge or expensive churches; they were willing to do penance, and were willing to suffer for their Catholic faith. Deep love of Jesus and Mary was in their hearts.
15. Station Island
16. While Patrick was there, he had a vision of Purgatory.
17. Around the year 1150, the knight had a vision of Hell, Purgatory, and Heaven. The vision so overcame him that he could not move, and his friends had to carry him out.
18. The British ordered that all the religious buildings on the island be torn down, and that the cave be filled in.
19. They were to be fined or whipped. Queen Anne
20. They gathered on the shore and prayed and fasted as if they were on the island itself.
21. The pilgrimage lasts three days. Each pilgrim must go barefoot and is allowed only one meal of tea and toast per day. An overnight vigil is kept and many, many prayers are said.
22. Answers will vary.
23. Answers will vary. People undergoing persecution must be able to accept God's will wholeheartedly, and they must not be afraid of suffering. These virtues are not very evident or appreciated in today's culture. Catholics make them present to the extent that they live a faithful life and try to make reparation for their sins and the sins of the whole world.

Chapter 15: Wife, Mother, Foundress
1. She lived from 1303-1373 in Sweden. She was born into a noble family, and was related to the king.
2. She saw a vision of Our Lady, in which Mary offered her a crown.
3. She saw a vision of Christ crucified.
4. "I give her to you to honor and marry; to share your bed, your locks and keys, every third penny and all legal right. In the name of the Father, and of the Son, and of the Holy Ghost. Amen." They believed in the sacredness of marriage, and recognized God's place in it.
5. No. "Frugally" shows that.
6. They both adhered to strict fasts.
7. They built a hospital on their estates. Bridget herself cared for the sick. They gave dowries to poor girls.
8. because after six years of steady exhortation to improvement, they could see none
9. eight
10. Scandinavia
11. She went to the monastery of Alvastra.
12. He was a Cistercian monk at Alvastra. As a result of two revelations he became her director: Christ told Bridget that Peter was to record and translate her visions; when Peter decided he was unworthy, he was struck down until he realized that God desired him to do what Bridget said.
13. The order would have strict enclosure and a special devotion to Mary. There would be 60 nuns and 25 monks, all in the enclosure. The nuns would wear white linen crowns, with five red spots arranged in a cross, in order to symbolize the five wounds of Christ.
14. Vadstena
15. Rival families had turned Rome into two armed camps. Buildings were collapsed, streets were quagmires.
16. She wrote him a letter, chastising him for his worldliness.
17. The special Office of Our Lady, known as the "Angelic Discourse," was dictated to her by an angel each day after Mass.
18. It was a chastisement for sin. Her work at Vadstena was undone.
19. Katherine was Bridget's daughter. She made a vow of obedience to Peter of Alvastra.
20. Count Orsini was a Roman; he tried to kidnap her twice. At the second attempt, he was struck blind, which made him realize his sin. He accepted the punishment and confessed to Bridget and Katherine. This eventually led to his cure and his becoming one of their most faithful friends and supporters. Also, Bridget later saved his son from death.
21. She cared for the sick in her own home.
22. She would develop a bitter taste in her mouth, and would smell an intolerable odor.
23. Bridget related a message from the Blessed Virgin. She told him that he was following the Evil One by returning to Avignon, that he would grow very ill and die if he continued there.
24. Gregory XI

25. He died of a serious illness which he developed because of Bridget's prayers that he die rather than persist in mortal sin. Mary appeared to Bridget to tell her that before, during, and immediately after death, Charles had been in the Blessed Mother's protection. While on pilgrimage to the Holy Land, Bridget saw a vision of her son's judgment. He was saved because he had had an ardent love for the Mother of God, and because Bridget had offered so many prayers and good works.
26. Nativity
27. Our Lord told her in a vision that she would die within five days, and she did, committing her soul into His hands.
28. The Order of the Most Holy Saviour, popularly known as the Bridgettines.
29. He drove them out of Sweden.

Chapter 16: Trading Crowns
1. Christiana lived from 1626-1687 in Sweden until 1554, after which she moved from around Europe.
2. Lutherans
3. Because her father was killed in battle, and she was his only child. She was trained as if she had been a prince, rather than a princess, to be very intelligent and curious
4. Anyone who converted was to be exiled and his property confiscated. Anyone teaching Catholic doctrine was to be banished as a traitor. Catholic foreigners were not allowed to have Masses in their homes.
5. She abolished the law forbidding foreigners to have Mass in their own homes.
6. She wanted to wait because she wanted to wait until she was crowned and no one could prevent the marriage. She was preoccupied with her responsibilities, enthusiastic about ruling, and was not interested in marrying except for love.
7. Because he had put more power into the hands of the nobility at the expense of the crown.
8. She made him commander-in-chief of the armies, successor to the throne, and hereditary prince.
9. Because this meant that he would have power over the nobility, whereas if he had married her, he would not have gained any special privileges or powers.
10. because she wanted to be sure there was a capable successor, without her having to marry
11. She got the Estates, the assembly of commoners, on her side, and this forced the Council (the noblemen) to have to go along with her plans.
12. philosophy, science, and mathematics
13. The mathematician, Descartes, came to help Christiana in her studies. She came to realize that Catholicism could be the true religion, and that nothing in the Catholic faith was contrary to reason.
14. Father Macedo
15. He carried a letter to the Jesuit general in Rome, asking for two priests to come secretly to Stockholm to instruct Christiana in the faith.
16. Is there such a thing as Providence? Is there really a difference between good and evil, or does it all depend on effects?
17. Lutheranism; how to remain queen and become Catholic
18. She would lose any guarantee of security for the rest of her life. If her conversion became known, a revolt could break out. She could be imprisoned or killed.
19. because she wanted to convert
20. The public reasons for her abdication were that it would be in the best interest of the country, of Charles, and of herself. The country would be a stronger country with a male leader. Charles would be relieved of uncertainty. And Christiana would have the time to devote to her intellectual pursuits.
21. She left Stockholm, sent most of her suite home, cut her hair, dressed in men's clothes, and crossed into Germany. From there, she went to the Low Countries, which were ruled by Spain.
22. She was received into the Church in Antwerp on Christmas Eve of 1654.
23. She entered Rome on December 23, 1655. She was met by a royal reception.
24. She involved herself in diplomatic negotiations with France and Spain.
25. St. Peter's Basilica

Chapter 17: Conversions in the North
1. Norway, Sweden, Denmark, Iceland, and Finland
2. It became almost completely Lutheran.
3. They continued in their pagan ways and their raids on the rest of Europe.
4. St. Anskar
5. St. Anskar lived from 801-865. He was born in France, but as an adult, spent most of his years as a missionary to the Scandinavian countries. His mother died when he was five, and he was sent to be brought up by monks. While still a child, he started having visions.
6. He dreamed that he was trying to reach a fence on the other side of a muddy field. A beautiful woman stood on the other side, surrounded by other women, including Anskar's mother. The lady asked him if he wanted to get to his mother, and when he said yes, she told him that he would if he worked hard, because there was no room for laziness where she was. From that day on, he was a very hard worker, and spent much effort on his studies.
7. He did not appear to have much success either in Denmark or Sweden, but his labors bore fruit later.
8. The city was completely destroyed, but the people were saved because Anskar had organized their escape.
9. He made friends with the Danish king, who allowed him to continue with his missionary work. Out of the ruins of the city, St. Anskar then built a church and a school.
10. Anskar asked King Olaf for support for his mission. Olaf did not want to give his support without getting something in return. Anskar would not promise him anything, so the king told him he would have to wait until the assembly of councilmen could vote on the matter. The vote was in Anskar's favor, and a Swedish mission was set up.
11. Eleven years, until his death in 865
12. He lived an ascetic life. He practiced strict tithing (10% of his diocese's income to the poor). He fed two poor men and two poor women every single day of every Lent; he redeemed prisoners with his own money.
13. Harold Bluetooth
14. He was the son of Harold Bluetooth. Missionaries had to go underground because he was a pagan and persecuted the Christians.
15. Canute the Great was a younger son of Sweyn Forkbeard, and he came to power after his father and older brother died. He had accompanied his father on an invasion of England, and after their victory over England, began to practice Christianity. He came to an understanding with the English bishops, and became an ardent champion of

221

Christian religion and culture. He made Christianity the dominant religion in Denmark, and used his influence to make the other Scandinavian countries tolerant towards the Christian religion.
16. Queen Emma, Canute's wife, assisted in the foundation of many monasteries.
17. He realized that he was sowing the seed that others would harvest.
18. St. Olaf was a King of Norway who was a strong Christian, and who strenuously fought paganism in his country. He lived from 995-1030.
19. eighteen
20. by fighting the battles for his country against the Danes under the sign of the Cross
21. He brought in missionaries and teachers from England. He built churches. He declared Christianity the official religion of Norway.
22. Russia
23. On August 31, 1030, he led his men into battle against the pagans. There was a total eclipse of the sun, and in the darkness, his enemies overcame him and killed him.
24. because he fought so many battles for the Church, and so many miracles happened at his tomb.
25. King Olaf I of Norway sent Norse-speaking missionaries to Iceland.
26. The first known missionary in Iceland was the Saxon priest, Friedrich, in 981.
27. The people were so impressed by the missionaries that when Parliament met to discuss the matter of Christianity, the majority vote was to adopt Christianity, and the idols were ordered to be destroyed. The first native bishop was Isleif in 1056.
28. Catholicism was declared illegal by the conquering Protestant Danes. No Catholic priests were left because they were all killed, and so the people were unable to hold onto their faith. The country became completely Lutheran.
29. We can pray, and we can support missionary efforts in Scandinavia. If any of our ancestors were from these countries, we should ask them to help the Catholics living there now.

Chapter 18: Switzerland's Heroes
1. Meinrad was a Benedictine monk who lived as a hermit in the early 800's in Switzerland. He was clubbed to death by two wandering men, who were later captured.
2. Einsiedeln was the site of Meinrad's hermitage. A Benedictine monastery was later established there. It means "hermit."
3. Einsiedeln now has 10,000 residents, not counting the pilgrims. The townspeople have a habit of greeting every stranger, to let pilgrims know that they are welcome. The monastery has a basilica with two bell towers. There are workshops, barns, and stables.
4. On September 14, 948, a vigil and fast were held as preparation for the following day when the church was to be consecrated. As the bishops and people knelt in prayer, Christ suddenly appeared at the altar. Angels and saints accompanied him. When the bishop started to consecrate the church in the morning, an angel stopped him, telling him that it had already been consecrated the previous night by Christ, himself.
5. The Black Madonna was a wooden statue of Mary that Meinrad had brought with him to the spot of Einsiedeln. It was destroyed by fire in 1464, and a new one was put in its place. Centuries of candles have darkened it.
6. The monks buried the statue in the hills, and then took it to Austria. The French army seemed to follow, so the statue was moved again, and this kept happening until eventually the French army returned to the church, and took a statue that had been put in place of the real Black Madonna.
7. Nicholas von Flue lived from 1417-1487 in Switzerland.
8. He was elected a councilor and a judge at a very young age. He fought in a war against Austria, during which he was made a captain of the Swiss army. By papal invitation, Nicholas fought against Duke Sigismund, who had been excommunicated for aggression towards a bishop.
9. A war is justified if in defense against an attack, or if it is waged to defend the innocent, or to correct some great moral evil. The war must have some chance of success; the good to be done must outweigh the harm; the war must be proclaimed by just authority; and moral means must be used in the waging of it.
10. He practiced mental prayer and mortification, as well as contemplation. He kept a rosary with him at all times. He fasted four days a week, and throughout all of Lent. Meanwhile, he never abated any of his duties or activities. He experienced mystical prayer and symbolic visions.
11. He was happily married to Dorothy Wiss. They lived on a farm and had five boys and five girls.
12. because the court system was making unjust decisions, and he was disgusted with it
13. He had a vision of three noblemen, Who were the Blessed Trinity. They asked him to give himself completely, body and soul, into their power, and told him that if he would loyally persevere in God's service, he would be assured of a place in heaven.
14. When he reached the monastery, it appeared as if engulfed in flame. He saw this as a sign that he was supposed to return to his native land.
15. Ranft
16. He would sleep for two or three hours, getting up at midnight to pray. He had no table and no chair. His bed was a log, and he went barefoot and bareheaded all year round.
17. Agents of the government; the Bishop of Constance
18. Visitors of all sorts came to ask his advice. The local governments of the cantons sent deputations to ask his help and advice.
19. the Eucharist
20. He had telepathic knowledge. He told a farmer it was wrong to suspect a woman of bewitching the cattle.
21. He recommended that they retain their individual values, but work together when threatened from the outside.
22. He died in 1487; he was 70.
23. This statue still stands in the building that houses the federal assembly. Also, Switzerland has continued to follow in the peacemaking/peacekeeping footsteps of St. Nicholas. It has remained an oasis through two world wars.

Chapter 19: Master of Music
1. in 1770 in Bonn, Germany
2. He started school at age six. At eight, he gave his first recital. At thirteen, he took over his music teacher's position as the organist for the 6 A.M. Mass. At fourteen, he became a music teacher for the Breuning family.
3. Vienna

4. Haydn
5. The classical style was very complicated and intellectual, with little or no emotional influence. The romantic style was extremely emotional.
6. He was a procrastinator and disorganized. He was awkward and absent-minded. He was also very generous to close friends and family.
7. It was the essay written by Beethoven in 1802. It shows his courage and determination in the face of great trials, especially his hearing loss.
8. Beethoven's third symphony, one of his most famous works
9. The main character, Florestan, is a prisoner. His wife, Leonore, is warm and faithful. The opera communicates the pain of imprisonment and the eventual joy of liberation.
10. because Vienna was under attack from Napoleon
11. arrival at joy through suffering
12. human hopes and fears
13. the praises of the Creator
14. human pain and sorrow
15. prayer for inner and outer peace
16. He died of pneumonia in the middle of a large thunderstorm, after receiving the Last Rites, in 1827.

Chapter 20: Earthly and Heavenly Loves

1. in the tenth century, with the conversion of King Stephen
2. She was born in 1207. Her parents were King Andrew and Queen Gertrude of Hungary.
3. four
4. St. Boniface
5. They educated her in the domestic arts, academic subjects, and horsemanship.
6. 1221
7. He had great concern for the poor and the unjustly treated. He had a high sense of honor. He respected God's laws absolutely.
8. When it was time for the church ceremony after the birth of her child, she imitated Mary by dressing in simple clothes, walking barefoot to the church, and carrying her own child. In general, she was very attracted to the Franciscan emphasis on poverty and simple piety.
9. At Mass, she had a vision of Christ crucified.
10. She assisted poor women in labor, cared for the sick in the worst conditions, paid the debts of the poor, and made baptismal robes for poor children. She washed the feet of lepers, and dressed their wounds.
11. She distributed the food of the court and housed the sick in a building attached to the castle. She visited the sick several times a day, and sold her own possessions to buy food and medicine for them.
12. He died in a fever epidemic at age twenty-seven.
13. Conrad of Marburg
14. He took the revenues of her dowry, which was unjust.
15. She was mocked and humiliated, and became ill from lack of food and shelter.
16. She wore simple clothes, abstained from meat four times a week, fasted on Friday, and from All Saints' Day to Easter, said the Divine Office, and continued in her work with the poor.
17. She established a hospital.
18. She died shortly after midnight on November 17, 1231.
19. Her body remained supple and gave off the scent of roses. After five years, it was still incorrupt.
20. 1235
21. wife, queen, mother, and servant of the poor

Chapter 21: Captive Cardinal

1. He lived in Hungary for most of his life. He was born in Mindszent in 1892.
2. He diverted a crowd's attention from a Communist speaker to his own leading of the Angelus. When arrested and forbidden to return to his parish, he immediately returned after being released.
3. He turned all of his religious houses into refuges for Hungarian Jews hiding from the Nazis.
4. He led fellow priests to say Mass every day while in prison. He made sure that the imprisoned seminarians finished their studies, and ordained ten of them while in prison.
5. They organized multiple Communist political parties and infiltrated and dominated the labor unions. They threatened to outlaw all organizations that did not cooperate.
6. He organized relief by appealing to the charity of other nations, especially the United States. He started a movement for prayer and penance, and set an example with intense prayer and fasting.
7. He personally led pilgrimages and proclaimed 1947 a Marian year with special rallies, pilgrimages, and other observances.
8. They refused to issue railroad tickets to Marian celebrations. They stopped all traffic on the pretext of epidemics. They set power failures to prevent public speaking. They operated loud machines near churches during masses.
9. They forbade any religious institution, organization, or school from receiving government financial support. Religious publications were forbidden publication. No Christian political party was allowed.
10. Only the parties in the Provisional National Assembly (of Communist construction) were allowed to run candidates. The only non-Marxist party was the Smallholders party. Catholics voted for the Smallholders candidate, who received the majority vote, but the party's weak leaders were pressured into giving the Communists 50% of the Cabinet positions.
11. In 1947, they increased their power by fraudulent elections, and persecution of opposing parties. In 1948, all Catholic schools were seized, and courses in Marxism became mandatory in all schools.
12. Brainwashing is a Communist technique whereby they put a man through such physical and mental stress that he can no longer think clearly. They repeat Communist doctrines over and over again until he can think of nothing else.
13. He was arrested on December 6, 1948. The Communists questioned him day and night, and forced him to stand with his hands over his head in blinding light for days at a time. On the verge of a complete breakdown, he signed a confession on January 11, 1949. Under his signature, he put the Latin abbreviation for "I signed under force. They gave him drugs, and brainwashed him for forty days, after which they held a trial. He was so weak he could barely stand or talk. He recited a memorized confession, which the judge would finish for him if he forgot a line. Mindszenty was convicted of treason and sentenced to life in prison.
14. They raided monasteries and convents. They passed a regulation abolishing the teaching of any religion in

schools, except when parents specifically asked for it. When almost 100% of the parents did make such a request, the Communists fired the religion teachers, and warned that students taking religion classes would not be allowed to go to college. Textbooks were re-written according to Communist doctrine. All non-Communist youth organizations were disbanded. Religious were expelled from hospitals, orphanages, etc. Religious orders were dissolved, and all members were forced to go into secular life.

15. It was led mostly by young people. The Communist government was temporarily overthrown, and Mindszenty was freed, but Hungary's freedom was very short-lived. The Soviet Union sent troops and tanks into the streets of Budapest, and since no help came from other countries, Hungary's Freedom Fighters were destroyed.
16. Negotiations between the Vatican and the Hungarian government resulted in permission for Mindszenty to leave Hungary. He did not want to, but in obedience to the Pope, he did, living in Vienna until his death in 1975.
17. Pope Paul VI
18. The Freedom Fighters
19. He stood for justice, human rights, peace, and most especially the Catholic Church.
20. Answers will vary (Pray for them. Make sacrifices for them.)

Chapter 22: Christ in Ukraine and Russia
1. She married Ihor I, Duke of Kyiv. She was baptized in 958 in Constantinople.
2. She tried to convert her son and heir to the throne of Kyiv.
3. Volodymyr was Olha's grandson, a brutal and bloodthirsty ruler. Originally a pagan, he was baptized so that he could marry Princess Anna, the sister of the Byzantine Emperor, and he reformed his life, and converted many of his subjects. He is now looked up to as the patron saint of Russia and the Ukraine by both Catholics and Orthodox.
4. He received a call for help from the Byzantine Emperor, but would not help without being promised that Anna would become his wife. In turn, the Emperor would not send Anna unless Volodymyr promised to be baptized Catholic. So the agreement was made, and in 988, Volodymyr was baptized.
5. He put away his former wives. He tore the idols from their pedestals, and had them dragged into the river. Shortly before he died, he gave away all his personal belonging to his friends and to the poor.
6. from Ukrainian monasteries and ecclesiastical institutions
7. refusing to be obedient to the pope
8. Russian Orthodox and Ukrainian Orthodox Churchs
9. Eastern
10. beliefs
11. The Mass in the Eastern rite involves more singing from the priest and the congregation.
12. Processions and incense are used with much greater profusion in the Eastern rite than in the Western rite.
13. Blessed Mother
14. at Baptism
15. at Baptism
16. icon screen in front of the altar
17. changed
18. icon
19. St. Luke
20. the spiritual side of life
21. flat; present
22. everyday
23. glorification
24. conventions
25. iconostasis
26. wood
27. jewels
28. holy object
29. *Our Lady of Kazan*
30. miracles
31. They spent three days in prayer and fasting before the icon of *Our Lady of Kazan*.

Chapter 23: Jadwiga's Wedding Ring
1. Hungary
2. Jadwiga
3. Hapsburg
4. They feared that Poland would be united with Hungary and lose its independence.
5. She was so young that the Poles thought she would constantly be returning to Hungary and leaving them without a ruler.
6. They would accept Jadwiga as their ruler if she would promise never to leave the country, and if she would promise not to marry William Hapsburg of Austria.
7. Cracow
8. to "respect all the rights, the liberties, and privileges of the people"
9. the businessmen and the merchants
10. She received state visitors from all over Europe, continued her education, sat in council meetings, encouraged the improvement of manners at court, and did needlework for recreation.
11. She loved William Hapsburg of Austria. Jagiello was twenty-five years older than she. He was a pagan barbarian. As a Lithuanian, he had a reputation for brutality.
12. He would unite Lithuania with Poland. He would restore Poland's lost lands. He would release Polish prisoners. He would become a Christian and bring his whole country into the Church.
13. She was not opposed politically, since she had not particularly desired a union with Austria. She understood her daughter's fears, however, and left the final decision up to Jadwiga and the Poles.
14. He told her that her duty to the Church and to her country was to marry Jagiello, and that this must outweigh her personal feelings.
15. The union of Poland and Lithuania
16. They made a four-month tour of the country.
17. He smashed the pagan idol Perkinas, and extinguished the perpetual fire that had burned there. He planted a cross in its place and knelt before it, singing the *Te Deum*. He cut down the country's sacred forest of sacred oaks, and killed all the snakes that had been living there. He destroyed the pagan temple, and laid the cornerstone of a cathedral in its place.
18. He signed a document which secured to all men property rights and equality before the law, protected workers and their families, outlawed forced labor, and provided for just judges.
19. Vilno. The Teutonic Knights attacked Vilno. Polish

knights drove them out.
20. The union of the two countries, the conversion of Lithuania, the rebuilding of Vilno into a Christian city with many churches, the remodeling of hospitals, schools, monasteries, and churches, the translation of the Scriptures into Polish, the reformation of the Church in Poland, and a general entrance into a golden age of art and culture.
21. A sick beggar covered in sores was healed because Jadwiga washed him. A boy who had drowned was brought back to life when Jadwiga spread her mantle over him.
22. They did not want to engage in any war, except for defense.
23. Complications after childbirth
24. One half went to the university; the other half went to the poor.
25. creator of divine culture, protectress of the Church, administrator of justice, servant of all virtues, humble and beneficent mother of orphans

Chapter 24: The Black Madonna's Fort
1. St. Luke
2. Tartar
3. Czestochowa
4. Jasna Gora
5. A large church and monastery
6. The Hussites
7. They slashed it twice with a sword
8. Walls and a moat.
9. Charles Gustavus
10. Warsaw and Cracow
11. Stephen Zamoyski
12. Abbot Augustine Kordecki
13. Four thousand
14. He said Mass before the altar of the Black Madonna. Then he carried the Blessed Sacrament in procession, blessing the weapons and ammunition.
15. General Muller
16. They sang hymns.
17. Sir Peter Czarniecki
18. They threatened to kill them if Abbot Kordecki would not surrender; they sent them to try to talk him into giving up.
19. The invaders were murdering priests and profaning churches.
20. Abbot Kordecki. Because he trusted God, refused to surrender and encouraged all the defenders to remain firm through every difficulty.
21. Stephen Zamoyski
22. They laughed and sang and had a big celebration.
23. He saw Our Lady.
24. Because when Our Lady appeared he concluded that he was fighting an enemy much stronger than he was.
25. It inspired them to rise up against the Swedish invaders.
26. Queen and Mother of Poland

Chapter 25: Suffering Poland
1. twenty; 1939
2. Columns of tanks and other vehicles, supported by aircraft, speed ahead of the rest of the troops wiping out everything in their path.
3. Soviet Union
4. They divided it.
5. One and a half million
6. In ghettoes
7. At the Katyn Forest
8. No. In Paris
9. The Home Army
10. They set up radio transmitters and receivers, provided education, disrupted Nazi food shipments, smuggled food to their own people, sent information to London, helped Jews outside the ghettoes, sabotaged German vehicles, and encouraged the Polish people.
11. The Jews were forced to live in ghettoes.
12. They sent them west to the concentration camps where they were killed.
13. He was educated in the Franciscan seminary and in Rome.
14. Knights of the Immaculata; to bring the entire world under the Immaculata's rule of love
15. He founded a minor seminary, printed thousands of booklets, built an airstrip.
16. Auschwitz concentration camp
17. He was martyred in place of another man.
18. A small group of Jews routed a larger German force without a single casualty of their own. They detonated a large mine turning the Germans back again. The Germans then decided to burn them out.
19. They went through a tunnel to a Franciscan church.
20. They were taken into captivity. Warsaw was destroyed.
21. Many Poles were killed and their capital city was destroyed. Poland stayed under their rule for over forty years.
22. The Communists built a new city that they intended to be godless, but the Poles attended Mass at a small chapel on the edge of town. They harassed the government until they were allowed to build a church. They built it themselves, mixing the cement by hand and working on it after long days spent at the steel mill. It was named in honor of Mary, Queen of Poland.
23. It is crowded every Sunday. Each of five Masses is attended by 10,000 people. *Corpus Christi* processions draw 40,000 participants. In May, nearly 2,000 children receive First Communion.

Chapter 26: Survival of the Faith
1. 1549
2. colonies
3. monks
4. baptized
5. powerful
6. 500
7. Sumurai
8. churches
9. city
10. Portugal
11. Nagasaki
12. Jesuits
13. Kyoto
14. That Portugal intended to conquer Japan by means of the Christian missionaries
15. He believed that the Christians were adoring the souls of those for whom they prayed.
16. All missionaries must leave and all Japanese Christians must give up the Catholic faith.

17. Their churches were burned; they were ordered to give up their Catholic faith.
18. They prayed and processed through the city.
19. They were torn down and burned.
20. 1614
21. Twenty-three Christians were burned at the stake, and 22 others were beheaded along with their wives and children.
22. They were persecuted, tortured, and killed.
23. It began as a protest against exploitation of peasants in the city of Arima. The government overwhelmed and then pardoned everybody except the Christians. 35,000 Christians were killed because they refused to give up their Catholic faith.
24. People were forced to trample on a picture of Jesus or Mary to discover if they were Christian.
25. The Japanese were forbidden to go abroad lest they become Christian, and very few ships were allowed to land in Japan.
26. Father Sidotti was captured and imprisoned for 7 years. When he converted his guard, he was moved to a dark cell were he died of starvation.
27. They were thrown in jail and beheaded because they refused to give up their faith.
28. They had secret lay catechists who taught prayers and doctrine. Designated people baptized children. Others carefully kept the Church calendar. Certain leaders announced feast days and days of fast and abstinence. They passed down prayers to their children. The Jesuit book *Doctrine* was memorized and passed on. The *Treatise on Contrition* was copied and passed down to children. Holy objects were guarded and hidden.
29. Commodore Perry persuaded Japan to negotiate a trading treaty with the United States.
30. French citizens
31. Father Mermet; make converts
32. The underground Christians started coming to his church.
33. They came early or late or in bad weather so people wouldn't notice.
34. imprisoned and tortured them; 3,290 were deported from one city alone
35. end the persecution of Christians
36. In 1889. 14,000 Christians
37. Nagasaki
38. 8,500 Catholics were killed by the atomic bomb

Chapter 27: Forbidden Country

1. Italian; Jesuit
2. He was gifted in math.
3. clocks, maps, spheres
4. That they were inferior; barbarians
5. So that they would be more welcome
6. Speak Chinese, dress, eat, and observe only Chinese clothes, foods, and customs. They had to marry only Chinese, and not bring any more foreigners to China.
7. baptized him and cared for him
8. swampy, unhealthy; Fr. Almeida became ill and died
9. He adopted customs of a Mandarin
10. Nanking
11. Wore an ankle length robe and black hat;let his hair grow
12. God appeared to him and asked him if he was going to destroy the religion of the country and establish a new one; God promised to help him

13. His amazing memory
14. a trip to Peking; no
15. James Pantoja
16. No
17. Taught them how to work clocks
18. No
19. He made his first converts
20. *A True Disputation About God*
21. Christian beliefs proved through natural reason
22. 1610
23. The Chinese Government issued an Edict of Toleration; 300,000
24. The Jesuits had dressed like the Chinese and adopted some of their customs other missionaries who came to China believed the Jesuits had compromised on Catholic doctrines. The issue was taken to the Vatican, and the Vatican commission of cardinals ruled against the Jesuits. Christianity lost respect in the eyes of the Chinese court and nobility and among the common people; Chinese Catholics left the Church in great numbers; however, in 1939, the Vatican reversed its decision, and Catholics increased to 3,000,000
25. The Chinese Communist government arrested, tortured, and killed every member of the Legion of Mary because they were locating fallen-away Catholics to convince them to return to the Church. They expelled foreign missionaries and permitted only the state-controlled "Catholic" church.

Chapter 28: Teacher of Reality

1. Hinduism; Buddhism
2. St. Thomas the Apostle
3. St. Francis Xavier
4. He was an Italian nobleman, of the Jesuit order.
5. Portuguese; Goa
6. Castes
7. that the converts to Catholicism had to quit the caste system
8. by joining the caste system
9. De Nobili became exhausted due to his efforts to change his lifestyle, but he managed to impress the Hindus and to become accepted by them as a Brahmin.
10. Some of the issues debated by Fr. de Nobili with a local teacher were the unity of God, unity of body and soul, and the true meaning of suffering. The first person baptized was the local teacher, given the name Albert.
11. Father de Nobili entered the Brahmin class. His special insignia was an insignia of threads, with three gold ones for the Trinity, and two of white for the body and soul of Christ.
12. The *Vedas* of India are the great epic poems. Father hoped to show the relationship of their good aspects to Christianity.
13. Individuality, reality, truth, good and right, even existence were denied by Hindu beliefs.
14. Teacher of Reality This title contrasted with the Hindu religious teachers who denied reality.
15. a seminary; first church
16. Because they did not believe in truth or reality, anything could contradict.
17. Baptism
18. social
19. a nayak or local king

20. untouchables
21. nayak
22. churches wherever he pleased
23. middle
24. 2,500
25. Teacher of Reality

Chapter 29: Roses in Winter
1. Our Lady of Guadalupe.
2. Juan Diego
3. Mexico City; Tepeyac Hill.
4. "ever Virgin Mother of the true God"
5. a church built in her name on Tepeyac Hill.
6. She wanted the church built in her honor, and to spread her love and protection.
7. The Lady said that men loved her, trusted her, and sought her aid.
8. to tell the local Bishop about her desire for the construction of the chapel
9. a sign of proof of the authenticity of the vision that Juan said that he had seen
10. Juan didn't want the Lady to see him, since he was ashamed of failing in his mission.
11. roses
12. The sign that Juan was to give the bishop was the roses in his tilma.
13. an image of Our Lady, miraculously imprinted on the tilma
14. The picture remains clear and bright despite the long years that would normally destroy the garment.
15. Mariana was born October 31, 1618.
16. poverty, chastity and obedience
17. Mariana cared for the poor and the sick, and aided those with personal problems.
18. The miracle of the loaves was a basket that Mariana had, from which she dispensed a never-ending supply of loaves for the poor.
19. Quito suffered a series of natural disasters, such as plagues, earthquakes, and a volcano eruption.
20. to offer himself as a victim, to spare the populace any more disasters
21. to offer herself as a victim so the priest might live, and to save the lives of the townsfolk
22. She returned home, after which she became so ill that she never left her home again.
23. the earthquakes ceased, the plagues disappeared, the volcano became quiet
24. the people of Quito repented, and went to confession & Holy Communion in great numbers

Chapter 30: Our Lord's Grandmother
1. French; Catholic
2. in 176, during the French & Indian War
3. Quebec, the original settling place of French Catholics
4. French sailors from Europe
5. in thanksgiving for her intercession in their dangerous sea voyages
6. He was a crippled farmer in the area of the Church of St. Anne de Beaupré, the chapel of the French sailors. When he placed several stones in the foundation of the chapel then being built, Louis was miraculously cured.
7. Bishop François de Montmorency Laval; a fragment of her finger
8. on March 12, 1670
9. the Jesuits
10. the Huron tribe; 1671
11. the Algonquins, Montagnais, Iroquois, and others
12. Admiral Phipps; 35 ships, 2,000 men
13. Pierre Carré, who led his men to kneel and pray at the Shrine of St. Anne
14. The small band of French soldiers won a resounding victory due to their bravery. This bravery confounded and scared the English, who retreated in disorder.
15. General Montgomery. Under his leadership the English burned most of the houses on both sides of the St. Lawrence River, and destroyed several churches as well.
16. It burned to the ground.
17. The people of Quebec built a new church on the site, the basilica of St. Anne de Beaupré.